PRAI...

GRII. _ _...

BASEBALL'S INTREPID INFANTRY

⭐

"*Grinders* is the story of the men that make baseball special. It is the guys that fight tooth and nail to get that one day in the big leagues. This book is the story of the guys that savor every at-bat and love the life of being a ball player. In many ways Mike Capps is a grinder. He has spent the last twenty-three years calling every game for the Round Rock Express, honing his craft and entertaining thousands and thousands of baseball fans. Grinders play for the love of the game and this book will paint the picture of what "love of baseball" is all about."

—REID RYAN, Baseball Executive and Founder of the Round Rock Express

"*Grinders: Baseballs Intrepid Infantry* is a peek behind the curtain of professional baseball and the "bit" players, or "grinders" that make the game operate smoothly and effectively on a daily basis. While the author, Mike Capps, spins the tales of the many overachievers, cup of coffee'ers, and once-in-a-lifetime players, what Mike fails to do is to reveal himself as the "ultimate grinder." When it comes to identifying a grinder, the old adage, "it takes one to know one" certainly applies here. Through the course of his storied career in news and sports, over and over again, Mike has done many things that exemplify his single-minded penchant for going over and above to achieve the means to an end. Who, for example, would give up his job as a CNN foreign/war correspondent to become a one-man show for three to four hours a day broadcasting minor league baseball? Only our Mike Capps!"

—TIM PURPURA, former general manager, Houston Astros

☆ ☆ ☆

"What Mike Capps has done in encapsulating what a true base "grinder" is with the people that are written about in this book is simply amazing. Readers will truly enjoy these great stories about amazing baseball men and baseball families."

—GENE WATSON, vice president and assistant general manager,
Kansas City Royals

"Baseball is a game of heroes—about a few hundred Hall of Famers, a smaller number of legends, and countless milestones, all captured in timeless books and films. Yet, none of these sources address the 'grinders' of the game. Author/broadcaster Mike Capps pours decades of baseball knowledge and passion into the dust of dreams that represent tens of millions of people, people who once proudly brandished a uniform, pounded a glove, threw a ball, or swung a bat. In *Grinders,* Capps shares the stories of dreamers, those who made it up and down the baseball ladder, and those whose hopes exceeded their actual performances within the baselines. Through adept storytelling, Capps delivers a different level of hero, the Everyman who perpetuates the game, from the physically gifted to those with the power to overcome the lack of physical gifts, from one generation to the next. Through scores of stories from a broad collection of mouths, hearts, and minds, Capps shares the unique stories of Grinders—individuals whose success is measured not necessarily in a box score or a baseball card, but through the abundance of will that possesses not one iota or ounce of quit. Grinders covers every experience of anyone who's heard the crack of a bat."

—CHARLES KAUFMAN, President of B'nai B'rith International
and professor of journalism at Texas State University

"Those who live and breathe baseball do so in part because they truly embrace the daily grind of a long season. It's what sets apart the game from all the others. To the casual fan, the players in this book are mere footnotes in baseball history. But without these players, the game simply can't exist. *Grinders* gives these men their proper due. Every grinder has a great story, and Mike and Chuck bring those stories to the forefront to show what makes these players special and why they are so important to baseball."

—ALEX FREEDMAN, broadcaster, Oklahoma City Dodgers

"Armed with a lifelong love of baseball and a reporter's attention to detail, Mike celebrates some of the game's unsung heroes by telling us their story in his own distinct voice. This is a great read by one of the ultimate grinders.

—MICHAEL COFFIN, broadcaster, Corpus Christi Hooks

"The ultimate fictional grinder, Jimmy Dugan, taught us 'the hard is what makes it great.' This book is a celebration of that mantra. Baseball is hard. Really hard. Baseball is also great, and the greatness of the sport is reflected in the stories it inspires. I can't think of a better person to tell these stories than Mike Capps. A grinder himself, with a Rolodex to make us all envious, Capps is a gifted storyteller. These diverse stories will make you laugh, make you smile, inspire you to grind away in your own life, and make notes in your scorebook for players to remember the next time you're at the ballpark."

—JOSH SUCHON, author and Albuquerque Isotopes broadcaster

"Mike Capps has been a storyteller for decades and he tells inspiring stories in *Grinders: Baseball's Intrepid Infantry*. From journeymen players to longtime managers to those who have overcome physical challenges, fans will read about the highs and lows of those who have dedicated their lives to the game."

—TIM HAGERTY, author and broadcaster

★ ★ ★

"Mike Capps has searched the four corners of the baseball world to put together this unique roster. He calls them 'Grinders.' They are people who haven't been given anything in making baseball their life. How do you know a Grinder when you see one? Cappy is about to tell you, and he ought to know because he is one of them, both in life and in baseball. I saw this personally as we teamed up to broadcast minor league baseball. Sit back and enjoy meeting these contributors to the great game of baseball."

—STEVE SELBY, former broadcaster, Memphis Redbirds

"No writer who has ever lived has properly captured the glories of America's great game of baseball. But Mike Capps' new book on grinders comes real close. He does it by turning his experienced eye away from the superstars and onto players whose love of the game is bigger than the Yankees' payroll. These are the stories of the "Grinders," struggling to make The Big Show, never giving up, always doing the hard work, and loving every blessed moment on the diamond. They make baseball what it is, and Capps knows them as well as he knows our great game. You don't need to love baseball to love this book. Capps has hit a two-out, bottom-of-the-ninth walk-off homer."

—JAMES MOORE, New York Times bestselling author

"People always ask me who my favorite players have been in my twenty-seven years as the broadcaster in Salt Lake. I usually give them names like Mike Trout, David Ortiz, and LaTroy Hawkins. I would then let them know a large part of my heart has gone to the guys that gave it their all, but either Triple-A was the end of the road or would have an all too brief stint in the big leagues. They are the Grinders, and Mike has captured their essence in this book."

—STEVE KLAUKE, broadcaster, Salt Lake Bees

"In *Grinders*, Mike Capps tells some of the stories of players who might play in the shadows and who might not have everyone's attention. These captivating stories show how essential these everyday players are to the game. Just as his grandfather told nine-year-old Mike about how baseball as we know and love it couldn't exist without these grinders, Cappy invites us to pull up a chair and learn about these players who changed the games as much as the biggest stars."

—GILBERT D. MARTINEZ, Commissioner of the Rogers Hornsby Chapter (Central Texas) of the Society for American Baseball Research and senior lecturer in the School of Journalism and Mass Communication at Texas State University

"Growing up, I lived and breathed baseball and, when I began working in sports, I remember watching Chuck Hartenstein pitch. He was shaped like a soda straw and, whenever I saw him, I wondered over and over how in the world he kept getting hitters out. After reading this story, I now know how he did it—heart."

—NORM HITZGES, author and host at KTCK SportsRadio 1310 The Ticket

"Finally, a book that honors the difference makers in the game. I have a thought that 90 percent of all players have the same physical ability. The players that have intangibles that others don't possess, are the ones who become the difference makers. Go Grinders!"

—JIM GILLIGAN, former Lamar University coach, and manager, Salt Lake City Trappers

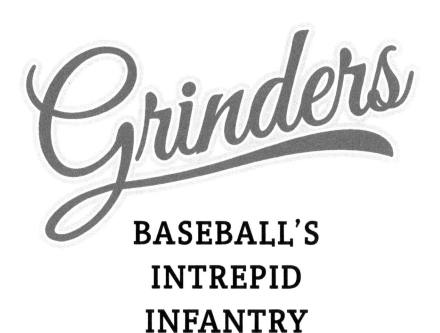

Grinders

BASEBALL'S
INTREPID
INFANTRY

MIKE CAPPS *and*
CHUCK HARTENSTEIN

STONEY CREEK PUBLISHING
stoneycreekpublishing.com

Published by
Stoney Creek Publishing
stoneycreekpublishing.com

Copyright © 2022, Mike Capps
Distributed by Texas A&M University Press

ISBN (paperback): 978-1-7368390-4-1
ISBN (ebook): 978-1-7368390-5-8
ISBN (audiobook): 978-1-7368390-6-5
Library of Congress: 2022908747

Cover & interior design by TLC Book Design, *TLCBookDesign.com*
Cover by Tamara Dever; Interior by Monica Thomas

Cover imagery: Sam Hairston catching for the Indianapolis Clowns courtesy of the Hairston family; Sliding into home photo courtesy of the Round Rock Express Baseball Club; Sam Agnew, Wikimedia Commons, 1918, Library of Congress; Baseball, UnlimPhotos; White jersey fabric, ©Kwangmoozaa/Bigstock.com.

Printed in the United States

CONTENTS

WHAT'S A GRINDER?

BASEBALL—much like other sports, the movie industry, and all forms of entertainment—is star oriented. The stars are the focus, the lead. They get the fame, the adulation, and the headlines. The supporting cast—the extras and the bit players—generally goes unnoticed and performs in relative obscurity.

There have been slightly more than 20,000 baseball players attain the pinnacle and appear in a major- league baseball game. Through 2021, only 261 have been enshrined in the National Baseball Hall of Fame. Their stories have generally been well documented. Books have been written about many of them. Their names, their accomplishments, and their personal lives are familiar to most ardent followers of the game. But what about the others? What about those who have ground it out in an effort to achieve their dream?

When I first became a fan, I was fortunate to live near a major-league city—Boston and, then later, Philadelphia. Those teams—the Red Sox, the Braves, the Phillies, and the Athletics—had stars like Ted Williams, Bobby Doerr, and Robin Roberts who became Hall of Famers. They were featured in the daily newspapers and on the radio broadcasts. But my interest went beyond these greats. After all, Ted and Bobby would only get up to bat every two or three innings and Robin would only pitch every fourth day.

I wanted to know about the other players on the roster like Catfish Metkovich and Putsy Caballero, whose very names intrigued me. I would wait earnestly for monthly publications like *Baseball Magazine* and *Baseball Digest* to hit the news-stands in hopes I could read more about some of the unsung players who also took the field and captured my interest.

Mike Capps has clearly recognized that void that still exists. He understands the human interest in the life stories—the trials and tribulations—of so many players who have strived in the face of sometimes unrelenting odds to achieve their goal of getting to The Show and getting to perform, if only briefly, on the big stage. As the radio broadcaster for the Round Rock Express since the club's inception in 2000 and as an interviewer nonpareil, there is no one better equipped to profile these "grinders" and tell their fascinating stories than Mike Capps.

—TAL SMITH, former Cincinnati Reds executive and
Houston Astros President

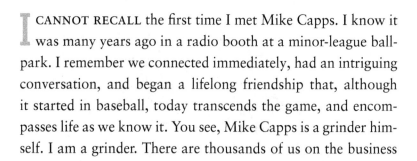

I CANNOT RECALL the first time I met Mike Capps. I know it was many years ago in a radio booth at a minor-league ball-park. I remember we connected immediately, had an intriguing conversation, and began a lifelong friendship that, although it started in baseball, today transcends the game, and encompasses life as we know it. You see, Mike Capps is a grinder him-self. I am a grinder. There are thousands of us on the business side of baseball. So, when you have a grinder writing about grinders with a grinder, Chuck Hartenstein, you have a true account of what makes baseball, and especially minor-league baseball, such a compelling part of America.

Minor-league baseball has served as the game's proving ground for centuries. It is where players learn to play, learn to be a professional, learn the fundamentals of the game, learn to grow up as men, learn how to work hard, and learn what it means to be a part of a team. Minor-league baseball teaches players to respect the rules of the game, respect the opponent, respect the umpires, and respect the fans. In the minors, players learn to respect the game's history and understand the responsibility they have to the game, to their teammates, and to all those players that came before them. For the fortunate few this journey results in big-league time—maybe that "cup of coffee" callup or a string of appearances over several years. But they always grind to get to The Show.

Minor-league baseball is where young boys and girls first see professional baseball. Eighty-one percent of America lives within fifty miles of a minor-league stadium. The minors provide millions of Americans their first touchpoint for professional baseball and in many cases the minor-league teams are the only touchpoint Americans have to this great game. Everyone can spot the superstar. It is those fringe players, the grinders, that capture the heart and feed the imagination of every little kid to think that he can someday play pro ball, too.

Minor-league baseball is where grinders start. It is where a young man gets a chance to chase that dream of being a big-leaguer. It is where sacrifice, hard work, talent, and some good luck converge for the one-in-a-million sandlot player to be given the privilege to don a professional baseball uniform and play the game he loves. But never underestimate the grind of being a middle-of-the-road talent in a demanding sport. Short on baseball tools and God-given talent, grinders have an exceptional heart and unparalleled passion that keeps them chasing that dream.

Mike and Chuck have assembled an incredible list of grinders who symbolize the term but more importantly illustrate what a grinder is, what it takes to be considered a grinder, and how being called a grinder is the ultimate compliment for a professional player. After almost forty years in the business, I have personal connections to many of the players in this book. Some played for teams I was associated with while I have crossed paths with others in the various minor leagues. Memories flood my conscience as I think back on what these players went through to be a part of professional baseball. These are men of exceptional character. Some are just plain characters, but they are all part of a rare and honorable fraternity of players who played professionally, players who played hard every day and players that endured the grind.

Minor-league baseball is a life and not just a lifestyle. I hope you enjoy reading the accounts of these players trekking through professional baseball. Their stories are inspiring and speak to the magic that is baseball and exposes the love affair America has with the game.

—**PAT O'CONNER**, former minor-league President

Aut inveniam viam aut faciam
(I shall either find a way or make one)

THIS MOTTO was first attributed to great Carthaginian general Hannibal when his generals told him there was no way for is war elephants to cross the Alps into Italy. It was also the motto of the great Arctic explorer Robert Peary, as well as a number of U. S. military services.

It also might well express the motivation of the baseball grinder, of which there have been a multitude over the long history of the game.

Fans of the baseball are dazzled by the extraordinary talents of the most accomplished players. Who would not appreciate the feats of the many great players baseball fans have watch and rooted for since time beyond memory?

Yet without the grinders of the game, where would the stars be? Those grinders fill out every roster at every level and have from the beginning of the game—players who plug away, year after year, persevering and succeeding through tenacity and grit.

Aut inveniam viam aut faciam

It may as well be the motto of every player, coach, umpire, scout, and front office worker who has ever persisted, continued, and stuck with it when others told them it might be time to do something else with their life.

I think anyone that has been in the game for a while could put together a list of their own personal favorite grinders: the player who lost a hand in a farming accident that went on to a noted scouting career, the umpire who spent parts of nineteen seasons in Triple A before getting a full time major- league contract, the hitter who had a lifetime average below the Mendoza line who became a successful and much emulated hitting coach. I could go on and on.

They are all the personification of the motto:

Aut inveniam viam aut faciam

You will read in this book the stories of a few of the grinders that have found a way or made one, exhibiting not just grit, but bravery, honor, and style as they have slogged away at their chosen endeavor, doggedly, happily, even joyously, doing what they loved, even when others may not have fully appreciated their dedication, endurance, or contributions.

All credit to Mike and Chuck for bringing attention to the individuals that have been highlighted in this book. They, and so many others, are deserving of the overdue recognition for their dedication, sacrifice, and steadfast efforts to better the greatest game ever invented.

— **TOM KAYSER**, former Texas League President

INTRODUCTION

T HE IDEA for this book began literally decades ago, when I was nine years old, on a brutally hot and humid summer night in Texas. Seated in rickety old, built-in-1910 Burnett Field, across the Trinity River from the twinkling lights of an about-to-explode downtown Dallas, my grandfather and I waited for the start of a Triple-A game between the Dallas–Fort Worth Rangers, an affiliate of the old Kansas City A's, and the Minneapolis Millers, who were part of the Red Sox system. Transfixed watching infield and outfield drills, my grandfather finally spoke.

"See that kid, that left fielder?" he asked excitedly. "That kid, that Yastrzemski kid, you will hear a lot about him in the future, he has All-Star written all over him."

Not to mention future Hall of Famer. When I glanced at my grandfather's scoresheet, something else caught my attention. He penciled check marks alongside names of six or seven players for both clubs.

"I also want you to pay attention to the names I have checked here," he continued. "These guys will travel back and forth between Dallas and Kansas City and Minneapolis and Boston all summer. You'll even see their names in the box scores. They aren't stars, but they are the engine that drives baseball's bus."

"Drives baseball's bus...engine that...*drives baseball's bus?*"

That emphatic grandfatherly declaration buried itself in my psyche for decades. Sixty plus years later that small yet integral snippet still ignites memories of my grandfather's love for the game and for me. His heart, his sporting soul, revolved around it. He'd talked to the Pirates, looking forward to playing after World War I. My grandfather, Miller Ekas, Jr., manned an artillery post in World War I's Meuse-Argonne offensive, won six Battle Stars, but suffered a hearing loss affecting his balance and ultimately any chance at playing for money. Years later he found in me a kindred baseball spirit, absorbing all he said.

Those dudes my grandfather called baseball's "engine" we now call "grinders." In the modern world, grinders are everywhere. They populate all walks of life, all colors, creeds, and persuasions. Look at it this way: If you're not the company CEO, and you willingly display passion for your work, turning that forty-hour week into sixty "because the company needs me," you are a grinder. If you're a single parent, working at a job or maybe two, battling to make ends meet, congratulations, you're automatically a member of The Grinders Hall of Fame. If you own a small business, constantly battle payroll commitments, obsess over taxes and an avalanche of government regulations strangling your company, you my friend, g-r-i-n-d!

Baseball-wise, every future grinder dreams the dream. Every single one. Millions of youngsters from the U.S., Canada, Mexico, Japan, the Caribbean, Cuba, Venezuela, and Australia all share it. They, more than anything else, want to play baseball in the U.S. major leagues. Chances of that happening? Any sane Las Vegas bookie races away from the odds.

"Imagine the player pool in the entire world," states former Cincinnati Reds executive and Houston Astros President Tal Smith. "We're talking literally millions of young men...millions. Then imagine the player pool as a funnel, from Little League to PONY League to high school to collegiate ball, that funnel narrows significantly to the point of a trickle."

A trickle? Research conducted by the National Collegiate Athletic Association reveals only one in six thousand high school players ever sniffs Major League Baseball. That number essentially represents no chance at all.

Since the game's birth, fans have jammed ballparks worshiping superstars. Sports writers from every generation extolled stars from Wee Willie Keeler to Mike Trout. Big names sell big tickets, big merchandise, placing billions in major-league owners' coffers. That said, would you guess which group, stars or grinders, comprises more major-league rosters?

"Let's be real," notes Smith, "the majority of guys coming into the major leagues don't have what we know as superstar talent. So many of them relentlessly love this game as a part of their very soul, so they simply decide nothing will stop them. Those are the grinders."

Grinders ride a mentally draining roller coaster, up and down, back and forth between the minor leagues and that holy grail, a big-league call up.

"Grinders play this game very, very well," insists former major-league grinder Jim Adduci, whose son, also Jim, represents a second generation. "They're blessed with world-class talent in a lot of ways, so when they come up and play, their teams never miss a beat."

Where does this inner voice originate; to survive and thrive, after constant criticism and disappointment, and incessant bouncing from the minor leagues to Major League Baseball?

"Some people simply are born with something within their psyche that says, 'no one can ever tell me I cannot,'" said Dr. Hillary Cauthen, a sports psychologist in Austin, Texas. "And those folks succeed where others with similar talents simply do not."

While grinders possess, as Jim Adduci says, "world class talent," differences obviously exist between superstars and grinders.

"Most all of us who played any significant time in the big leagues knew in our heart of hearts we had to battle our asses off every day just to stay on the train [major-league roster]," said Ron Swoboda, a nine-year veteran major-leaguer and member of the 1969 world champion New York Mets. "It struck fear in us if we didn't go all out, all day every day. Hey, I could do some things talent-wise. But I didn't have superstar talent, so every day I spent in The Show, I knew I had to go all out or go home."

We don't claim we're profiling every grinder who ever played. No way! You could start with those who played in the early, early days in the 1860s, 1870s and 1880s, when players rode to games on buckboards or on horseback or ambled into ballparks totin' their shootin' irons. How about those intrepid dudes, into the late 1950s, riding trains all over the major leagues, American Association, International League, and Pacific Coast League for hours on end then walking, rubber legged, to the yard, strapping on wool uniforms, and playing in intense summer heat? So many battled on, overcoming injuries that would've incapacitated lesser humans. Baseball's bus riders, traveling millions of miles, sometimes stranded in the middle of nowhere, especially in the Jim Crow South, faced harassment and death threats. Don't forget players who went to war overseas; many made the ultimate sacrifice.

"Thank you, thank you, for writing this book," said grinder Travis Driskill, an Austin, Texas, native whose baseball pitching career led him all over the U.S., Canada, and Japan. "Those superstars always had tons of stories told about them. But you know what? They had to have competent teammates [grinders] who played alongside. The superstars live differently than us. They just do. And speaking for grinders everywhere, thank you for telling our stories because lots of great stories come from our ranks, because at the end of the day, we represent the common man in baseball."

Travis and I were radio partners on Round Rock Express broadcasts for almost ten seasons, and his tale? Well, wait until you read it. That said, let's add a little more flavor to grinders' psyches, hearts, and souls.

From the movies, both "Rudy," and "Rocky" represent the essence grinders—constantly knocked down, bloodied yet unbowed by opponents, coaches, promoters, or life itself. Again and again, they rise, Phoenix-like, from disappointment's flames, kicking the odds' ass, ultimately winning self-respect while showing courage, determination, and plain old guts. That's the world Rocky, Rudy, and Baseball's Intrepid Infantry inhabit.

"And this is why," Smith said, "this game is so doggone beautiful: players whose relentlessness, love and passion for the game tend to move mountains, and these guys we're talking about became the player and man no one but themselves knew they could become."

Put it this way: If MLB stars struggle, managers and the front office tread lightly with a simple, "It's okay, he's a pro, he'll come around." Not for a grinder. He winces hearing the familiar refrain, "You have to work out this slump in Triple A," or worse, "You know we got this kid in Triple A or Double A who's a five mil bonus baby we gotta look at." Hating the words, "we have to send you down," the grinder phones his, he hopes, understanding family, giving them the bad news, then dejectedly heads back down.

"Same old story," Smith said. "When management needs a spot on its twenty-six-man [daily roster], ninety-nine times out of a hundred, it won't be the young superstar who goes back to the minors."

Back and forth it goes, the grind bringing them back up to the big leagues, amped and believing that *this time I'm staying.* Then, for whatever reason, the numbers game, a trade, or management excuse, the roller coaster whiplashes them downward, back to minor-league reality.

"The fact these guys can do this time after time," Smith marvels, "says so very much about their love for the game, their ability to play it well, and their dream, their chance to be at the top, even if it's for a short time."

"And so many," noted former MLB player and Texas Rangers General Manager Tom Grieve, "don't care about the money, but simply getting that one chance for that one moment to wear a big-league uniform."

Chuck and I proudly share tales of relentless determination, overcoming steep odds, beating cancer, war wounds or other physical handicaps, or proving any scouting report wrong that says a young man "cannot." *Grinders* also proves that humans from all walks of life can still dream and achieve more than they ever believed if they whip the disappointment sting and hang on and battle for all they're worth. So here we are, ready to tell fantastic tales of tenacity, over the top desire and heart, and unmatched courage.

Enjoy our ride up and down the grinder's trail please, and our richest blessings from Austin.

—MIKE CAPPS

Chuck Haretenstein pitching for the Dallas-Fort Worth Spurs

(Photo courtesy of The Dallas Morning News)

MEET THE INFANTRY

Tribute to
CHUCK "TWIGGY" HARTENSTEIN

CHUCK HARTENSTEIN and I began this project in his living room in early January 2018. Having been a grinder himself and loving his baseball life, Chuck beamed with anticipation, playing a huge role in deciding this book's profiles.

Sadly, on October 3, 2021, while broadcasting the final game of the Round Rock Express' 2021 season, a text arrived from Chuck's son, Chris, telling me his dad had passed away. Stunned beyond belief, I announced my dear friend's passing, and from that moment the rest of the game and the day remains a blur.

As a kid, I watched Chuck pitch for the old Double A Dallas-Fort Worth Spurs. The fact my cousin Billy signed him for the Cubs thrilled me to death. Later, meeting him in person in 2000, he and his wife, Joyce, became dear friends. My wife, Karen, and our family love and appreciate the Hartensteins and that's why we dedicate this book and the entire *Grinders* project to Chuck and Joyce.

On November 21, 2021, I spoke at a memorial service for Chuck in his hometown, Seguin, Texas. The basic premise?

"Chuck did it right," in his baseball life, his life with friends, former teammates, his college alma mater, and most especially his family. I finished this way:

> "A member of the [University of Texas] Athletics Hall of Honor, Chuck remained a passionate, loyal Longhorn. For decades he maintained that same passion about you, his friends, and his teammates from Little League, through professional ball. Chuck and I have been working for a couple of years on a book about players like himself. We're dedicating the upcoming book to Chuck's memory, to his family, and his rich, wonderful baseball life. His name will appear as a co-author on other books we write as a memorial to the man, husband, father, grandfather, and great grandfather he was. You see, you do not replace Chuck Hartenstein, you keep him alive by telling others about him, because he was so special and because, of course, Chuck did it RIGHT! Godspeed until the other side my trusted friend. Godspeed."

Just six months after Chuck's passing, his beloved wife Joyce Engleke Hartenstein followed. Joyce loved baseball and its people but not those owners who tried to take advantage of players. Joyce followed Chuck through all baseball's ups and downs. The baseball grinder Chuck certainly married a baseball and life grinder in Joyce. Perhaps no baseball wife could grind with Joyce.

While she certainly missed Chuck during the months she taught school in Texas while he played or coached, raising two great sons by herself for several months a year must have been a tough road to follow. But Joyce long spoke about joyous vacations once the school year ended. She'd load up her sons and travel to Hawaii, or Canada, or U.S. destinations where Chuck was pitching or coaching. Once Chuck ended his baseball career, baseball people never left the Hartenstein's lives. Joyce and Chuck loved entertaining and visiting with Chuck's high school and Texas Longhorn teammates, and his freshman coach at UT, Roy Enderlin. Joyce loved cheering the Longhorns in person with Chuck, and she also treasured her own golf outings with friends.

Most especially, she was head over heels in love with her two sons, her daughters-in-law, her five granddaughters, and her great-grandson, as well as her beloved dog, Buster. Her smiles and warm conversation in the midst of dinners at home with friends are legendary. Karen and I will miss her beaming countenance, there's no question about that. And one final note: Our message to friends at Chuck's memorial service, "Chuck did it right," most assuredly applied to both Chuck and Joyce. Godspeed to both of you until the other side!

Now, to Chuck's amazing grinder's tale, which features beautiful, sweet Joyce!

CHAPTER 1

CHUNKS ROCKS

A THOUSAND DIFFERENT professional baseball players tell a thousand different stories about how they made it in this game. Some tales stand as too hard to believe. Not this one. Chuck Hartenstein, veteran MLB pitcher, pitching coach and co-author of this book, grew up chunkin' rocks. Small town Texas kids, especially in the 1950s and 1960s, chunked rocks.

A lot of rocks.

Guys chunked 'em at a myriad of targets. Chuck's targets were different. Rock chunking helped him learn by himself how to handle a baseball pitcher's role. He created imaginary strike zones, with imaginary hitters trying to beat him in game situations.

"Like runners at first and third and less than two outs," he remembered. "Or with bases loaded. In my mind, my job is to get out of each jam by striking out someone or getting a hitter to ground out or fly out. And you better bet I never lost one damned game!"

Relentless rock throwing, underneath a covered carport near his home, strengthened his arm, and set the stage for success. Chuck also swung a mop-stick bat, aiming for imaginary fences. No money for baseball equipment as a kid? No problem. Chuck's inventive nature, his heart and soul drove him to success.

"Twiggy," a nickname given the five-foot, eleven-inch, 155-pound righthander by Cubs teammate and Hall of Famer Billy Williams, thrived in a fourteen-year playing career, with equal amounts of swagger and relentlessness. Chuck's baseball life also included several seasons as a major-league and minor-league pitching coach and scout. Every day in baseball, in uniform or out, Chuck "brought it."

"I didn't know any other way, because that was my life, baseball twenty-four seven," said Hartenstein.

Three seasons at the University of Texas as its star pitcher, a two-time College World Series ace in the early 1960s (his ERA still ranks among the tops in CWS history) under the legendary coach Bibb Falk, we view a clearer picture of the man and pitcher, Chuck Hartenstein. Before UT, Chuck and his Seguin Matador teammates earned a Texas high school championship in 1960, with Hartenstein pitching and winning the final two games in as many days. A grinder? No doubt!

"Grinders know instinctively," says fellow grinder and former Hartenstein major-league pupil, Dan Plesac, now a star on MLB-TV, "it's full bore, all the time, and that was one of the lessons we learned from Chuck Hartenstein."

Chuck coached Plesac for three seasons with the Brewers. But let's back up a bit and examine where it all began for Hartenstein in his hometown. Seguin, for more than 140 years, stood as a working-class burg. Its population base, German, Czech, and Hispanic, ground out a living working on railroads, city service jobs, or agriculture. In football country's dead center, Seguin residents pride themselves as truly baseball savvy.

"Grown men played on semi-pro teams all around us," said Jeep Kiel, Hartenstein's Seguin baseball teammate. "Some played pro ball and were good guys. We were lucky they wanted to help us learn how to play the right way."

Perhaps no one in Seguin owned a more unquenchable thirst for baseball than Chuck Hartenstein.

"He amazed us as kids with that rock-throwing routine," laughed Hartenstein's Matador teammate and catcher, Yankee Camarillo. "Every day was the same: grab some rocks and throw, throw, throw. That turned him into a hell of a pitcher."

In high school, Chuck and the Seguin Matadors overpowered almost everyone they played in 1960. Led by their coach, the late Bill McElduff, the Matadors and Hartenstein won their first game in the state tournament in Austin.

"After the game, sitting in the stands watching the other semi-final game," Hartenstein remembers, "our trainers rubbed my arm up and down with hot analgesic balm as a means of helping me recover."

The Matadors returned to Austin the next evening, looking for a state championship, but Chuck had been told he wouldn't start that game.

"When we got to Austin," said Hartenstein, "I began to throw, and I said to Coach McElduff, 'wait a minute, I feel okay, and I wanna start,' so I put a little extra into the last few, gave 'em some real pop. I felt great. Coach said 'OK,' and away we went."

"Damned if he didn't pitch a no-hitter," marveled his catcher, Camarillo. "He was nervous and had thrown a lot in that first game. In the final, he forgot nerves or being tired and mowed 'em down. And not once did he shake me off, *not once!* Wildest, damnedest thing you ever saw!"

Chuck flatly refused to take credit for the win.

"Hey, I had a great team behind me," he said. "That team *got it done!*"

"Yes, we had a great team," remembers Matador teammate Curly Tigett, "but let it be said clearly and explicitly that *Chuck Hartenstein won that state championship.* His pitching in back-to-back games motivated us all."

Hartenstein's calm demeanor, and his sinking fastball, didn't go unnoticed by Falk, the former major-leaguer and legendary UT coach. Falk saw both games and locked in on Hartenstein exclusively. After a quick visit with Chuck after the championship game win, the coach invited the eighteen-year-old to visit the UT campus.

"At a steak dinner with me and my mom, Coach Falk asked, 'well, you comin' here or not?' I told him I had to have a scholarship," Chuck continued, "and Bibb said, 'I can offer you a full four-year scholarship, but I have to have your word you'll be with me the entire four years and not sign with a big-league team.'"

"Where do I sign?" Hartenstein said.

"You don't sign anything," said Falk, "you and I do business with a handshake."

"All Bibb wanted was my pledge that I'd stay at UT four years."

While freshmen weren't allowed on varsity teams back then, UT's freshman coach, Roy Enderlin, watched Falk's direct approach to Hartenstein.

"Bibb knew what it took to make a big-league player," Enderlin said. "From the first day, Coach got Chuck ready for life as a big-league pitcher. Sure, Chuck was scrawny, but he was convinced he could retire any hitter he faced. By the time Bibb finished with him, Chuck was ready."

With dominating success after his junior year, the Phillies offered excellent pre-draft money.

"I promised Coach Falk I'd stay four years," Chuck said stoically. "I was not about to break that promise."

After his senior season at UT, Hartenstein scrambled to find a professional chance. That was until veteran Chicago Cubs scout Billy Capps stepped up, initially offering Chuck five hundred dollars a month.

"I just couldn't do that," Hartenstein said. "So, Billy went back to his bosses, got me fifteen hundred dollars as a bonus that allowed me to buy a car."

Once in pro ball, Hartenstein described his pitching repertoire to Dallas-Fort Worth Spurs announcer Bill Mercer, later the original voice of the Texas Rangers, in Bill's book, *Play by Play: Tales From A Sports Broadcasting Insider:*

> "I had two kinds of fastballs—a worm-killing two seam sinker, a four-seam fastball which was very straight, and it got [hit a long way], a noon to dirt curve, and a slider that, if someone got a good swing on it, endangered fans sitting in the outfield bleachers. I was essentially a sinker-slider pitcher who worked from slow to slower," Hartenstein grinned.

"When we faced him, we'd always ask ourselves, 'how in the world did this guy ever get us out?'" marveled former UT star catcher, minor-league player, and manager Tommy Harmon. "But I tell you this, Chuck Hartenstein had guts, guile, and believed in himself so much, he *had* to succeed."

On a hot, muggy June night in 1965, pitching against the Austin Senators for the Spurs, the Cubs' Double-A team in Dallas-Fort Worth, Chuck Hartenstein sealed his reputation, throwing eighteen innings of a twenty-five-inning loss.

"I gave up one run in the ninth," Hartenstein bristled, "on a double and a single, and it really pissed me off. It made me so damned mad, I told my manager, Whitey Lockman, that I'm staying in this game, and I'm gonna finish it."

Inning after inning he battled with no offensive help.

"We just couldn't hit the ball that night," apologized Spurs first baseman John Boccabella. "I was a power guy, and it was almost embarrassing."

The fight continued until Hartenstein finished off Austin in a scoreless top of the eighteenth, then trudged to the dugout.

"I told Whitey that I'd had enough," Hartenstein said.

"On the one hand, I felt for him," Spurs announcer Mercer noted, "but on the other, my God, what an effort!"

Without overpowering stuff, Cubs bosses recognized the Hartenstein tenacity, his "worm burning sinker," his confidence, and his Texas League-leading ERA over more than two hundred innings of 2.18. When his Double-A season ended, Chuck received his first major-league call.

"September 9, 1965, I walked into Dodger Stadium, and watched Dodgers' future Hall of Famer Sandy Koufax warm up to go against a pretty good lefty the Cubs had in Bob Hendley," said an overwhelmed Hartenstein.

What a match up. Through seven, both pitchers had no-hitters. Koufax throttled the Cubs with the only perfect game of his four no-hitters. Hendley pitched extremely well, surrendering a run on three hits. The Dodgers won the historic game on an unearned run, featuring an MLB record for fewest baserunners in a perfect game (two), marking the only perfect game in MLB history with the winning team sending fewer than twenty-seven hitters to the plate.

"I sat there watching intently," said an exhausted Hartenstein, "thinking what in the hell am I doing here?"

In three Cubs seasons, Chuck's best came in 1967: 9-5 with a 3.08 ERA in forty-five MLB relief appearances. Two seasons with the Pirates, and parts of seasons with the Cardinals, Boston, and Toronto turned into a whirlwind. In Pittsburgh Hartenstein made a career-high fifty-six appearances in 1969 including ten saves.

"I was in my element, and every time they sent me to the big leagues, it was like a trip to heaven," he smiled.

Grinders make those "trips to heaven" courtesy of their own ability, but so many have wives and children to thank. Wives become mom and dad for months every year, kids remain separated from fathers they dearly miss. Chuck's wife of almost sixty years, Joyce, also fits the grinder's profile.

"Chuck told me one time that if I had to get out [of our marriage] and couldn't take all the sacrifices, he'd understand," Joyce remembered. "But I stuck with it and with him. Sure, there were hard times. But I always knew even back in our University of Texas days that baseball is who he is, and that ultimately, he'd succeed."

"Our mom became dad and mom," said son Chris. "The only thing we didn't like was guys who didn't believe our dad was a professional player. I always carried his card in my pocket and pulled it out to prove what I said."

Both regret that their dad never saw them play Little League.

"But vacations were great," son Greg beamed. "Especially when he was pitching or coaching in Hawaii. We spent summers there, chasing foul balls and being around great guys like Doug Rader, the Islanders manager."

"Not only did they vacation in Hawaii but in Puerto Rico and Canada," Joyce continued. "They loved being at ballparks, in clubhouses with players and their dad. That gave all of us lifetime memories."

As an ode to her husband's career, Joyce wrote a poem, "The Life of a Ballplayer's Wife." Here's part of it.

"There are so many memories of events in my life that
I have experienced as a ballplayer's wife."

"When Chuck and I married in 1961, we were both UT students and life was just fun," she said.

"He loved what he was doing, and I learned to love it too. Juggling my life as a wife and mother, it was all so new. I love you Chuck and am proud to be your wife. We've been blessed with a beautiful family and happy memories I'll cherish the rest of my life."

Mired in Triple-A three straight seasons, Chuck needed an extra few days for a better MLB pension. Then one day, great news. A bullpen spot opened with the brand-new Toronto Blue Jays in 1977. The job came courtesy of Chuck's long-time friend and Blue Jays Manager Roy Hartsfield.

"You deserve those days. You worked hard for them and you're gonna get 'em," Hartsfield told Chuck.

"Roy Hartsfield was one of my all-time favorites and I owe that man so much," Hartenstein said. "You cannot imagine how much he means to me and my family."

Appearing on Opening Day in Toronto in 1977, and in Montreal on Opening Day at Parc Jarry in 1969, Hartenstein became the only MLB player in a big-league uniform for franchise opening games in both Canadian cities. After Toronto came pitching coach stops with the Pirates at Triple-A Hawaii, MLB in Cleveland in 1979, and for Milwaukee from 1987 to 1989.

"I had been preparing for a coaching career since the days I spent with my freshman UT baseball coach Roy Enderlin," Chuck said. "I took something from every coach I had and applied it to pitchers in the bigs and minors."

"Chuck wasn't just a great pitching coach," said former major-league third-baseman Doug Rader, who managed the Hawaii Islanders during the 1980s. "I always thought he could do anything in baseball—manager, general manager, anything he wanted. He did it because he loved baseball so much. It owns his heart."

"I did a lot of pitching coaching in bars and lounges," Hartenstein laughed. "Now that may sound funny, but I wanted to know my pitchers' insides, what made 'em tick. I figured if I knew who they were, where they came from, their likes and dislikes, all that information would help me in helping them achieve success."

"Baseball's a loud game," said eighteen-year veteran MLB and grinder Dan Plesac. "With thirty or forty thousand in the stands, the last thing a pitcher in trouble needs is some pitching coach complaining about 'arm angle problems,' or 'your foot plant is wrong.' A pitcher simply needs to slow down, take a deep breath, and hear a word or two of encouragement. That's what Chuck was all about."

"Every time I came out, I said 'hey, you're okay, you know how to get this guy, so go get 'em. And then I'd give 'em a wink," said Hartenstein. "The wink *always* worked!"

"The most beautiful thing about Chuck Hartenstein as far as I was concerned: we always had no secrets," said Brewers Trainer John Adam. "If he thought a pitcher had physical problems, we talked about it. And if I spotted something physically that didn't look exactly right, we talked it over. Communication—Chuck did that so very well."

That's Chuck Hartenstein, a slender Texas firebrand who loved baseball with his heart and soul—a man who did things right and never accepted the words "you cannot."

CHAPTER 2

LORENZO BUNDY

*"If Lorenzo is not in this book...
there shouldn't be a book."*

"I GOT RELEASED from the Texas Rangers in spring training before the '82 season and found myself in a nightmare after my first year in the game," Lorenzo Bundy said.

A nightmare only the most passionate baseball operative could overcome.

Before the Rangers, Bundy's childhood favorite, the Orioles, took him in 1977's twenty-third round of the draft. He chose not to sign, instead accepting a James Madison University baseball scholarship.

"They had great hitters—Billy Sample and others—I followed," Bundy said proudly, "and my folks could come see me play, plus my coach, Brad Babcock, was the best. He'd never seen me play before I got there and took a leap of faith."

Lorenzo Bundy as manager for the Albuquerque Isotopes in 2012.
(Photo courtesy of the Albuquerque Isotopes Baseball Club)

Undrafted after his senior collegiate season, Bundy turned down a chance with the Dodgers as a free agent. He visited with Rangers' scout Joe Brunzell who asked, "Will you fly down to a Rangers tryout camp in Asheville, North Carolina and bring enough clothes to stay?"

"Not 'yes,' I told him but 'hell yes!'" Lo laughed.

In thirty games for Asheville, Bundy hit .291 and the Rangers invited him to spring training in 1982. After hitting well that spring, Lo received his first professional baseball slap in the face.

"They told me they had no money invested in me, and those words quickly taught me about the business of professional baseball," he said.

Stunned and heading back to his native Virginia to take two courses he needed to graduate while helping his former coach

Babcock work with James Madison hitters, Bundy discovered another option.

"I was working out with the team," Bundy remembers. "When veteran Pirates minor-league manager John Lipon, who had seen me in a tryout after I was released by the Rangers, recommended me to the Pirates."

No one from the Pirates had promised him anything, but Lo, bursting with hope, hopped a bus on his own dime and headed south, traveling more than a thousand miles from Virginia to Bradenton, Florida, where Pittsburgh trained. A tepid welcome awaited.

"Pirates Farm Director Murray Cook recognized my name from the Lipon recommendation," Bundy said seriously. "He told me he had no spot for me in the camp and certainly no room or board."

Bundy made a lifetime decision that day, no doubt saving his baseball career. In an overwhelmingly huge leap of faith and courage, steeled with absolute belief in himself, he asked: "What if I paid for my own room and board for the entire training camp?"

"Cook said OK, but promised no money or spot on a team," Lo recalled.

The Pirates return message? "You can draw a uniform, but after that, it's on you."

"That was good enough," Lo smiled. "I just needed a chance. Look, I didn't have a standout tool. I couldn't run, couldn't throw, but I could hit and with occasional power. All I needed was a chance."

Bundy settled into his living quarters and his routine—a twenty-dollar-a-night room and a daily six-mile round trip walk from the hotel to Pirates camp and back. Initially dejected but now proudly wearing a Pirates spring training uniform, he played very little at first. Once given a chance, he hit and hit hard.

"I was on a mission," Lo laughed, "I was relentless. I had to make a team!"

Near spring training's end, the Pirates changed farm directors, hiring Branch B. Rickey, the son of a former Pirates general manager (Branch Rickey, Jr.), and grandson of the legendary president of the Pirates, Dodgers and Cardinals, Hall of Famer Branch Rickey.

"He still couldn't promise a roster spot," Bundy said, "and at that point, they had no money or contract for me, but I continued walking back and forth from hotel to training camp. Once there, I pounded that baseball every chance I got."

During his first spring training game, future Hall of Famer Willie Stargell stopped Bundy after he sharply lined an RBI-base hit to right.

"Hey, kid, I'm Willie Stargell," the big man announced.

"I know," Bundy responded.

"I just wanted to tell you," Stargell continued, "that's a great swing you have, and I want you to keep it up."

"That little visit, just those few seconds from Stargell," Bundy grinned, "gave me a big boost of confidence."

Future Hall of Famers didn't pick Pirates' minor-league squads, however. With his professional baseball life on the line, with spring training hours and innings slipping away, Lo still had no place on a roster.

"I was nervous," he now laughs. "But I knew I had played well, hit well and hustled my ass off."

During the last three days before team assignments were made, Rickey and Bundy met again. Rickey asked the young player to meet with Assistant Farm Director Tom Kayser.

"Tom asked me, 'what's the closest airport to your hometown in Virginia?'" Bundy recalled. "I thought 'that's weird,' but I told him Richmond, Virginia. Then he asked, 'Did you keep receipts from your hotel stay?' And I answered, 'yessir.'"

Kayser, who later became Texas League president, explained what happened next.

"We [Pirates] always took care of our people, and after Branch told me to pay his room and travel costs, I relayed that to Lorenzo."

Thrilled?

"Oh my God yes," he beamed. "The man recommending me to the Pirates, John Lipon, told his bosses that he'd take me on his team, so they assigned me to Alexandria in the Carolina League. That's where I got back on track."

"Can you imagine Lo's courage?" Kayser asked. "Talk about a study in persistence!"

"Determination, character and a man who spent less time complaining than anyone I ever saw," Rickey remembers, "Lorenzo Bundy is a today guy with a yesteryear reverence for the game of baseball."

The "today guy" hit like a fiend: .291 in 116 games at Alexandria, with twenty-five homers and eighty-eight RBIs. Bundy's eight-year playing career ultimately topped out at Triple-A stops in Hawaii, Mexico City, and Indianapolis. His playing days only scratched the surface of Lo's ultimate baseball life, beginning what must be one of the best resumes among baseball lifers in the game's history.

Playing Career

◆ Four college seasons at James Madison University, where he's still the second-leading home-run hitter in school history

◆ Six seasons with the Pirates organization and two with the Expos:

   • High A, Alexandria, Carolina League

   • Double A, Nashua, Eastern League

   • Triple A, Hawaii, Pacific Coast League

   • Triple A, Indianapolis, International League

   • Triple A, Mexico City (Mexico City held working agreement with the Pirates and then the Expos)

Managing/Coaching Career

◆ 1990: Player coach, Jacksonville Expos (Double A, Southern League)

◆ 1991: Manager, Sumter (Expos), Single A, South Atlantic League

◆ 1992: Manager, Albany (Expos), Single A, South Atlantic League

◆ 1993-94: Manager, Burlington (Expos), Single A, Midwest League

◆ 1997: Manager, Brevard County (Marlins), High A, Florida State League

◆ 1998: Minor-league Base Running/Outfield Coach, Florida Marlins

◆ 1999: Bullpen Coach, Colorado Rockies under HOF Manager Jim Leyland

◆ 2000-01: Minor-league Base Running/Outfield Coach, Colorado Rockies

- 2002: Triple-A Hitting Coach, Pawtucket Red Sox, International League
- 2003: Double-A Hitting Coach, El Paso (Arizona Diamondbacks), Texas League
- 2004: Interim Bench Coach, Arizona Diamondbacks
- 2004-2006: Triple A Hitting Coach, Tucson (Arizona), Pacific Coast League and Triple A Champs .289 team batting average in 2006.
- 2007-08: Manager, Triple A Las Vegas (Dodgers)
- 2009: First Base Coach, Arizona Diamondbacks
- 2010: Manager, Rookie League Dodgers
- 2011-13: Manager, Triple A Albuquerque (Dodgers), Pacific Coast League Manager of the Year,
- 2014-15: Third Base Coach, Los Angeles Dodgers
- 2016: Outfield/ Base Running Coach, Miami Marlins
- 2018-19: Manager, Mexican Triple A Summer League
- 2020: Manager, Double A Binghamton (New York Mets), Eastern League

Manager in Mexican Leagues (Summer and Winter Leagues)

1991-2020:

- Won three championships:
  - Navajoa, 1999-2000 (Winter)
  - Hermasillo: 2006-07
  - Mazatlan: 2008-09
- Two-time Mexican Winter League Manager of the Year

In a career year in Mexico in the summer of 1986, Lo hit forty homers, striking out only nineteen times. His Mexico playing career set the stage for a remarkable run as a manager.

"Playing in Mexico taught me the feeling of managing big-game, big-time pressure situations," he recalled. "That factor became a huge learning tool for me."

The winter of 1986 marked the beginning of Bundy's marvelous coach/manager life. After he returned home from winter ball to look for a summer job in 1987, Expos Assistant General Manager Dan Duquette called to ask if Bundy had signed with anyone.

"No, not yet," responded Lo. "I have an offer from Double A, and maybe I can go back to Indianapolis in Triple A."

Bundy told Duquette he heard Mexico City's owner wanted him back. At that point, Duquette raised the conversation's stakes.

"Listen, Lo," Duquette followed up, "besides playing, I also understand you are an excellent coaching/managing candidate. Is that right?"

"That's right up my alley," Bundy laughed, "and I am definitely interested. Dan then offered me a two-year minor-league deal, which I had never heard of, and he said he wanted me to go to spring training and win a Triple-A job."

Bundy hit five spring training homers, driving in nineteen runs while winning a pinch hitter's job at Triple-A Indianapolis. One afternoon while running sprints before a game in Syracuse, he received a message to call Duquette in Montreal.

"He said, 'Lo, will you go to Double A Jacksonville for us?'" Bundy said. "We have two very young top prospects, Marquis Grissom and Delino DeShields, making big jumps to Double A.

They're struggling, so would you play for us down there and help them get going?"

With an immediate yes, Bundy dropped a notch in league classification yet found himself aimed in the proper direction for himself: coaching and managing.

"They both were in trouble," he said, "Grissom was only hitting .210 when I got there. The manager in Jacksonville, twelve-year veteran big-leaguer Alan Banister, turned both Grissom and DeShields over to me."

God blessed both young men with tremendous speed. So, trying to simplify, he asked them individually, "Have you ever thought about bunting?"

Neither had, but the first time Grissom tried it, he came up with a base hit.

"Even though it wasn't a good bunt," Bundy grinned, "with his speed he beat it out by a mile."

That bunt and constant assurance from Bundy was all Marquis needed to turn his offensive game around. In August 1989, Grissom, hitting at a .300 pace in Double A, received his first call to the big leagues.

"[The manager] Banister called me over with Grissom's news," Lo remembered. "And he said, 'Lo, you go tell him he's going up.' I told him nah, that's your job, and he replied, 'listen, you're the guy who turned him around, you give him the good news!' What a thrill!"

Grissom became Montreal's lead-off hitter, speed demon centerfielder, and All-Star. He spent seventeen big-league seasons with the Expos, Atlanta, Cleveland, Milwaukee, Los Angeles, and San Francisco. He led the National League in stolen bases in both 1991 and 1992 and won the MVP award for the American League Championship Series in 1997. In World Series play Grissom owns the second-longest Series hitting streak—fifteen games.

On the street in 1994 after new Expos' ownership fired existing minor-league brass, Lo immediately placed a call to old friend John Boles, by now the director of minor-league operations for the Florida Marlins.

"Thank God for friends," Bundy laughed. "John Boles brought me in as his minor-league base running and outfield coach. Fortunately, I learned a lot about those skills from former MLBer Dave Nelson in Montreal and I used that knowledge with the Marlins."

Bundy made sure his Marlins minor-leaguers knew when to run and why, and how to defend opposing hitters. Accountability, he says, separates those who buy into the system from those who don't. As a player, Lorenzo never made it to The Show. He's held five MLB coaching jobs, his playing career aiming at coaching/managing goals.

"I was always close to the action," he noted, "at first base or DH. While watching and playing I asked myself how I'd handle certain situations. In my head, I made pitching changes, positioned infield and outfield defenses, always paying strict attention to how my manager filled out his lineup card, and worked with the pitching coach setting up a rotation and maneuvering a bullpen."

Lo's first MLB coaching gig came in 1999 as Colorado Rockies bullpen coach under Manager Jim Leyland. Awaiting Leyland's call, Lo and his wife found themselves extremely nervous.

"My sweet wife dealt with nerves by saying her prayers, then making a deal with God that if I got the Rockies Bullpen

Coach job, she would shave her head," Bundy laughed. "I guess I never understood why shaving your head pleased God regarding your husband's job. While I was on the phone with Leyland, she kissed me goodbye, drove to the mall, shaved her head and by the time she got back, the Rockies had a new Bullpen Coach—me. So, I guess it all worked out okay."

Bundy also made it to the bigs as Arizona's interim bench coach in 2004 and as first base coach in 2009. Joining the Dodgers as third base coach in 2014-15, he then moved back to the Marlins in 2016 as outfield/baserunning coach. Although managing Dodgers Triple A affiliates in Albuquerque and Las Vegas, twenty-five Mexican Winter League seasons really proved Lo's managerial skills.

"I've had quite a run there, and I really loved it," Bundy grinned. "Owners there are intense, fans are well schooled and know baseball well, plus they are as loud as it gets."

While admittedly experiencing problems in the past finding work in his home country, in 2021 he managed the Mets Double-A affiliate in Binghamton, New York. In 2022 he was set to handle the Chicago White Sox club in Winston-Salem, North Carolina, his first single A managing assignment.

"I am looking forward to it," Lo beamed. "It's all baseball and youngsters need veteran guidance."

In his early sixties, Lorenzo Bundy smiles as he has over the past forty baseball years, playing, teaching and never spending a day not appreciating his baseball blessings.

JACKIE MOORE

"A sixty-year love affair..."

EARLY JANUARY TEMPERATURES in downtown Houston's concrete canyons—thirty-three degrees and thirty-mile-an-hour "Blue Norther" winds—mark the opposite of the city's blistering, boiling summer steam baths. On this frigid January night, warmth awaited at Minute Maid Park.

The warmth? Celebrating the eightieth birthday of Jackie Moore, a sixty-year veteran baseball player, coach and manager.

"Is there anyone who doesn't absolutely love Jackie Moore?" asked Mike Maddux, the Cardinals pitching coach and a former Moore pupil.

Moore's wife, Jo Ann, Houston Astros President Reid Ryan, Reid's dad, Nolan, and Jackie's two youngest sons, Jonathan and Spencer pulled off a near-impossible feat in baseball's chatty world. They assembled two hundred members of what Jo Ann calls "Jackie's extended baseball family" for a surprise party.

"Jackie Moore means the world to me," said former Astros' pitcher Chris Sampson.

"If Jackie told me to jump off a bridge," insisted former MLB pitcher Travis Driskill, "I'd find the nearest one soon as I could."

As baseball carried Jackie far away, his growth as a player, coach, and manager paralleled Houston's. In Jackie's youth, legendary freeway traffic didn't exist. No monolithic concrete, steel and glass office towers burst from its skyline. Three marked population explosions, and worldwide import as an

Jackie Moore managing the Round Rock Express.
(Photo courtesy of the Round Rock Express Baseball Club)

international city loomed in the future. The Houston Colt 45s, later the Astros, represented nothing but Judge Roy Hofheinz's unachieved dream.

"We had the Houston Buffs, the Cardinals team in the Texas League, that was our big leagues," laughs Moore. "We rode our bikes to that old park. We were members of the Buffs Knothole Gang, and the Buffs were our big-time heroes."

Names like Ken Boyer and Don Blasingame prepped in Houston for the bigs in the 1950s and loved visiting with kids like Jackie. He and his friends stayed together from Little League to high school.

"I pitched and played outfield," Moore said. "The American Legion coach needed a catcher, so I stepped in, and strapping on that gear increased my value to scouts interested in me."

After high school graduation, Jackie signed with the Detroit Tigers, playing his first campaign in rookie ball, then onto Triple A. Eight seasons later came his first MLB game—and what a debut! Say, Jackie, how about you catch twelve innings of a thirteen-inning marathon game with the Angels on Opening Day 1965?

"It dawned on me," remembered Moore, "I had found the end of the rainbow, achieving my dream. I was a *big-league player*. All those minor-league bus rides, all that hard work, made me realize my good fortune. A huge part of my life came together that day. Lives come together when dreams come true."

Ultimately, his MLB regular starting catcher dream never came true. Perennial All-Star catcher Bill Freehan had plenty of good years left in Detroit

"So, in 1967," lamented Moore, "I finished my playing career for the Red Sox Triple A team in Toronto, and when my bosses asked me if I'd like to manage the next season, I said 'Well heck yeah!'"

No death-defying, runaway carnival ride served up more twists, turns and sheer excitement than Jackie's coaching and managerial career. Successfully managing an A ball club led to a bullpen coaching job with MLB's Seattle Pilots. By spring training 1970, the Pilots headed elsewhere.

"As spring training ended," Jackie remembered, "new Milwaukee owners told equipment truck drivers leaving camp to call for directions a few hours down the road. When they

called, the owners told them 'steer northeast to Milwaukee.'
We went from Pilots to Brewers."

The land of beer and brats lasted three seasons then Jackie
changed again. His friend Whitey Herzog hired him in 1972 for
his first of five stints with the Rangers. The next season, Billy
Martin took over the Rangers and no surprise, all hell broke
loose. In June 1974, after a Rangers-Cleveland "10-Cent Beer
Night" Arlington Stadium melee, the clubs met a week later in
Cleveland, on the Indians' 10-Cent Beer Night!

"Our infielder Lenny Randle and some Cleveland players
teed it up in Arlington and that led to the first brawl," Moore
remembered. "We found out later a Cleveland radio shock
jock continually begged fans to come out and 'pay back the
Rangers.' They sure did."

After concessionaires sold an estimated sixty thousand cups
of beer, alcohol-addled young people intent on mayhem charged
the field. Fending off the drunken throng, Rangers right fielder
Jeff Borroughs clobbered a drunk who'd grabbed him as a riot
ensued.

"Billy Martin saw it," Moore remembers, "and he yelled to
his players 'hey, Jeff's in trouble, we gotta go get him, grab
some bats and let's go!'"

Cleveland players followed. In riot gear, police wielding
night sticks battled the mob, while escorting players to safety
in nearby dugouts.

"That mob was relentless," Moore continued. "They threw
anything they could find at us. One grabbed a steel bullpen
chair slamming a Cleveland relief pitcher over the head before
police could stop him. Fortunately, the pitcher wasn't seriously
injured; more fortunately, no one died."

The riot ended, but Jackie's whirling baseball carousel continued. Ending the 1976 season, the expansion Toronto Blue Jays' General Manager, and Jackie's friend, Pat Gillick, hired Moore to coach third base for manager Roy Hartsfield.

"Pat and I went back decades and had a Houston connection," Moore explained. "And what a ride this one turned out to be."

Moving into brand-new major-league territory in Toronto, while returning from road trips, Hartsfield, Moore, and the Blue Jays needed help. Canadian Customs agents had no idea they had a major-league team in Toronto.

"Agents asked us who we were and what our purpose was for being in Canada," Jackie laughed. "The question surprised us, and we said, 'We are members of the Toronto Blue Jays Major League Baseball team, and we play our home games right here in Toronto!"

"What is a Toronto Blue Jay?" the customs officer asked.

Toronto opened its first season in the old fairgrounds ballpark. They battled the White Sox, and since nothing happens easily on Opening Day, a driving snowstorm delayed the first pitch.

"Good thing they had Astroturf," Jackie laughed. "With snow and twenty-two degrees, a grass field would've been a mess. We won it on a three-run homer from our first baseman Doug Ault who became a fan favorite."

After a second stint in Texas, Moore joined his old friend Billy Martin in Oakland for the 1981 season as the A's first base coach.

"When Billy managed the A's," Jackie remembered, "Charley Finley had sold out to Levi Strauss, and they improved the organization. When Billy left, I became manager."

For two seasons, Moore's clubs struggled. Midway through the 1986 season, A's management handed him walking papers, but baseball pals came to the rescue, sending Jackie back to Canada in 1987, coaching third base for Montreal. Three seasons later, becoming Cincinnati's bench coach in a World's Championship season became a lifetime opportunity.

"That club had very special chemistry, coaches, players, and manager," Moore recalled. "Players fed off Manager Lou Pinella's tremendous energy, and it all came together. A lot of 'experts' predicted an Oakland sweep. What the Reds pulled off, in my opinion, was one of the biggest upsets in professional sports history, and we had fun making it happen.

After Cincinnati came another trip south to the Rangers. Then, Jackie went on to Colorado for three seasons coaching for Texas native Don Baylor, now managing the Rockies.

"Don's reputation as a fighter carried into the dugout," Moore remembered. "As a manager, while that fire remained, he fully realized his responsibility to all twenty-five players. [He] kept that fire under control, and players knew he was with them all the way."

Once the three Colorado seasons ended, and with Jackie's fiftieth year in professional baseball approaching, he faced the tough question: "do I stay or go?" He found himself conflicted.

"With all the managers I had," Moore remembered, "and all the opportunities I learned from, I had a lot to offer."

While mulling his next move, Jackie learned that his friend Nolan Ryan, Ryan's son Reid, and Houston financial expert Don Sanders put together a group buying the Double A Jackson (Mississippi) Generals in the Texas League and intended to move the club to the Austin area.

"They were gonna become the Astros Double-A affiliate in Round Rock, north of Austin," Moore remembers vividly. "So, the Ryans, and Jay Miller, who I knew as the Rangers ticket manager when I was there for the fourth time, wanted me to come look at it."

With thirty-seven years of Major League Baseball behind him, one of the last things Jackie wanted was long bus rides around Texas, Oklahoma, Louisiana, and Kansas.

"So, with the urging of my wife JoAnn, Jay, Nolan and his son Reid, I went down there," Moore grinned. "What they showed me was a big hole in the ground and I said, 'yessir, you got it started.'"

Skeptical, Moore tried talking himself out of dropping back two baseball levels as a manager. JoAnn knew before her husband did that Round Rock offered a perfect situation.

"I said, 'I'm gonna go one year, get it off the ground and then we're out.'" Moore said.

One year turned into eight. Jackie, his wife, and the entire Round Rock Express ownership, major- and minor-league officials and other experts could never have forecast:

- ◆ The biggest franchise opening in minor-league history.

- ◆ Obliteration of Texas League attendance records, attracting more than 650,000 rabid fans to Dell Diamond.

- ◆ A Texas League title in the Express' first year.

- ◆ Introduction of future MLB players like Roy Oswalt, Morgan Ensberg, Brad Lidge, Jason Lane, and Chris Burke to Round Rock fans.

"Add to that," beamed Moore. "We also moved up from Double A to Triple A after the first five seasons, and to this day Round Rock and its wonderful people remain so special to JoAnn, my family and me."

Former Astros General Manager Tim Purpura praised Jackie's presence and effect on young Astros prospects.

"First off, they had a chance to learn from a former major-league manager and fifty-year baseball veteran," Purpura noted. "That and the fact that Jackie related to those youngsters so very well really paved the way for them moving up."

Leaving the minors for good in 2008, Jackie returned to Houston as bench coach for manager Cecil Cooper. Three very successful Astros seasons later, back to the Rangers he went, for a fifth time, as Ron Washington's bench coach. Three straight Rangers playoff appearances and two World Series trips highlighted his final professional baseball stint.

"What a ride," he laughed, "and how fortunate am I to have spent most of my life around people I love in a game I love?"

To this day, Jackie Moore keeps in close touch with dozens of his former players and teammates.

"It's a people business," he smiles, "and it's all about the people in that dugout, the people in the front office and most especially those wonderful people in the stands who pay our salaries. And that's only a small part of why this game remains, despite its flaws, the best game ever!"

DEACON JONES

"Allow no one to take away your dream!"

RAISED IN GREENBURGH, New York, Grover "Deacon" Jones has been a mainstay in professional baseball for sixty-five years, playing, coaching, managing, and scouting. But the pain of his early years, cutting his professional teeth as a young black player amidst the ugliness and violence of the Jim Crow South, have stayed with him over the decades.

"When I think back on those days, I still hurt from fear and rejection," Jones vividly remembers. "My wife and I went through so very much. We came through some really, really, close calls."

Deacon Jones at a ceremony to retire his number with the
Sugar Land Skeeters, August 2019.
(Photo courtesy of the Sugar Land Space Cowboys)

During a road trip in Georgia in the early 1960s Deacon's minor-league White Sox teammates Jim Hicks and Don Buford (both black) joined white teammates in a roadside cafe. Sensing danger, the pair headed back to the bus. Deacon went inside for a soft drink, and while moving toward white teammates, trouble erupted.

"I heard the N-word growled loudly at me," he remembered. "It jarred my soul. Then I heard, 'I got a gun and will blow your goddamn head off if you don't get outta here.' It was the Devil himself."

Veteran manager Les Moss raced inside aiming to stop trouble. Moss told the gun-toting redneck the team wanted no trouble, then ordered his players back to the bus. Moss found Jones stunned.

"Next stop, I raced for the telephone," Deacon said.

Calling his folks in New York, Deacon's mom told him, "God will take care of you." His angered father grabbed the phone growling, "hey you finished crying?"

"Yes," came Deacon's reply.

His father continued gruffly, "I'm only saying this once, but you are to never allow any man or group of men to determine where you go in life or ruin your dream of playing in the big leagues. EVER!"

His dad slammed down the phone, and a dial tone came up.

"His words rocked my soul," Deacon whispered, "but I became a man that day. And I have often wondered what would've happened to me if I hadn't had parents who were such role models."

Later, Deacon's wife Tiki, and Buford's wife, Alescia, became great friends and followers of Dr. Martin Luther King, Jr., his Freedom Riders in the South, and his entire civil rights efforts.

"They came to the park in Savannah one Sunday afternoon," Deacon explained, "initially sitting in assigned, 'Colored Only' seats in the heat and sunshine. After a while we couldn't spot them, until we looked directly behind home plate in the shaded 'Whites Only' section, talking things over with the Savannah general manager."

Not knowing he'd encountered two rabid Rosa Parks followers, Tiki and Alescia, the GM listened as the wives expressed indignation over their seats in the sunshine and heat. Both told the GM, "Wives of the two best players should not be forced to sit in such."

"If you don't leave," replied the GM, "I'll lose advertisers and be forced to move from Savannah."

"Not our problem," the wives flatly stated, staying in the shade. Advertisers revolted, the Savannah club was forced to move, and NAACP members asked Tiki, Alescia, and their husbands to join their marches.

"They took care of the situation pretty well, I thought," Deacon grinned.

A star high school player in upstate New York, Jones later thrived at Ithaca College. Before Ithaca, he gained notoriety putting on a hitting show in an American Legion game pitting his New York-based team against a California Legion outfit starring future MLB infielder Billy Consolo and MLB Manager Sparky Anderson.

"I hit a grand slam homer in that game," Deacon remembers, "and I won American Legion Player of the Year, in 1951. The Yankees, Dodgers, and Giants had scouts there and Branch Rickey and Jackie Robinson were there too. Mr. Rickey invited me to a workout at Ebbets Field."

Working alongside Roy Campanella, Billy Cox, Duke Snider, and Carl Furillo excited the eighteen-year-old.

"Imagine me, a kid really, working out with those guys," Deacon beamed, "And when it ended, Jackie told me, 'Grover [his given name], I'm telling you, you will play in the big leagues someday.'"

Jones' American Legion Player of the Year trophy now sits in Baseball's Hall of Fame, making him technically the first black player honored by the Hall. After scouts from Pittsburgh, Philadelphia, and the White Sox showed interest, Chicago stepped up, inviting Deacon to a private tryout witnessed by owner Chuck Comiskey, Manager Marty Marion, and GM Frank Lane. Deacon's work blew 'em away.

"Lane said to me, 'Grover, we are not going to let you leave here without signing, so what do you want from us?'" Deacon remembered. "Keep in mind in those days if clubs offered more than a twenty grand bonus to any young player, rules required that player be kept on a major-league club's twenty-five-player main roster for a year, but there they were opening the coffers."

A youngster not worldly at age twenty-one and just out of college, Deacon reacted quickly.

"I told them I wanted seven thousand for my parents," Deacon smiled, "Marty Marion's brand new, brown-and-yellow convertible and twelve to fourteen grand for myself. They told me they'd bonus me four thousand up front, and the car, then I'd have to come to Chicago after my season ended to pick up the rest of the money.

"When my season ended in Waterloo, Iowa, hitting .318, I drove back to Chicago, picked up the cash, fourteen thousand dollars, then scared to death, drove as fast as I could to my parents' home in New York."

Returning from a severe shoulder injury the next season, Deacon played in a hundred games at Dubuque Iowa, slamming Midwest League (Single-A) pitching at a .409 clip, homering twenty-six times, while winning the Louisville Slugger Silver Bat award.

"I missed the next two seasons in the U.S. Army," Jones noted. "While I was playing Army baseball at Fort Benning, Georgia, the Executive Officer asked to have my Silver Bat sent to our base so troops could stage a full-battalion ceremony honoring what I did. I thought that was cool."

Deacon made his MLB debut with the White Sox in September 1962, coming up with a pinch-hit single in his first at bat against the Washington Senators.

"When I got to first," Deacon recalls, "Don Gutteridge, the coach, spewed a bunch of situational stuff, but I was so overwhelmed by the size of the crowd, the ballpark itself, and the noise, I was scared to death."

Back and forth between Triple A and MLB over the next few years, Deacon and his friend Don Buford played winter ball together in Venezuela and Puerto Rico. Two of those seasons in Puerto Rico featured Pirates future Hall of Famer Roberto Clemente.

"Bobby, we called him," Jones laughed. "If you think Latin American ballparks are loud as hell, which they are, when Clemente played you couldn't hear yourself think, the noise was so deafening."

And Clemente loved strategy. Before a Deacon Jones at bat, "Bobby" whispered, "Hey, Jonesy, you get on, you run first pitch."

"I got a single, then three times the pitcher threw to first, disrupting Bobby's timing." Jones laughed. "Next pitch, I took off, Clemente tomahawked a line drive to center, and I scored the winning run after running through the manager's stop sign."

After an hour celebrating the win with fans, "Bobby" came back to the clubhouse saying, "Hey, Jonesy, I said run first pitch, next time you run first pitch, will work out better."

"I wasn't so sure about that," Deacon said, "Les Moss [the manager] already chewed my ass for running through his stop sign and the only way I saved myself was telling him, well hell, I scored the winning run."

Back in the states, along the minor-league trail in the Atlanta airport, Deacon and Jackie Robinson reconnected.

"I reminded him who I was, and about the Dodgers tryout camp," Deacon beamed. "He asked if I went to college, and I said yes and told him I was in Triple A with the White Sox. His response? Jackie said, 'I am so proud of you.' That man literally gave his life so I could play, and he openly re-ordered American societal consciousness. That's profoundly earth moving."

Jones went on to coach MLB hitters in Houston and San Diego. One of his pupils, future Hall of Famer Tony Gwinn, in a tight game at Dodgers Stadium learned a Deacon Jones lesson.

"I asked Tony to give me one pitch in his next at bat, and look for a fastball middle in," Jones explained. "Tony said okay, and I said, 'you're up first in the top of the ninth against Valenzuela, really turn it loose and see what happens.'"

As Deacon predicted, Valenzuela delivered a fastball mid-dle-in on the first pitch, Gwinn unloaded a tremendous drive to the Dodger Stadium Pavilion, tying the game at one apiece.

"You snowed me," Gwinn laughed at Deacon. "It's almost as if you knew what was coming."

"Think about it for a moment," came Deacon's response. "Valenzuela's got great command, in a tight game [he] wants to get ahead in the count and doesn't believe you can pull one aimed at your hands. He did what I thought, you did what I thought you'd do!"

At age eighty-seven, Deacon Jones' baseball career continues as a special assistant for the Astros Triple A team in Sugar Land, outside Houston. Friends frequently ask him why he still works.

"My quick response is [that] I was with the Astros and remain loyal and I get a charge out of watching these kids at Triple A growing into major-leaguers," Jones said. "Plus, minor-league baseball is fun, and fans enjoy the atmosphere at our park."

Baseball lifer he is, Deacon insists MLB should be more active in telling its story to young black athletes. MLB he says, should:

- Tell every young black athlete MLB doesn't have the catastrophic injury problem football has

- Tell them MLB offers longer careers, better pensions, and insurance programs than any other sport

- Remind young black athletes failure is okay

"Hall of Famers failed a lot," he points out. "We've gone too far teaching kids not to fail. We all fail and always will."

One more thing: Major League Baseball should tell the Deacon Jones story, and the stories of others who battled Jim Crow, battled racial hatred and bigotry and still succeeded as major-league players. It's a history lesson not only for current and potential players, but a lesson for us all.

JACK MCKEON

"Trader Jack, and the gifts that keep on giving...."

Jack McKeon, who, at age ninety-one, still serves as a baseball consultant, instantly commands respect in any room he enters.

"All eyes and ears are on him," said Jay Robertson, the special assistant to the Washington Nationals general manager. "He's had so much success and he's done it all from the ground up: player, coach, scout, manager, general manager—it doesn't matter, he's been successful."

As we begin our discussion highlighting Hall of Famer "Trader Jack" McKeon, let's take our own private honesty test. Please examine your conscience and answer truthfully.

- With professional baseball scouts knocking down your door, and your father insisting you must go to college first, would you go on to college, then "pray twice a day to the Blessed Virgin Mary" that your baseball dream comes true?

- Once in pro ball and realizing after a handful of seasons you wouldn't hit enough to play major-league ball, would you then become a player-manager, honing your managerial skills, keeping that MLB dream alive? "Ah, hell," McKeon laughed, "I hit .300. I was a switch hitter, and I hit .150 from *both sides!*"

- Would you have continued after three separate times being promised jobs, only to be told when you arrived at spring training that, "sorry, a mistake has been made and we have no job for you," or that the league you were headed for had folded up shop?

♦ Would you have been willing, in your off-seasons, not only to work an almost countless list of jobs—including cop, basketball referee, the night shift at a hosiery factory, TV and refrigerator salesman, drive-in restaurant owner, taxicab driver, and mechanic—just to make ends meet? But not only that, would you continue work to finish your college degree, a promise you made to your father if he'd allow you to sign a pro contract?

♦ Would you have had the persistence to continue if the legendary Branch Rickey refused to hire you for your first manager's job, insisting instead that you finish your college degree first?

♦ Would you have the patience and resilience to battle through the twenty plus years of hard times and hanging in long enough to achieve your dream of managing a big league team at age forty-two, continue bouncing up and down between MLB and the minors, before, at the advanced age of seventy-three, winning a World Series for the first time with the 2003 Florida Marlins and then, eight years later, sign on as interim manager for the Florida club?

♦ Would you, at age eighty-eight, after all you accomplished in the game, sign a deal giving you the title of senior adviser to the general manager of the Washington Nationals?

The above provides a mere skeleton of Jack McKeon's prolific baseball life. Jack McKeon stands way beyond special and a Hall of Famer in the annals of baseball's lifetime grinders.

Jack McKeon, left, with son Kasey.
(Photo courtesy of Jack McKeon)

"I didn't know any other way," McKeon said. "I always knew I loved this game and vowed to stay in it."

Imagine today's young players, with the advantages they have, racking up millions of miles of ten- or twelve-hour rides on non-air-conditioned buses, playing for rock-bottom pay on teams with rosters so small (sometimes as few as seventeen players) that players were sometimes forced to play with pulled muscles, broken fingers or ribs, or open cuts simply because they had no one else to fill in? In fact, one of McKeon's rugged seasons almost concluded disastrously. After suffering a serious knee injury and changing his minor-league team's paid-for train ticket home, McKeon took a different train and arrived home safely. The train his initial reservation was on exploded coming into the train station, killing thirty-three passengers. Such was life in the minor leagues for Jack McKeon, and so many others of his ballplaying generation.

"Ah hell," he laughs, "All those years spent in the minors were worth it. I set the goal of managing in the big leagues by age forty-four or I was done. Fortunately, I made it two years before."

We'll talk about McKeon's Magical, Mystical Major-League Managerial ride later, but for now as we examine his extremely lengthy baseball life, his incredible journey proves beyond a shadow of a doubt the assertion made by my grandfather years ago that "these lifetime baseball guys are the engine driving baseball's bus."

Quite simply, Jack McKeon represents the epitome of a baseball lifer:

> He allowed no injury, no release, no disappointment of any kind, to temper his fire and passion to succeed. He played, managed, or occupied front offices over an astounding eight decades. The ups and downs, wins and losses, disappointments, and victories he's experienced would've tested the most patient monk or mystic. His refusal to buckle, to give in, or quit, as he pursued his dream stands as a testament to an ironclad will and hard-headed Irish determination.

"This game is so much of who I am," McKeon smiled.

His wife of sixty-six years, Carol, has been right alongside most of the way. The two met while Jack spent several seasons rotating between teams in North Carolina and states as far away as Montana.

"I am so fortunate to have a wife who understands the lifestyle of baseball people," McKeon smiles. "Carol got it from the start. And she passed it on. Once, I told my daughter Kristy to never marry a baseball player. Well, she did—former MLB pitcher Greg Booker. Unfortunately, we lost him several years ago, and were lucky to have had him. But my wife has her own life when I'm gone, and she's done so well."

Most people, by the time they've reached ninety-one and have had a long and satisfying career might decide to slow down. Not McKeon, the ultimate grinder. He still loves baseball so much he can't give it up.

"He's been down a lot of roads, playing, managing and being a general manager," said his son, Kasey, who's the Nationals' director of player personnel. "When he sits down, he's one of us."

At first sight McKeon stands as the youngest looking, fastest talking, most passionate ninety-one-year-old baseball lifer you'll ever meet. Blessed with a striking presence, the McKeon aura includes a tanned, grizzled baseball face, topped off with a glint of mischief in his eyes. Of course, McKeon enhances the presence package, chewing his omnipresent cigar, lighting up everyone around him with a caustic wit, sometimes bizarre sense of humor, and rapid-fire takes and stories. "Trader Jack" spins hundreds of intriguing, sometimes profanely funny baseball tales, especially around his fellow Washington Nationals front-office staff.

"He has special gifts as a leader," said Jay Robertson, the Nationals executive. "He's done it his way, and the Nationals brass and a lot of other baseball people know Jack McKeon did what he did in this game—always, *always* for the good of the team and not himself."

Robertson admits he and fellow National staffers find themselves addicted to McKeon's stories. It's not just memories of his

World Championship 2003 season with the Marlins or tales of becoming the oldest manager ever to win a World Series. His much younger counterparts want to hear his "road stories" about twenty-plus years in the minors and the rugged conditions from bus rides and less-than-adequate places to sleep at night.

"We just shake our heads in disbelief," laughs Robertson. "Look at it this way, when I played forty-plus years ago, we had occasional road trips or bus rides or hotels that were tough, but the stories Jack tells, my God, they make our eyes bug out and forty-year-olds in our group simply shake their heads in disbelief!"

Always known in baseball circles as a man who could pick out talent others missed, McKeon retains that special eye.

"It absolutely is special," says former Nationals Executive Terry Wetzel. "He's just gifted with an incredible knack for seeing potential in players. To watch him is amazing. He loves to walk away from the group, maybe rest his arms on the top of a chain link fence, or whatever and just watch, just take his time and look. I think he sees things differently than a lot of guys, but at the end of the day, he knows who can and cannot play."

"I didn't always know exactly what it was I saw in players, but sometimes I just had a feeling," McKeon said. "I always believed in and had faith in my players. It was all about them. And then I work my ass off to make 'em better. It was all about them."

But perhaps McKeon's greatest talent is how he relates to players and front office staff, no matter their age. He stands as a bridge from baseball generation to generation.

"Jack knows no hierarchy," marvels Robertson. "He knows what all these young people we have are going through—scouts, front office staff, player personnel staff—because he's been there and can relate. He'll just pull up a chair with a younger staff member and say, 'let's sit down and talk about it,' and when he talks it's always about the other guy and not Jack McKeon."

Robertson especially enjoys listening to the passion McKeon retains in discussions with other Nationals staffers concerning players.

"Now, if he debates with us, we know where he stands," Robertson insists. "There's no doubt about that. But if you're in a debate with him, you better come to the party with a stout belief in your position. You have to strongly state your case and maintain it. If he feels you're cowering or unable to defend yourself, forget it."

He got the moniker "Trader Jack" from overseeing more than twenty-five different trades, involving 120 or so players, during his wild and wooly general manager days with the San Diego Padres, where he once traded future Hall of Famer Ozzie Smith (living to tell and laugh about it later). During those Padres years, he also played a dual role as San Diego's manager and general manager. While "Trader Jack" became McKeon's calling card, if you had nicknamed him "Intrepid," "Relentless," or "Maniacal," those labels would've also fit like a glove.

McKeon and his brother, who later became a player in the Braves minor-league system, were raised in South Amboy, New Jersey, a town of 9,000 along the Raritan River near the concrete ribbon called the New Jersey Turnpike. Their father, Bill McKeon, who owned and operated a garage and taxi service, raised his boys with a relentless work ethic.

"We watched how hard he worked, how much his business meant to him," Jack said quietly. "And the impact he made on us was so huge, especially when he created a Boys Club there in South Amboy. When he did that, he opened our eyes to a whole new world."

The new Boys Club meant every kid from South Amboy who had ever dreamed of one day playing baseball now had the chance.

"My dad loved baseball so much," McKeon remembered, "that he wanted my brother and me and all our friends to have a place to play. That Boys Club turned out to be a dream come true for all of us."

In so many ways the Boys Club launched Jack McKeon on a lifetime journey. Not only did he become a first-rate catcher for the Boys Club and his local high school, but he also became a manager for the first time at age fourteen.

"My dad turned me loose," he laughed, "to find and recruit players, build the team, make out lineups, and run the game as I caught it."

With the advent of his manager's job, Jack McKeon in essence owned a road map that, unbeknownst to him at the time, paved a path to an eight-decade career. By the time he entered his sophomore year, Jack McKeon's baseball enthusiasm and light beamed brightly, and it did the same for almost a dozen of his friends and teammates. While major-league scouts tracked his development as a catcher and leader, they also found other prizes on the South Amboy squad. Of the fifteen players on his high school team, ten, including his brother, Bill, Jr., played professionally. Three made it to the big leagues.

"We had a lot of excitement and a lot of inspiration to do well," McKeon grinned. "Our idol was a South Amboy guy named Allie Clark who played seven years in the big leagues for the Yankees, Indians, Philadelphia A's, and Chicago White Sox. He gave us the idea that we could do it, that we could play professionally. We thought everything Allie did, including his service in World War II, was great. Plus, we had a lot of guys who really loved it and would do anything it took to improve. That made for some really good times."

An All-State catcher in New Jersey his senior season, professional baseball stood as Jack McKeon's biggest dream. Scouts who'd been watching McKeon and his teammates in South Amboy began showing up, becoming more serious about signing McKeon after hearing about the young catcher and the overall talent pool in South Amboy. Proud father that he was, Bill McKeon loved watching his sons grow up playing baseball. He also took great joy watching scouts observe his sons. Jack had several teams ready to sign him after his senior year ended. Oddly, Bill McKeon wanted young Jack and his brother to go to college instead of signing a contract with a major-league team.

"His reason," McKeon said, "was because he didn't want us to have to work as hard as he did all his life."

So, devoted son and Catholic, Jack McKeon obeyed his father's wishes. Much to his own consternation and that of several professional scouts, he headed to College of the Holy Cross in Worcester, Massachusetts, where he played for a former major-league infielder, Jack Barry. McKeon's body may have been at Holy Cross, but his heart, mind, and soul were already in professional baseball.

"Every single night after dinner," he remembers with a huge smile on his face, "I would stop at the Shrine of the Blessed Virgin Mary and pray that she would talk to the Good Lord and help me convince my father to let me sign [a professional contract.] When I came back home for Christmas vacation, the scouts came back to see me and my father."

Young Jack's prayers obviously were heard in heaven and relayed to earth.

"My father asked me, 'you really want to sign, right?'" McKeon vividly remembers, "and I said, 'yes,' and he said, 'well, okay but you have to promise me you will finish your degree, okay?' I promised, I signed with the Pirates and off I went."

Several years into his professional career, Jack honored his father's wishes, completing his degree at Elon College in North Carolina. The fact McKeon hadn't finished his college degree actually kept him from leaving the player-manager ranks and becoming a full-time manager.

"Well, with the work ethic he gave us, and the promise I made him that I'd get my degree," McKeon laughed, "I was not about to let him down. It took some hard work and balancing things in the offseason, but I got it done."

Here's how this incredibly blessed man armed with rock ribbed, concrete determination blazed his personal path to Major League Baseball.

Let's start with the hundreds of thousands of miles Jack McKeon travelled in his minor-league playing career, then switching to player-manager six years into his career at such out-posts and long-gone leagues as, the Alabama State, Interstate, Western Association, Three-I, and Canadian-American. He moved among cities like Greenville, Alabama; York, Pennsylvania; Hutchinson, Kansas; Burlington and Fayetteville, North Carolina; Missoula, Montana; Dallas-Fort Worth; Atlanta; and Richmond. Throughout his seventeen years, managing and as a player-manager in the minor leagues, McKeon's teams won.

"I still call my biggest managerial break the four years I spent in Omaha as manager of the Triple A Royals," McKeon said.

"Those were great young teams full of up-and-coming stars like hard throwing righty Steve Busby, lefty Paul Splittorff, speedy outfielder Amos Otis, future Hall of Famer George Brett, and power hitting first baseman John Mayberry—guys I managed later with the Kansas City Royals. My ego simply wasn't just winning the American Association Championship while I was in Omaha. I was all about developing championship players for the Kansas City Royals."

Royals ownership and front office brass watched McKeon's player development success, and in 1973, after twenty-six minor league seasons, he became the Royals' manager.

McKeon's first Royals club, led by the same "kids" he managed in Omaha, put on a show during his first season. Busby pitched the first no-hit game in Royals' history against the Tigers in late April. Splittorff won twenty games that year, and Otis hit .300. Otis, Mayberry, and Brett, a rookie who went on to a Hall of Fame career, later played on Kansas City teams that made the American League playoffs seven times between 1976 and 1985. McKeon didn't get to enjoy those years. After the 1975 season, the Royals released him, and he went back to the minor leagues to keep managing. Did the drop to a level below the big leagues bother him?

"No sir, not at all," he said intently. "I managed for the Braves at their Triple A spot, Richmond. My whole deal with that was, hey, I need to stay busy managing, at least at the Triple A level so I'd be ready when a big-league manager's spot came open. A lot of guys don't want to go down, but I didn't mind. Working at Triple A kept me learning and kept me sharp."

By the time the 1977 season rolled around, the Oakland A's picked him up for parts of two seasons, but by 1979, McKeon was back in the minors. This time it was Denver in the American Association, the Triple-A affiliate of the Montreal Expos.

The stories of seventy-one years of professional baseball adventures, from Miami to Missoula, from Burlington to San Diego, from Dallas-Fort Worth to Denver, and from Arecibo and Vancouver to Kansas City and Cincinnati, astound all those around him.

"When I was managing the Twins Triple-A affiliate in Dallas-Fort Worth in 1963," McKeon remembers, "I had Tony Oliva there. What a talent. A St. Paul newspaperman asked me, 'can Oliva play?' I said, 'hell, yes, he can play. Now, I can't promise he'll hit over .300 in the big leagues, though. Well, damned if he doesn't spend his rookie year leading the AL in hits with 217, hit thirty-two home runs while hitting .323 and winning the American League Batting Championship in 1964. How about that?"

Not only did Oliva repeat the AL Batting Championship the following year, he did it again in 1971.

Then there's the story of pitcher Lee Stange.

"Lee had a lot of trouble early in his career, struggled a bit in parts of two seasons with the Twins," McKeon said. "In '63, they started him in Minnesota, then sent him to me in Texas. He got to the clubhouse at five p.m. after driving seven hundred-plus miles and he said, 'Skip, I'm worn out. Gimme a day.' I couldn't. So, he pitched and lost. Then four days later he was ready and won his next ten straight. Best pitcher in the league, and back to Minnesota he goes, and pitches well. Writers ask, 'what did ya do to turn him around?' I said, I just gave him the damned ball every four days and told him to win."

McKeon believed so deeply in Stange that he hired Stange as his pitching coach in Oakland.

"One more pitcher story," he said happily. "I had seventeen-year-old—Jim Kaat, the tall, slender lefty—in the minor leagues. Everyone got scared when he threw 251 innings, pitching at age seventeen on a full season professional team that only carried seventeen players. Writers said, 'Come on McKeon, you'll wear out his arm.' Well, his arm wore out after twenty-five years, so I guess those 251 innings as a seventeen-year-old didn't hurt him much."

One of the best television baseball analysts of our time, after his 283 major-league wins, Jim Kaat deserves a place in Baseball's Hall of Fame.

McKeon has trouble remembering where he latched onto that first real managing job, perhaps because Jack had so much success in the dual role of player and manager.

"I was asked to take over the Fayetteville, North Carolina, club in 1955," he said, "and as player manager I took them from last place to first. They had a veteran club and I caught and managed guys who were much older than me."

For the next three years, McKeon took his catching-managing road show to Missoula, Montana, and found that the club had lost its minor-league affiliation. Not only did McKeon catch and manage for Missoula, but because he had only two players under contract, he became general manager and chief scout, building the club from the ground up.

"When I came home to South Amboy, New Jersey, sometimes in the off season," Jack said proudly, "I'd run into friends of my folks and they'd tell me how proud they were of my baseball success, and that really charged me up, and it kept me battling."

Son Kasey followed his dad's path into professional baseball as a light-hitting catcher, and now, as the Nationals' scouting director, he remains amazed at his father's absolute immersion in baseball for more than seventy years.

"After all these years, the names and situations he remembers are incredible," marvels the younger McKeon. "All the way back to his first season. Think about it. He's been around thousands and thousands of players, hundreds of thousands of game situations, and they're all clear as a bell to him."

But the determination and tenacity instilled in Jack by his father is still with him.

"My whole deal has always been my work ethic," McKeon said. "Very simply, I sold myself to baseball brass, I sold them my work ethic. I did it my way, and I think that has to be my legacy, and I want to be remembered by people who say, 'Jack did it his way!'"

Perhaps his son Kasey sums up best, his father's magnificent, life-altering, baseball marathon extravaganza.

"I just don't completely know how to put all this in words," the younger McKeon said. "But I truly believe he deserved everything good that's happened to him. He's worked hard his whole life; years and years in the lower minors, always believing, never giving up hope. My dad had the ultimate will to succeed and never had one thing handed to him."

Perfectly stated, from the heart of a son who received his baseball baptismal from a father who immersed himself in baseball, and in its people. A man who, for the whole of his life, set the iron-clad example that passion, fire, and dogged determination always sets the stage for excellence.

DR. TOM HOUSE

The good doctor is in!

S EATED IN THE DUGOUT, Texas Rangers Manager Bobby Valentine and Pitching Coach Tom House watched intently as future Hall of Famer Nolan Ryan, unlike most times in his career, struggled mightily against the Cleveland Indians.

"Bobby told me," House grinned, "Hey, go out there and check him out. And I said, 'Me, why me?' Bobby continued, insisting, 'you're the pitching coach,' so out I went."

The visit lasted mere seconds, and back came House much faster than he went out, after a conversation between Pitching Coach and future Hall of Famer went something like:

House: "Hey Nolan, how's it going?"

Nolan: "What're you doin' out here?"

House: "Just worried about you, how you feelin'?"

Nolan: "Terrible, but I'm better 'n what you got warmin' in the pen now, get outta here!"

House: "Uh, gurgle, okay."

Yikes.

Breathing a sigh of relief that a brutal murder had not occurred on "Nolan's bleeping mound," the shellshocked House sauntered back to the dugout. So, later in the game with no improvement, Valentine himself popped out of the dugout, ostensibly to remove Ryan from the game. He thought.

Valentine: "Nolan, how you doin?"

Nolan: "Bobby, leave me alone, and listen, one of us is gonna leave this mound and it ain't gonna be me."

Valentine: "Uh, okay, Nolan.

And off Valentine trotted, back to the dugout, and sat himself once again, beside his pitching coach. A few quietly uncomfortable moments later, Valentine broke the silence.

"Tom, I'm telling you now," Valentine winced, "we gotta come up with a better plan."

The two did, indeed, develop a better plan. From Day One, Ryan embraced House's "radical for the times" workout schemes, including throwing a football before games (an unheard of and much-ridiculed exercise for pitchers in those days), functional weight training, biomechanics, and postgame cardio. Those practices often labeled House as heretic, but not with Ryan. During his Hall of Fame speech in July of 1999, Ryan praised his former pitching coach.

"I'm fortunate to have my Rangers pitching coach, Tom House here," Ryan told the crowd assembled in Cooperstown. "He was always on the cutting edge, and with Tom pushing me, I think I got into the best shape of my life when I was with the Rangers."

Fair to say that at age forty-six when he retired, Ryan did in fact benefit from House's coaching techniques.

"We were shooting from the hip," House grinned. "Nolan was willing to try new stuff. He bought into what we were doing, and at that point this was all new and criticized by old school scouts and pitching coaches. Look at how long he played; twenty-seven years total, the last five seasons, from age forty-two to forty-six, with the Rangers. That's almost unheard of."

House strongly believes his plan would not have worked if Valentine and Rangers General Manager Tom Grieve refused to buy in completely.

"Look, Nolan Ryan would've been a Hall of Famer," House said, "without me ever showing up. What I did for Nolan helped lengthen his shelf life."

While Hall of Famer Ryan certainly benefited from House's training regimen, he wasn't by himself. Other Rangers pitchers in that era also bought in.

"Jamie Moyer, Bobby Witt, Darren Oliver, Mitch Williams," noted House, "pitched well into their forties. Remember in those days, average MLB pitchers retired between thirty-three and thirty-six. We had eight Texas Rangers who retired after their fortieth birthdays."

An eight-year veteran MLB pitcher, pitching twelve professional seasons, House began his upward trek by pitching for legendary University of Southern California coach Rod Dedeaux, including one season alongside future Hall of Famer Tom Seaver. Fifteen of House's twenty-five teammates, including Seaver, Dave Kingman, Steve Busby, and Bill Lee, ultimately made it to the big leagues.

"There I was throwing 82-83 tops, and striking out guys with curve balls," House recalls. "But there I stood next to a big old workhouse like Seaver and other guys who could throw tomatoes through locomotives at 93 or 94 miles an hour. I said to Coach Dedeaux 'well, if you're looking for me to do *that*, I can't do it."

Dedeaux, perhaps the best college baseball coach of all time, won twelve National Championships in his tenure at USC, told House, "Son, you're not that guy, and I want you to worry about being yourself, and I will be responsible for making it all work."

The Atlanta Braves drafted House in the third round in 1967. Making his MLB debut in 1971, his best year came in 1974.

Pitching out of the Braves bullpen, Tom sported a 6-2 record in fifty-six National League appearances in 103 innings pitched, with an incredible WHIP of 0.98.

"Dan Frisella went down, and the [closer's role] fell into my lap," House said modestly. "I was an innings eater, a slightly below average major-league pitcher. What I was most proud of that year was that I was given the opportunity and took advantage of it."

Always looking for the edge, House succeeded in doing the little things.

"I had an excellent move to first base," he said. "I always held runners close, and I picked off a lot of runners. Always doing things by analytics, I knew holding runners close increases double play chances."

Perhaps the personal highlight of 1974 for House came on Atlanta's opening night on April 8 at Fulton County Stadium. House's teammate, Hank Aaron, needed a single home run to break Babe Ruth's all-time home run record.

"In the bullpen we drew straws," House told MLB-TV, "to see which ten-yard space in the bullpen we'd get. And we promised to respect the territory of others."

Aaron smoked a pitch from Dodgers' lefty Al Downing into the Braves bullpen for his record-breaking home run. House made the catch. He told MLB-TV he remembers almost nothing until he arrived at home plate with the baseball for Aaron.

"I've said it a lot that the good news is that [catching Aaron's record homer] was the highlight of my career," he laughed. "I've also said that the bad news was it was the highlight of my career."

Once his MLB playing career ended, House headed back to USC, earning a bachelor's degree, an MBA, a master's and a doctorate in Sports Psychology from Alliant University.

"When I finished playing, I signed a ten-year deal with USC to be their pitching coach for five years and [to be] a researchist for the entire ten," House told GQ Sports.

Besides USC, House also served as MLB pitching coach for the Texas Rangers and San Diego Padres in the U.S. and the Chunichi Dragons and Chiba Lotte Marines in Japan, furthering his experience and research. But it was at USC where he applied exact science to the experience as a professional pitcher to using exact science.

"I simply had to know why," he told GQ Sports. "I wanted to provide help and not some opinion from what we did in my generation. I think we've succeeded."

Now known as "The Father of Modern Pitching," House uses a variety of means to connect with youngsters from age fourteen through the professional ranks. Nationwide pitching clinics and camps at his southern California research center set the stage. Pitchers, quarterbacks, golfers, and tennis, volleyball, and even cricket players have benefitted. The process analyzes timing, sequencing, and mechanics, as well as the movement of hips, shoulders, and arms. It also includes nutritional, mental, and emotional training, combined with personalized data.

"We're not guessing," he told GQ Sports. "We're operating from science."

Terms like "exit velocity," although relatively new in current baseball parlance, have been a part of House's vocabulary for forty years. As has his digital-age equipment, including high-speed cameras, recording an athlete's movement at up to one thousand frames per second, enabling House and his staff to show each pitcher, quarterback, or other athlete exactly what's happening in their delivery step by step.

"It's not what we think and see," he insists. "It's what's actually being done."

"Old school pitching coaches and managers," House told Fangraphs, "knew what, but didn't know why."

MLB pitchers like Randy Johnson, Nolan Ryan, and hundreds more came to House for help, along with broken-down minor leaguers trying to stage comebacks, MLB wannabes; collegiate pitchers looking for an edge in catching the attention of MLB scouts, and scores of high school athletes hoping for college offers.

"We can tell you what you are today," House told The Guardian. "And if you do this with legs, torso, and arms, we can tell you in six to twelve weeks how hard you'll be throwing."

The six-foot, ten-inch-tall Hall of Famer Randy Johnson, pitching for the Mariners in 1992, struggled mightily with walks. A quick visit with House, then pitching coach for Ryan and the Rangers, provided the remedy.

"It was a simple solution," House said. "Instead of landing on his heel, we had Randy adjust and land on the ball of his foot. It obviously worked."

Instead of fearing being sent down to Triple A, Johnson and his overpowering fastball overcame the walk problem, and he became a Hall of Famer in 2015. While baseball remains House's lifeblood, football entered his stratosphere working with then-San Diego Chargers quarterback Drew Brees. Brees' injured shoulder, rebuilt by veteran sports surgeon Dr. James Andrews, would have shelved most quarterbacks, the doctor said.

"One of the reasons [Brees] has been able to maintain success," Dr. Andrews told 'En Fuego', "are the exercises Tom House has him on."

Over the course of his twenty-year career, Brees remained a constant devotee of House's approach. Another sure-fire football Hall of Famer, Tom Brady, follows House's umbrella approach as well.

"We have," House noted, "dealt with twenty-eight of thirty-two NFL quarterbacks, 100-plus from the collegiate ranks, and hundreds from high school."

Enter the newest Tom House array of teaching tools, The Mustard app. Via cell phone, subscribers maintain access to House's seemingly endless knowledge. Mustard followers first learn how to record pitching motion videos to be critiqued by House and his staff.

"[We put] training information," Tom told Fan Nation, "into the hands of anyone who wants it. Anyone with a phone has the ability to get the same information and instruction we give in person."

Motion analysis, an important part of House's training since the 1980s, and the use of artificial intelligence provides important tips, feedback, and improvement drills. House and his Mustard staff also provide sleep and nutritional advice as well as mental and emotional assessment. Mustard equals digital-aged coaching, all aimed at three goals: "Inform. Instruct. Inspire."

"This is just like having Coach House with me every day," said a Miami Marlins draft choice on the Mustard website.

Critics still exist, of course. But from after more than fifty years in and around major-league Baseball, from his work, research, and analysis through the National Pitching Association to his new Mustard app, Tom House experienced runaway success. Mustard app's website indicates: a thousand MLB pitchers and seventy-one NFL quarterbacks have used his services. House's reasons for the creation of Mustard go much further than simply teaching optimal ways of becoming MLB pitchers or NFL quarterbacks.

"Most kids," he told Fan Nation, "stop playing sports at age fourteen, 80 percent of them. Mustard can allow kids to play longer, getting the same information as elite athletes, keeping them more involved. Kids just need to play and develop their mind and body."

Since his days as Texas Rangers pitching coach, using footballs to warm up pitchers and position players, opinions and criticism have rolled easily off Tom House's back. With what he's accomplished, it's easy to call his work and pursuits of athletic and mental excellence, "revolutionary" or "legendary." While those terms obviously fit the Good Doctor, he's far more self-effacing, far more likely to conclude, in a humorous tone, far removed from 3-D motion analysis, and life at a thousand frames a second with the following:

> "I've often thought of myself as the Forrest Gump of baseball, stumbling into things without having any clue why."

Truth to tell, he knows why his theories and practices work. He has science on his side to prove it.

CHAPTER 3

JERRY REUSS

"Bring in the Right-Hander"

SELF-ASSURED, iron-willed, and cocky since his elementary school days in Ritenour, Missouri, Jerry Reuss told his brother, "I'm gonna pitch in the major leagues." His brother's skeptical response was "The odds are a million to one!" "Maybe," Jerry recounted in his autobiography, "but I'll be that one!"

"Cocky, yes," remembered Reuss, "but I wasn't about to let anything or anybody stand in the way of my dreams."

Decades past retirement he still looks the part. The veteran lefty lights it up with a lean, athletic look, a miles-wide smile, and a positive attitude. Vigorous exercise, regular rounds of golf, and a lengthy, happy marriage keep it all intact. An outrageously edgy sense of humor propels him to action during any boring party. Reuss retains wackiness yet remains deadly serious about his life's passions.

"Work hard and play harder. That's what I've always believed," he said.

A relentless work ethic won constant battles against arm and leg injuries, career peaks and valleys and clashes with front offices. In twenty-two seasons pitching for eight different MLB teams, Reuss:

◆ Won 220 games

◆ Was one of only two 200-game winners who never won twenty in a season

◆ Pitched one of the most notable no-hitters in MLB history

◆ Threw a total of twenty-nine complete games over two seasons while playing for the Pittsburgh Pirates

◆ Threw a career high six shutouts in 1980

◆ Battled arm injuries for the last five years of his career, which included trips to the bullpen and journeys to new teams

◆ At age forty-one, after twenty-one big league seasons, pitched in amateur ball, auditioning for MLB scouts in an effort to "end my career on my own terms."

◆ Broadcast MLB games on ESPN, and for the Angels and Dodgers as well as minor-league baseball in Las Vegas

◆ Spent five seasons as minor-league pitching coach for the Chicago Cubs

Jerry learned the game from his older brother, Jim, who "took me out to the backyard to play ball for the first time and was

Jerry Reuss.
(Photo by Mike Kee Photo)

surprised that I batted and threw left-handed." Jerry constantly watched his big brother's baseball exploits, dreaming he'd be that good or better.

"Because I was bigger than most of the other kids," Reuss says, "and could throw harder, I had early success on the mound."

His first trip to Busch Stadium opened his eyes with its "sheer electricity." Frenetic workers scurrying through the concourse added another spark. Vendors, concessionaires, cleaning crews, the smells of popcorn, beer, and hot dogs upped the excitement Eyeing Busch Stadium's emerald playing surface provided "a profound sense of belonging, and bluest sky you ever saw,"

Reuss remembers. "The green pavilion roof shaded the right field seats, and a red cinder warning track surrounded the field. Players were busy hitting, fielding grounders or chasing fly balls. Right then I knew *I had to play!*"

Later, as a strapping six-foot freshman at Ritenour High, Jerry attracted attention. Former minor-leaguer turned-American-Legion coach John Ailworth watched Ritenour games, then invited Reuss to his team's tryout. Jerry made Ailworth's exceptional Legion team as its youngest player, much to the anger of some parents.

"Playing against players four or five years older always worked in my favor," Reuss mused.

Ailworth told disgruntled parents Jerry belonged because he had a "real chance" for a professional career. Reuss pitched his way onto an excellent Junior Varsity team his freshman year, and those JVs grew up, winning the 1966 and 1967 Missouri State Baseball Championships. Coach Lee Englert set a high bar.

"I talked frankly about goals and communication with coaches, fellow players, family, and friends," Englert said. "We also talked about loyalty to each other, families, country, and to the Good Lord."

At the end of every practice, Ritenour pitchers ran up and down an extremely steep hill nearby. An all-out sprint to the top and a backward jog downhill six times was a workout that strengthened legs, limbs, lungs, and back, providing an ironclad will to win. On a cold rainy afternoon while Jerry maniacally sprinted hills, a group of his friends stopped and made fun of his "work." Reuss' prophetic reply ended the idiocy.

"That's okay," he yelled back, "One day you'll watch me pitch in the big leagues."

Soon, major-league baseball scouts knew the Reuss name, which is not terribly surprising when an athletic, six-foot, five-inch, 195-pound seventeen-year-old throws extremely hard. When the Atlanta Braves came to St. Louis after Jerry's junior season, Braves scouts asked him to throw a bullpen session at Busch Stadium. First came a visit to the clubhouse.

"I tried to act as if I belonged," Reuss recalled. "That's a tough act to pull off when my knees were knocking, and I could hardly breathe!"

The whirlwind stunned him. Sitting quietly, he noticed the next locker belonged to future Hall of Famer Hank Aaron, who hadn't arrived. He spotted another future Hall of Famer, third baseman Eddie Mathews, quietly reading a copy of *Beau Geste*, the tale of English brothers enlisting in the French Foreign Legion after someone stole a family member's valuable jewelry.

"How's the book," the curious teen inquired?

"Horseshit," came the terse reply.

The reply started him. Jerry never heard the term "horseshit" before. He later laughed, "The Mathews exchange expanded my vocabulary, and later in my career 'horseshit' became a powerful word that, said loudly enough to an umpire, could get you tossed from a game!"

After shocking the youngster with his verbiage, Mathews offered, "They said you were really bringing it," repeating the Braves' scouts' reaction to the young lefty's bullpen session.

Upon Aaron's arrival he expressed good wishes to the wide-eyed Reuss. As scouts' interest peaked, Jerry and his family faced the issue: college or pro contract. Then as the 1967 base-ball draft began, St. Louis took him in the second round.

"The Cardinals drafting me was a huge surprise," Jerry remembered. "In looking back on it, their scouting director's son was a friend of mine."

Inside the Reuss household, heart-to-heart discussions involving family and coaches took the next step.

"In a normal situation," said coach Englert, "I'd recommend college. With Jerry I just simply said, 'this is something I think that is strictly up to you and your parents.'"

When the Cardinals, led by General Manager Stan Musial (in his only season as their GM), ponied up an additional two thousand dollars for Jerry's mom and dad to take a vacation (on top of the $35,000 bonus originally offered), their son's wildest dreams took wings.

"It was a chance of a lifetime," Jerry beamed. "Who knew if anything like this would ever come again?"

Rookie ball in Florida, then nine A-ball starts and a 1.86 ERA, led to a force-fed Triple-A baptismal under Tulsa manager and Hall of Fame lefty Warren Spahn. Afterward, with Vietnam military service threatening, Reuss enrolled at Southern Illinois University. Reporting late after his spring semester ended in 1968, he managed only sixteen Double-A starts for the Cardinals' club in Little Rock, Arkansas. Jerry found himself at a career crossroad.

"If I continued a heavy workload at school, other pitchers would pass me by," Reuss said.

Joining the Army Reserves helped. Even better, his St. Louis unit never received a call to Vietnam. His first full Cardinals spring training in March 1969 meant a wake-up call.

"I remember when Bob Gibson delivered a knockdown pitch to Tommy Agee on the first pitch of his first at bat with the Mets, in spring training no less. That opened my eyes."

After that adventure, Reuss went back to Triple A Tulsa for 1969 and on September 1, Jerry received his first major-league callup. Naturally the St. Louis native relished the fifteen-minute drive to Busch Stadium as a first-time big leaguer.

"There in the locker room I stood," Reuss smiled, "living that dream."

Reuss debuted on a cold, rainy late September afternoon in Montreal's Parc Jarry, recording his first win, helping himself with his first hit and big-league RBI. The military intervened again. Service time wiped out spring training 1970, resulting in a late report to Triple A Tulsa. A quick seven-win start and 2.12 ERA propelled Reuss to his first mid-season call to St. Louis.

"And it really opened my eyes, *again,*" he said.

Following Bob Gibson's hard-nosed lead, Jerry intentionally hit Expos' righty Bill Stoneman—payback for Stoneman knocking down the Cardinals' Jose Cardenal, then aiming at outfielder Dick Allen's head. Later came his first MLB complete game, but 1970 yielded a so-so 7-8 mark. A full 1971 season ended at 14-14 with a bulky 4.78 ERA. The Cardinals offered no 1972 contract. Apparently, owner Augie Busch's disgust at Marvin Miller's takeover of the Players Union and veteran Cardinals players' salary demands resulted in changes.

"[General Manager] Bing Devine and I never talked contract," Reuss said. "But if we'd had a face-to-face meeting, I believe we'd have reached an agreement."

Traded to Houston, given a fresh start and excited by Houston's offense led by power-hitting outfielder Jimmy Wynn and third-baseman Doug Rader, Reuss ended 1972 with a 9-13 record. Flourishing in 1973 with a career-high forty starts, 279 innings pitched, and boasting an outstanding 3.74 ERA— including six starts in Dodger Stadium—Jerry fell in love with Hall of Fame Dodgers announcer Vin Scully's voice.

"If the crowd was relatively quiet," Reuss remembered, "I could hear Vin's calls on radios from around the ballpark."

While staring in for a sign, Jerry heard the radio poet laureate telling one of his signature baseball stories.

"As a courtesy to him, I stepped off the rubber, grabbed and threw down a rosin bag. He delivered the punch line, the crowd laughed, and Scully continued, 'Reuss winds and the pitch on the way...'"

Dodgers' dream on the backburner, Reuss' bags were packed, and he was on the road again when the Astros traded him to the Pirates and their great clubhouse, led by power-hitting first baseman Willie Stargell—"The heart and soul of the Pittsburgh Pirates," Reuss called him.

Knowing how to win, veteran skipper Danny Murtaugh left his front office job for a dugout return. Winning World Championships in 1960 versus the Yankees, and in 1971 with Hall of Famer Roberto Clemente leading the way with a .400 plus average, whipping Baltimore, Murtaugh knew he had talent.

"He told me, 'If you can give me six innings every start, you'll win a lot of games,'" Reuss said.

Soothsayer Murtaugh's forecast proved spot on. Jerry won sixty-one games in five Pirates seasons, fashioning his first of three eighteen-win seasons in 1975, along with a sterling 2.54 ERA.

In Pittsburgh, Jerry befriended outfielder Dave "Cobra" Parker, All-Star outfielder and National League MVP, with a perfect body, ego to match, and a Star of David necklace. Asked if he was Jewish, Parker said, "No, but my name's David and I'm a star." After a game in Chicago the pair rode an elevator with Muhammed Ali.

"Well, Dave," Reuss said smartly, "why don't you tell him how you could 'whup' his ass like you bragged in the locker room?"

"Jerry, what the hell…," stuttered a flummoxed Parker.

Reuss tried introducing himself as Ali muttered, "I know you, you're the *instigator.*"

The champ and Parker had a friendly visit. A red-faced Reuss suffered "the longest elevator ride of my life."

For Reuss, 1978 became a nightmare. An ERA just below seven cost him a Pirates rotation spot. Pirates GM Harding Peterson violated Jerry's no-trade clause, but Reuss' agent asked for a buyout. Peterson refused, and Reuss sat. Pirates Manager Chuck Tanner told Jerry the Dodgers wanted him badly.

"At a fifty percent raise on a five-year deal," agent Jack Sands said.

Blown away, Reuss signed quickly, beginning the first of eight Dodger Blue seasons. The Pittsburgh disappointment became a West Coast adventure. Hollywood celebrities surrounded Reuss and his new teammates. Jerry's new manager, the veteran skipper and raconteur Tommy Lasorda, entertained himself around celebrities Frank Sinatra and Don Rickles.

"Outside of Lasorda, I never heard more enthusiasm," marveled Reuss. "When I told him I preferred starting to relieving he became business-like, saying he had five starters already, but he'd keep me in mind."

More career-high Reuss eighteen-win seasons followed, including an All-Star berth and a Comeback Player of the Year award. On an unusually warm June San Francisco evening, he no-hit the Giants, a throwing error spoiling a perfect game. Reuss' only career no-hitter stands as only one of ten in MLB history featuring no walks or hit batters, and only two strikeouts.

"I just missed a no-hitter with Houston," Reuss remembered. "But I will always remember the one against the Giants because I felt my teammates with me on every pitch."

Wackiness always erupted. Reuss and teammate Jay Johnstone changed into grounds crew gear, then helped drag the infield during a Dodgers game. Teammates alerted video crews to the over-the-top shenanigans. As Reuss, Johnstone, and company sauntered crisply, smoothing infield dirt, smiling, waving and inducing cheers, an apoplectic Lasorda blew a gasket.

"In one breath," Reuss recalled, "he used the "F" bomb as a noun, verb, adverb, and adjective."

The pair left taking bows, waving and high-fiving fans who were providing a standing ovation as the cameras of the local news crews kept rolling. Losing it completely, Lasorda ordered $250 fines and immediately sent Johnstone to pinch hit. He promptly homered and Lasorda cut his fine in half. "Your fine's still 250 bucks," Lasorda screamed at Reuss, "so sit your ass down here where I can see you and shut up!"

After an extremely hot 1981 start, Jerry and his Dodgers overcame a lengthy strike, winning the National League pennant, then beating Houston for a World Series berth. Losing the first two to the Yankees, L.A. came roaring back to win four straight (with Reuss winning Game 5), handing the Dodgers a World Championship.

"Success continued in '82," Jerry said. "I won two in one day at Wrigley Field, finishing and winning a 21-inning suspended game, and a half hour later threw five innings for the second win."

Elbow and hamstring issues lingered in 1983 and put a damper on the next season as well. The Cardinals ruined the 1985 Dodgers' campaign. By 1986, with many of his 1981 teammates long gone and at age thirty-seven, father time felt close.

"I heard whispers from Los Angeles writers," Reuss remembered. "[They'd ask questions like] do you see your role changing now that you're the elder statesman?"

Sick of "elder" chatter, Reuss decided he'd trade himself in Chicago. After a day game at Wrigley, he jumped in a cab with Dodgers' equipment bag in hand and bounded into the Yankees clubhouse at Comiskey Park. His target? New Manager Lou Piniella.

"Hi Lou, I'm Jerry Reuss," he grinned. "I want you to know I can pitch either in relief or as a starter for you."

After an expletive-laced tirade, a completely perplexed Piniella finally realized the joke.

"You know, you'd fit in here," Piniella laughed. "Sit down with me, I'm suspended tonight."

Going back to work in early 1987, knee and elbow pains continued, and in April the Dodgers set Reuss free. He went on to Cincinnati for three months before being released again. He immediately signed with the Angels, but even after winning three straight, Jerry's confidence disappeared.

"How miserable was 1987?" he asked himself. "Two teams released me, I spent time in the minors for the first time since 1970, and then wasn't asked back to the Angels."

Rebuilding strength and confidence, Jerry turned a non-roster spring training invitation into a 13-9 mark for the White

Sox. He split 1989 between the Sox and Milwaukee with a 9-9 mark. Neither team wanted him back, yet Reuss refused to give in. Auditioning for an amateur team impressed major-league scouts and former team the Pirates, who, after a short stint at Triple A Buffalo, gave Jerry a chance to "end my career under my own terms." Entering the Pirates clubhouse, he spotted Barry Bonds.

"We were just talking about you," Bonds laughed. "We didn't know you were still playing."

Three games remained on the Pirates' schedule. Pirates' manager Jim Leyland wanted to send the forty-one-year-old off in style, offering him a start in Pittsburgh against the Mets. Was Reuss up to it?

"Absolutely," Reuss said.

A crisp, cool fall morning greeted Jerry's melancholy walk from his hotel to the Pirates' Three Rivers Stadium. Emotion and memories from two plus decades enveloped him. After Reuss gave up three runs over the first six innings to the Mets, out came Manager Jim Leyland.

"It was only fitting that in my final game," Reuss wrote later, "I heard a manager say for the final time, 'bring in the right hander.' I shook Jim's hand and said 'thanks.' I said, do you mind if I keep the ball?"

"I could give a damn about the ball," Leyland beamed, "I'm proud to shake the hand of a man who pitched twenty-two years in the big leagues!"

Some 28,000 screaming Pirates fans stood and cheered. Fans upped the decibels as he moved to the dugout, bidding him a raucous, rousingly final goodbye. Mets TV broadcaster and Hall of Fame Pirate Ralph Kiner called Jerry's ovation, "Better than a gold watch!" Disappearing into the dugout, Jerry thought to himself, "I was the luckiest twenty-year-old in St. Louis on my first day in the big leagues, and I had a fairy tale ending on my final day twenty-two years later. I had come full circle and was ready to begin the rest of my life."

When he wrote his autobiography, the veteran lefty took the title from Leyland's call for his replacement: "Bring in the Right-Hander."

SCIPIO SPINKS

"Faster than Seaver"

So, how do you pronounce your name, Scipio Spinks? Is it "SKIP-ee-oh," "SKYPE-ee-oh," "Su-PEE-oh"?

"It's like takin' a cool sip of water," Spinks laughs. "I've been asked that question a thousand times. It's SIP-ee-oh! Cool drink of water, just a sip, that's me!"

God blessed this "cool drink of water" with an infectious smile, a laugh audible for miles and a raucous, sometimes borderline R- to X-rated sense of humor. His street background gave him a swaggering edginess.

"I was 'inner city' so much," Scipio laughed, "that, hell, the guy who helped us organize our kid baseball teams was "Shank." He carried a knife—a 'shank' he called it. That's what they called it in prison. Shank knew both—knives and prison. Sure woke us up!"

Scipio grew up on the south side of Chicago. That's important because as a quiet, humble youngster, yet rebellious at heart, he cheered for the northside Chicago Cubs, denouncing allegiance to the neighborhood White Sox. Why? Ernie Banks.

"Ernie lived only about seven blocks from my house," Scipio grinned. "Every chance I got, I sprinted to his house, and sat on his stoop and asked him for a ride to Wrigley Field. And he took me. I just loved that man."

Scipio and his southside friends had no Little League baseball, so groups of ten or eleven neighborhood youngsters formed teams, playing against other kids from nearby neighborhoods.

"Anytime we played against other guys," Scipio laughed, "it was put up or shut up. No smack talk, no screwing around."

With no high school baseball, Scipio proved that if a will existed, he would find a way. Playing Connie Mack ball on weekdays, semi-pro on weekends proved critical.

"At age fifteen, I started playing on a team with several ex-professional players," he grinned. "They were really tough, so the whole time playing against those older, better guys, made me a better pitcher and player."

Even then, Scipio had all the makings of a professional. In junior college, Spinks faced what scouts called "a big-time prospect." Scipio outpitched the prospect, hitting a homer and shutting out his team, 4-0.

"I asked one scout who walked by, 'Hey why don't you visit with me, didn't you like what I did?' The guy said, "Son, you will never make it.'"

The caustic, backhanded verbal dig completely stunned Scipio, creating a huge chip on his shoulder. Later, facing one of the top semi-pro teams, a regular finalist in National Baseball Congress' Wichita, Kansas tournament, Spinks put on a show.

"I shut 'em down," he laughed. "I mean fourteen, fifteen strikeouts, a couple RBIs, I had it going that day."

Afterward, Astros' scout Wally Liskowski came down for a visit.

"You ever think of playing professional baseball?" Liskowski asked.

"All the time," Scipio replied.

Liskowski and his newest prospect headed for Scipio's home to speak with his mother about an Astros contract.

"She wanted me to go to a four-year school," Scipio remembered, "but I didn't want to do that. When Wally said he'd give us $7,500, Mom and I looked at each other and said, 'where do we sign?'"

While all the money wasn't immediate, opportunity certainly was. Scipio's first pro stop came at Bismarck, North Dakota. Wide open spaces and extreme bus rides shocked the urban youngster. Places like Sioux Falls, Aberdeen, and St. Cloud boasted populations that combined were less than a tenth the size of his native Chicago, and summer temperatures often reached triple digits.

"You never heard me griping about sweating through a heavy wool uniform shirt," he remembered. "I didn't care about that. I proudly wore a professional uniform."

And he pitched that way. Against future Reds right hander Gary Nolan (later a National League All-Star who pitched for Cincinnati's Big Red Machine with Johnny Bench and Pete Rose), the pair went at it full tilt. Nolan struck out seventeen Bismarck hitters and Spinks took down twenty Sioux Falls batters. They set a Northern League record for total strikeouts by starters. Neither got a win.

"Can you believe that?" Spinks laughed. "Almost forty total strikeouts in the game, thirty-seven by the starting pitchers. A good old fashioned hardball game."

Single A Greensboro, North Carolina, in the Carolina League served as Spinks' next stop. His confidence over the top, he passed the Salem Pirates dugout, waving at everyone on the bench.

"I yelled, 'hey, I'm strikin' out every one of y'all twice today,'" Scipio recalled. "Well, they scorched my butt, scoring six runs, and I never got out of the first inning. The lesson learned? Shut up and pitch!"

The other lesson, more serious, dealt with racism. After shutting out a team from Rocky Mount, North Carolina, Scipio took a case of beer to a hotel housing only white players, intending to celebrate his shutout with teammates. Accompanied by six-foot, six-inch fellow starter Wayne Twitchell, Spinks found trouble waiting.

"Out of nowhere bolted this big white dude aiming a single shot shotgun at us," Spinks remembered. "He began screaming he'd 'shoot us dead' and yelling at the top of his voice that 'you ----- ain't goin' in that hotel."

Teammates grabbed the guy and the gun. Twitchell got a piece of the guy before police showed up.

The next Spinks stop, the High A Florida State League, brought a mishmash of teams playing at spring training sites all over Florida. Heat, humidity, mosquitoes, and an occasional alligator provided "good times."

"I tell ya, I don't want to talk about alligators," he laughed, "No sir. Wanted no part of those dudes."

At the All-Star break, Houston sent its flame-throwing A-ball right-hander to Turnpike Stadium in Arlington, Texas, to start for the Astros against the Double-A Texas League All-Stars. When Scipio looked at the Texas League lineup, he couldn't believe what he saw.

"I thought, damn it," he laughed. "Nate Colbert became the first legitimate San Diego Padres star with a couple of thirty-eight-home-run seasons, Bob "Bull" Watson, a nineteen season MLB vet, later GM in Houston, and New York. Top it off with future NL All-Star Dusty Baker, and one of the all-time great Dodgers outfielders, Willie Crawford. That was a load!"

Maybe not so much. Spinks went three shutout innings for the win. He finished the season at Double A Amarillo in the Texas League, unceremoniously.

"They told me they brought me in to stop a losing streak," Scipio winced, "and help them hang on and win the Texas League title. Well, I didn't, and I didn't!"

The next year, 1969, began a wildly out of control ride for the whip-armed righty. Starting at Oklahoma City, fashioning a so-so 7-11 record with an earned run average of better than 7, he made his MLB debut that year, arriving late in New York City.

"I jumped in a cab, raced to the Shea Stadium clubhouse, arriving with the game underway," he recalled. "I put on my uniform, ran to the bullpen and bam, just like that, I didn't have any time to take it all in because I'm in the game."

Face to face with the 1969 "Miracle Mets," Spinks received the call to the big leagues against the team that found themselves knee-deep in a come-from-behind run, overtaking the Cubs and snatching the National League Pennant.

"In front of 45,000 screaming Mets fans, who sounded like a million of 'em, there I am, hands shaking, teeth rattling, knees knocking and asking myself, 'what the hell am I doing here?'" Spinks recalled. "The hitter Ron Swoboda, who already heard I was wild and didn't dig in, yet I somehow got out of that inning without completely embarrassing myself."

Lack of confidence and inability to consistently throw strikes always hurt his chances with the Astros. Before his first callup, Scipio actually lost a no-hit bid in a complete game by walking a whopping eight batters and throwing two wild pitches.

"They knew I was wild as hell," he grinned.

The Astros assigned legendary pitching coach Hub Kittle to work with Scipio. A baseball lifer, Kittle upped Spinks' confidence immediately.

"When visiting players walked to their dugout in Oklahoma City, they passed by the home team bullpen," he grinned. "As I warmed up, Hub stopped visiting hitters saying, 'Hey buddy, watch that guy. Look at the fastball, how quick it is and how much it moves, and then ask yourself, how in hell am I ever gonna hit that? And you ain't even seen the curve!' Hub was my man!"

The Astros obviously had no long-term plans for Spinks. Before the 1971 season, Astros Manager Harry Walker, a son of the South, called Scipio and Bob Watson in for a visit. Watson made Houston's opening day roster; Scipio did not. After caustically breaking the news, Walker insisted Spinks sit down for ten minutes of batting tips.

"I was really pissed," Spinks said with a frown. "I told one of our coaches, Bob Lillis, that I had had it with Harry, that I was quitting and heading for home, that I couldn't stand him."

Lillis encouraged Scipio to chill, be easier on himself, while insisting Scipio had big league stuff.

"Later," Scipio said, "I came back to the Astros and pitched a complete game shutout in Atlanta and came away knowing I could pitch somewhere in the big leagues, if not Houston."

Spinks' dream came true shortly after baseball settled its 1972 strike. The Astros traded Scipio to the Cardinals for lefty Jerry Reuss.

"Once I met with Manager Red Schoendienst," Scipio said, "he told me simply, 'we know you can pitch, we like you, just conduct yourself as a St. Louis Cardinal, you'll do fine.'"

Later while walking into the Cardinals clubhouse before a Sunday afternoon game, Spinks spotted one of his all-time heroes, Bob Gibson.

"I was scared to death of him," Spinks said.

For three weeks, Gibson never acknowledged Scipio's presence. After three successful starts came a fourth on an extremely cold day in Montreal. After Spinks' complete game shutout, he broke the ice with his hero.

"Writers jammed my locker saying, 'you're another Bob Gibson waiting to happen,'" Scipio remembered. "I said, 'oh no, no I'm not. My name is Scipio, I'm proud and happy to be a Cardinal. Bob's in a league by himself. I'm just trying to win some games.'"

When writers walked away, Gibson finally approached his new teammate.

"All he said to me was, 'great job today, and you have to know that anytime some hard throwing, young black righthander comes to the Cardinals, they always compare him to me. It's about time someone here had the courage to be himself,'"

Spinks recalled. "He was talking about me, and that's how he broke the ice."

Later, Gibson invited his new protege to dinner. Spinks refused, saying he couldn't afford to eat at restaurants Gibson frequented.

"Who said that you had to pay?" Gibson asked.

While on the road during the season, the future Hall of Famer called Scipio's room asking his roommate's name. When Spinks told him "Donn Clendenon," Gibson insisted Spinks call the Cardinals' Traveling Secretary, "and tell him I, Bob Gibson, said you needed a room to yourself."

"And that's exactly how I got my own road room," Scipio laughed.

Gibson's advice kept coming, and as a result the young right hander pitched extremely well his first two months in St. Louis.

"I always say Houston taught me how to pitch," Spinks remembers, "but the St. Louis Cardinals and Bob Gibson taught me how to win. He never told me what to do, but Bob said he'd always be there to help."

Gibson's death in early October of 2020 upset Spinks immensely.

"Bob Gibson was a godsend for me," he said. "His lessons I remember well, and I keep him in my thoughts and prayers every day. He just meant so much to me, especially at that time in my life.

By July 4, 1972, Spinks found himself on a roll. In a start against the Phillies. All-Star shortstop Larry Bowa told reporters after a Scipio-dominated Cardinals win: "That kid throws harder than Seaver!"

Third in the National League in strikeouts and ERA, pitching well enough to be considered for the All-Star team, Scipio and the Cardinals met Cincinnati on a rainy, dreary day. Early in the game, he struck out Johnny Bench, then in a tight game in the seventh, Schoendienst let Scipio hit for himself.

"Bang right out of the gate I singled to left," he recalled. "Then Luis Mendez hit a rope to left center field and I was off to the races. Around second, I realized the outfielders hadn't reached the ball. I ran through the stop sign knowing the play at the plate would be close. I slid, coming down, my knee on his knee."

Trying desperately to get up, his knee buckled. The knee-on-knee collision severed Spinks' ligament, ending a hopeful, perhaps career-changing season.

"There I was, a wonderful world in front of me," Spinks said, tearing up. "Bob Gibson teaching me the ropes, me having found myself as a pitcher, and I kept asking myself why me, why me?"

The damage cost him all but three games in 1973. Doctors pleaded with Scipio to take the entire year to heal, but in his haste to compete, the knee never healed properly, leading to shoulder issues and eventually shutting down his pitching career.

"Well, I did pitch for my Cubs in 1974," said Spinks who was traded to his favorite team from boyhood. "I was glad to be there at Wrigley Field, but then they sent me to Triple A Wichita for treatments, and I never really came around."

Trials with the Yankees and Pirates and a couple of seasons as a minor-league pitching coach didn't work. Scipio found his niche scouting for the Padres. He and a handful of other scouts zeroed in on a Pine Bluff, Arkansas high school senior said to be a sure-fire big leaguer. As the prospect's uninspiring batting practice ended, Scipio locked in on a freshman pounding MLB-style rockets all over the outfield. During outfield drills the youngster showed an above-average major-league arm, and footspeed.

"I took him aside and told him, "You keep playing hard because you can play this game at an extremely high level and do not ever let anyone tell you that you can't!'" Scipio said.

The senior never played, but the freshman played seventeen major-league seasons, made five MLB All- Star teams, hit a whopping 353 career homers, and played a dynamic center field for the Twins and Angels. Oh, don't forget: Tori Hunter also won seven Gold Gloves.

"Seeing Tori," Scipio noted, "simply proves what old-time scouts always said: 'keep your eyes open and your mouth shut because sooner or later, you'll see someone you might not have noticed otherwise.'"

Spinks returned to his old organization, the Astros, and after seventeen years as a professional scout, he moved on to the Diamondbacks for five seasons before finally hanging 'em up. To this day, Scipio Spinks still helps young players.

"I am coaching a club program at the University of Houston Downtown," he said. "I want to take this program to either NCAA Division 3 or to the NAIA. We don't get the kids with big names or big bodies. But my kids have heart, and they don't mind driving to the rougher parts of town to work out because we don't have a real ballpark. All that's coming, though, and I want to make it happen for those kids."

Just like a Hall of Famer, Bob Gibson, did for young Scipio Spinks.

BRIAN MAZONE

"A rainy day goes away..."

"WHEN WE FIRST LOOKED at Brian Mazone, we said to ourselves, 'this kid can't do anything past high school,'" said Tom House, the longtime major-league pitcher and pitching coach who now trains players across multiple sports. (See Tom's story in Chapter 2).

Not the biggest, strongest kid on the block, nor armed with a big-time fastball, and certainly no professional offers out of high school, Mazone knew he faced a rough road to his ultimate goal—the major leagues.

"I went to the University of San Diego," Brian explained, "and I wasn't lights out as a pitcher. I both hit and pitched at USD. While I wasn't a particular standout on the mound, neither was I with a bat in my hands. Pro scouts were divided, and I didn't have a personal preference. Whatever they [the scouts said] that's the direction I planned to head."

"Brian worked so hard at it," House mused. "He hung with friends and teammates who were excellent athletes, who encouraged him, and they all had persistence in common. Brian certainly did, in abundance."

House's research in the art of pitching remains second to none, and he knows that all good pitchers have one trait in common.

"I did research and have a psychological perspective on persistence," he insists. "Successful athletes thrive on abundant persistence. You become persistent at your craft; you stay. Simple as that."

Mazone needed gobs of perseverance in facing and overcoming roadblocks and discouragement over an eleven-year professional career. As an undrafted free agent, signed by the Atlanta Braves, the young left-hander struggled during his rookie league season, then received walking papers. That bloodied professional lip lit a fire under Brian, so back to Tom House he went.

"Both Tom and the catching coordinator for the Dodgers at that time, Ryan Sienko, opened my eyes," he recalled. "Proper nutrition, proper workouts, working on proper mechanics, as well as proper mental toughness conditioning. I was with them throughout the three or four years I spent in independent ball, and it all came together, and I was so lights out, the San Francisco Giants signed me."

It's almost hard to believe that just a few years earlier Mazone couldn't find a job in organized baseball. Instead, the resolute Mazone was relegated to independent ball with the Zion Pioneers in the now-defunct Western League. Brian led the league in shutouts, but an injury shut him down in 2001. Then in 2002 he rallied back, leading the independent Northern League in wins at Joliet, Illinois, with the Jackhammers, notching fifteen victories.

"My manager and former MLB catcher Matt Nokes really opened my eyes about how to use my stuff," Mazone remembers. "And as a result, the Brewers picked me up and sent me to Class A."

A disappointing 0-7 mark with the Brewers High Desert club in the California League led to another release. But if you think the trauma of a release or two could stop Brian Mazone, think again. Back to independent ball he went, finding progress with manager Nokes.

"I was always a late bloomer," Brian grinned. "I didn't shave until I was a sophomore in college and really didn't hit any kind of mental or physical stride until I was twenty-five. For me, independent ball, and Matt Nokes, they were both avenues for me. Without those years in independent ball, I would have slammed headfirst into a dead end."

The Giants signed after he led the independent Northern League in shutouts, and sent him to Double A Norwich, Connecticut in the old Eastern League.

"When I left Joliet, I had only had one other Double-A start," he remembered. "But when I got to Norwich, I had eight straight scoreless innings, and within two days I was headed to Fresno in the Pacific Coast League, my first Triple-A experience."

Ever the fighter, Mazone made one start, pitching well and receiving an invitation to spring training with the Giants in 2005. Triple-A baseball did not, by any means, overwhelm.

"I really didn't notice a difference, between Double A and Triple A," he said. "As far as I was concerned, the advancement from independent ball to Double A and then Triple A in one season had to do with growing up and trusting myself and my stuff."

For Brian, 2006 led to a season of amazing highs and one incredible setback. Moving on to the Phillies organization, Mazone dominated International League hitters, recording a 13-3 mark for Triple A Scranton-Wilkes Barre, with an incredible 2.03 ERA, and 1.12 WHIP. His sterling work earned him "The Most Spectacular Pitcher in Triple A" award from minor-league baseball.

"Overall, a great season," Mazone grinned. "We were in Rochester, and I was called to our manager John Russell's room, and my pitching coach Rod Nichols was there. They told me I was headed to Philly for a start (and my major-league debut) because Phillies starter Randy Wolf had been hurt and would miss his next outing."

Seasons of disappointment were forgotten. Brian Mazone was going to The Show.

"John Russell and Rod Nichols were invested in me, and that was so cool to see when they gave me the word I was going up," Mazone smiled. "They were in tears; I was in tears. Everyone in Russell's room knew I had overcome impossible odds."

Brian's wife Amber and their two sons, fortunately, were with him on the Rochester road trip. He excitedly called her, and she began packing up their hotel room for the trip to Philadelphia. Then, Brian called his parents, the two people who had initially been with him through the roller coaster ride.

"No, Dad," he excitedly told his father, "No, this is the real thing, the real call-up."

Brian, immediately flew to Philadelphia, and his wife and sons drove there, assuring themselves plenty of time to get there from Rochester for the next night's start.

"Everyone in my circle was shocked," he remembered. "This is, real, this is happening, it's not a pipe dream."

Amidst the Mazone family's unbridled joy, it was in fact, raining in Philadelphia.

"Yes, it was, unfortunately," said Mazone. "And by the time I left really early from our hotel in Philadelphia to head for the ballpark, rain was still falling."

Brian refused to allow sheets of rain to dampen his spirit. Adrenaline-charged, he arrived extremely early for his scheduled start. Seeing the locker room—and his name on a Phillies uniform—stunned the veteran professional pitcher.

"Surreal," he whispered, "and really that's the only way to describe it. I had one of those split-second moments that took me back through college, through independent ball, through surgeries, being away from my wife and kids in winter ball, all that we went through seemed like nothing. It was all worth it."

At that moment, Phillies players began arriving in the clubhouse, greeting Brian, congratulating him on his call to the big leagues and his start. Mazone knew most of them, had been to spring training and had played with them there. Outside, torrential rains relentlessly pounded the Philadelphia ballpark.

"It helped having them in there," Brian said, "knowing about the call up, realizing the rains were falling harder and harder, but I had to maintain focus and go about my routine, rain or no rain. I still had to prepare. I had on my headphones, tried not to think about the rain and began concentrating on scouting reports. I put on my uniform, stretched, walked outside. It didn't look promising. So, maybe a two-hour rain delay, I hoped."

Hope ran out. Dreaded news followed. That night's Phillies game, the only major-league chance he'd ever received, was washed away by rain.

"Phillies players, every single one, knew how badly I felt," he remembered. "One by one, every guy in that clubhouse walked up to me, and told me how sorry they were, and they hoped I'd be back later in September."

Because Mazone did not occupy a spot on the Phillies forty-man roster, he received no September call, and not much else from Philadelphia brass. A lesser man crumbles under such a situation.

"Only my husband could come through this," Amber Mazone said stoically. "Only my husband could do this and be okay."

Brian feels doubly blessed with Amber as a baseball wife who understands the knock-down, drag-out life of a minor-league player.

"She always gave me a little more fire, and she always brought so much stability to me and what I was trying to do." he smiled broadly, "Knowing I had [Amber's] full support, and the fact that she was always ready to grind through this baseball life with me, made a huge difference. I took my work ethic more seriously because of her and my sons. I didn't run the streets until four a.m. like a lot of guys did, or try to drink my way out of problems, like others. She was always there throughout my career, through all the ups and downs, so I could focus on what I needed to do and that was work my ass off to succeed."

It may or may not come as a surprise that Brian Mazone holds no malice toward the Philadelphia Phillies for never giving him another shot at a major-league callup or start.

"To this day, I'm not bitter, I'm not hating anyone," he said quietly. "I'm really not."

The next year, Mazone took his talents to Korea, with the Samsung Lions. Returning from Korea with significantly more money than he would've made as a pitcher in Triple A, Brian signed on with the Dodgers, pitching at their Triple-A affiliate Albuquerque, finishing his career in 2010. How did he survive the disappointments and struggles, and especially the rainout of his only potential MLB start?

"I just guess it's because of the way I'm built inside, nothing really got me down," he insists. "Disappointments like releases only served to fire me up. I had a great work ethic, I believed in myself, had dogged persistence, and I always knew if I got knocked around in a start, I'd go right back to work the next day, working to improve."

The example Brian and Amber set for their sons paid off in spades. Their oldest son now plays collegiate baseball as a catcher at Washington University in St. Louis. The youngest stars in high school football in Southern California.

"I've taught them nothing comes easy," he grinned. "Nothing. Nothing worth having is ever handed to you. You don't deserve anything other than love and support from your mother and me. If you want something, you yourself have to earn it, and you must take responsibility for your actions. That's not negotiable."

JOE SLUSARSKI

Blue-collar pitcher, red-ribbon dad

"FOR ONE MONTH in my career, I drove 340 miles round trip each home game, to keep a Double-A job," remarked veteran MLB right-hander Joe Slusarski. "And I did it so my daughter, Meagan, knew I loved her."

Wait a minute. What? Hold on. *You did what?*

"Yessir," Joe said, "I drove back and forth from the Astros Double-A ballpark in Jackson, Mississippi, to New Orleans, every home game over a month's period of time in 1998.

Joe Slusarski with the Round Rock Express
(Photo courtesy of the Round Rock Express Baseball Club)

Why? "Family's always been important, and I needed a job and some money to stay active in a career I absolutely loved, so away I went," he said.

Let's be honest here. Yes, fathers love their children, but a commute like that stretches the imagination and sanity boundaries, even for the most intensely competitive athlete. So, it also comes as no surprise that Slusarski made those trips in an un-air-conditioned, four-cylinder beater—and only three cylinders worked.

"Yessir," he laughed, "it was hot and humid as hell, even at night, on the return to New Orleans, but I could not put baseball down and I could not ignore my daughter."

So addicted to the game and its lifestyle, having pitched in the big leagues for two clubs, Oakland and Milwaukee, he simply couldn't let it go. Joe's 340-mile daily trip, resulting from a call to Astros Triple-A manager John Tamargo in 1998. It was not the first time Joe Slusarski called up a New Orleans manager asking for a tryout. "After the A's released me, in '94 I called up Chris Bando, the Triple-A manager for the New Orleans Zephyrs [then a Brewers affiliate], right there in my hometown," Joe said. "That was in early '95. Bando liked what he saw, so did the Milwaukee brass, and I pitched in the bigs for the Brewers in 1995 and with the Brewers at Triple A New Orleans in 1996."

Let's back up a bit. Joe Slusarski starred at Lincoln Land Junior College in southern Illinois, under Coach Claude Kracik, who also sent pitchers Jeff Fassero, Pat Perry, and Mark Clark to the MLB. The six-foot, four-inch, 195-pound flame-thrower went on to the University of New Orleans, winning medals pitching for Team USA in the late 1980s, as well as competing on the U.S Olympic Team at the 1988 Seoul Olympics.

"Man, what a great bunch of teammates," Joe remembered. "Jim Abbott, Charles Nagy, Robin Ventura, Ted Wood, Tino Martinez—really great guys."

Drafted by the A's in the second round in 1988, Slusarski worked his way to Oakland, making his major-league debut in 1991, then spending parts of three seasons with the A's as a starter and reliever. Then he suffered a shoulder injury after a freak accident on a golf course. He tripped while searching for a lost ball and put his hand out to break his fall. Spines from a Jumping Cholla lodged in his right bicep and pitching hand. The result: tendon damage leading to shoulder injuries.

After pitching for Milwaukee in 1995, their Triple-A club New Orleans in 1996, off to Taiwan Joe went for the 1997 season. Working odd jobs as the 1998 season opened, he realized he couldn't stand being away from the game, so he picked up the phone again.

"I told some friends I was going to call [with] the Zephyrs [by then Triple-A affiliate of the Houston Astros] to see if I could try out with them, and maybe get back in the game and sleep in my own bed all at the same time," he grinned. "And it worked out, somehow."

Zephyrs' manager John Tamargo answered his call, greeted Slusarski, then handed the phone to the Astros minor-league pitching coordinator at the time, Dewey Robinson, who was in New Orleans observing and working with Astros' Triple-A pitchers.

"Dewey remembered me from my days pitching for the Oakland A's when he was with the White Sox," Joe continued. "A couple days after I made the call, there I was at Zephyr Field, throwing a bullpen session in front of Dewey, and the New Orleans pitching coach Jim Hickey, who later became pitching coach in Houston and Tampa Bay."

The Astros liked Joe's bullpen tryout, and he eventually made it back to the big leagues again, this time in Houston. But not before one of the wildest, most incomprehensible, circuitous commutes for a player from his New Orleans home to his new, short-term baseball home in Jackson.

"Well, that's right," Joe smiled, "but sometimes in life and in baseball, as the old saying goes, 'a man's gotta do what a man's gotta do.'"

The Astros' 1998 deal with Slusarski called for him to report to Jackson and pitch on a one-month contract for the Double A Jackson Generals in the Texas League.

"I figured the Astros and I could get to know each other over a month's time," he grinned, "so I signed up."

He decided against renting an apartment in Jackson. Instead, after at least fifteen home games, Joe climbed into his old beater and drove to New Orleans simply so he could take his daughter Meagan to school each morning. The drive, one way from Jackson, Mississippi to New Orleans took two and a half hours. On every postgame trip, a weary dad arrived back home in New Orleans sometime between three and four in the morning. After a quick nap, he joined his daughter for breakfast, then dropped her off at school.

"Meagan just needed to know that daddy was trying to be with her as much as he could," Joe smiled.

As soon as Joe had Meagan safely at school, back he drove, retracing the 170 miles to Jackson in time for afternoon batting practice.

"Sure, it was tough," he grinned, "but it kept me close to my daughter, and I don't regret it for a minute."

By the end of the 1999 season, Joe manned Houston's bullpen, pitching for the Astros and manager Larry Dierker. Working in the Astros, and later the Braves, bullpens for the next three seasons, helping both teams to the playoffs, Slusarski then took pitching coach jobs with both the Astros and

Rangers. Lately he's worked with DBat in Georgetown, Texas, and has become more addicted to coaching than pitching. A new challenge awaits Joe Slusarski in California. A college pitching coach's job.

"Yessir, in Southern California at Marymount College in Rancho Palos Verdes," he smiled. "One of my great friends in life and a former A's teammate, Ron Witmeyer, serves as head coach. It's a small school, but I'm gonna do what I do best. Give young guys everything I have, doing my best to help them become the best pitchers and men they can be."

Even if it involves making a twenty-two-hour drive from his Texas home to a new one in California.

CHAPTER 4

DARREN OLIVER

"The change did him good...."

"I WANTED TO make him our closer," insisted Kevin Kennedy, who managed the Texas Rangers in 1993 and 1994. "He had two dynamic pitches, was relentless and had a swagger."

During those seasons, nothing Darren Oliver did surprised Kevin Kennedy.

"I always believed he'd be great, late in a game," Kennedy continued. "And we proved that in a Sunday game, early in his career, against the Yankees. I had Tom Henke as the closer, but I brought Darren in to close the ninth. With two aboard, Darren got pinch hitter Mike Gallegos on a 6-4-3 double play to end it. [Darren] was amazing."

Signed as a 1988 third-round draft pick by the Rangers, and son of former nine-year veteran MLB power hitter Bob Oliver,

Texas scouts believed they'd found a sure-fire number one or two starter in Darren.

"That's how he profiled," said former Rangers General Manager Tom Grieve, "instead, he turned out to be more of a mid-rotation starter."

"Believe this or not," Darren laughed, "I was at high school, and someone came up to me and said, 'Hey, you got drafted by the Rangers,' and I said,

Darren Oliver with the Double A Tulsa Drillers, before getting called up to the majors.
(Photo courtesy of the Tulsa Drillers)

'Cool.' I really didn't know much about the baseball draft."

Darren did, however, find out about Port Charlotte, Florida, his first Rangers stop as a professional.

"Noon games in the ungodly heat and humidity of a Florida summer," Oliver grimaced. "If we weren't pitching, we'd be running, shagging flies, then taking a shower. After the shower, we'd be back sitting in hot aluminum seats watching the game. My worst experience in baseball, period!"

To Single A Gastonia, then Double A Tulsa, after forty-six appearances, a 7-5 record, 1.96 ERA and 1.255 WHIP as a reliever, Darren received his first call to the big leagues, remaining a bullpen operative in his first two trips to MLB. Then, in 1995, under the late Johnny Oates, Oliver made seventeen appearances, seven of those starts.

"At that point," he said, "I finally felt like I was doing what I was supposed to do."

The next season turned out to be the best he had as a starter. Oliver sported a 14-6 mark for the Rangers American League Division Champs in 1996. In 1998, after ten seasons in the Texas organization, the Rangers traded him to St. Louis.

"By that time, I needed a change of scenery," he said. "I loved my two seasons in St. Louis. In '98 that was Mark McGwire's seventy-home-run season. I pitched and won the game when he hit his record sixty-first in front of Roger Maris' family. That was wild. Besides all that, 25,000 people showed up at the park for batting practice every day and it all was great."

With thirteen wins over two seasons as a starter with St. Louis, Darren (still a starter) went back to Arlington for his second stint with the Rangers; two rough seasons for Texas and for Oliver himself.

"The team wasn't very good," he remembered. "We suffered a lot of injuries, and although we had a lot of veteran players, no one could put it together."

After eleven wins for Texas in 2001, the Rangers traded him to the Red Sox in December for outfielder Carl Everett. In 2002, Manager Grady Little used him as a starter and reliever, releasing Oliver in July. Visiting with former MLB infielder-turned-agent Jeff Frye at baseball's Winter Meetings later that year, Darren said, "Hey Jeff, I got no job for '03." Frye's cocky response, "Dude, I'll get you a job tomorrow."

Frye came through. Signing on with the Rockies, Oliver got back on track with thirteen wins.

"I tell ya, Denver's a tough place to pitch," he remembered. "At altitude it's tougher to pitch and workout, so I had to do 50 percent workouts."

Signed as a free agent by the Marlins in 2004, splitting the season in Miami and Houston at age thirty-three, Darren's relief role became more pronounced. Ten of Oliver's twenty-seven total appearances that season came from the bullpen. Out of baseball in 2005, while at the Winter Meetings back in Dallas that year and standing at a bar with agent Jeff Frye, New York Mets Assistant GM and former Rangers assistant Sandy Johnson posed a question.

"You ever want to pitch again?"

"Sandy, I'm so out of shape, I don't know," came Darren's reply.

"Let me know what you wanna do," Johnson replied.

"Jeff let him know I wanted to come back," Oliver laughed. "And I tell you the truth, Jenny Craig works. I knew they'd weigh me at spring training, and I was in legit panic mode, but Jenny Craig came through!"

Signing a minor- league deal with the New York Mets in 2006 turned out a bit of a problem initially.

"With five days of camp left, I asked GM Omar Minaya (who I knew from the Rangers) if he could tell me whether or not I made the Mets roster," Darren said. "I told him my mom was having cancer surgery and I was going."

Minaya couldn't promise a roster spot, but guaranteed they'd bring Oliver up from Triple A at some point.

"I told them I was not gonna do that," Oliver continued. "The next day they called and told me I made the team. And I was there for my mom's surgery."

Darren Oliver turned late inning reliever for the rest of his career. With the Mets in forty-five appearances, he shut down opponents with a 1.123 WHIP and 3-to-1 strikeouts-to-walks ratio.

As he aged and switched to the bullpen exclusively, his numbers made him appear physically stronger.

"I got wiser," he said proudly. "I paid attention to the analytics, what pitches guys could and couldn't hit, and who was hot and who wasn't."

Moving to the Angels in 2007, Oliver joined Nolan Ryan as the only two MLB players to play for all four original MLB expansion club—Astros, Mets, Angels, and Senators/Rangers. Back again to the Rangers for the third time, in 2010 and 2011 at ages thirty-nine, he appeared in five World Series games.

"I had so much fun with Manager Ron Washington and Pitching Coach Mike Maddux," Darren grinned. "Wash made you feel good. Maddux conducted some great, funny, classic pregame meetings and really made it fun!"

The Rangers lost those series to the Giants and Cardinals. In three appearances against the Cardinals Oliver had one victory. Two seasons in Toronto wrapped up Darren Oliver's twenty-year MLB run.

"I was forty-two years old, and I knew I could've gone on," he remembered. "But I just decided it was time."

"Think about this," said Grieve, for former Rangers GM. "For the last eight years of his career, going from mid-rotation starter to top-flight seventh- or eighth-inning guy, Darren averaged sixty plus appearances most of those years. I promise you he was better and made more money than he did before changing to the bullpen. That's pretty special."

Oliver now works as a special assistant to Rangers President Jon Daniels.

"It's still great to be around the players, managers and coaches," Darren says.

How would he like to be remembered as a pitcher?

"I hope they'll say he was tough to hit, a tough competitor, and the kind of guy who would battle to win."

CHUCK CRIM

"Big League Bassin...."

"BIG LEAGUE BASSIN," is the Facebook website title belonging to an unusually gifted man in two professional sports. Chuck Crim was a top-flight MLB reliever for eight seasons in Milwaukee, Chicago, and Anaheim, California—and he was a talented fisherman in different professional bass fishing organizations.

"As a reliever, I always tried to deliver the perfect pitch to the perfect spot," he grinned, "and make the perfect cast to the perfect spot where I thought fish were hiding."

Fishing and baseball lessons began at age three.

"My dad never forced either one on me," Crim remembers well. "He taught me extremely important lessons—hit my spots while pitching or fishing. He was really teaching me 100 percent focus."

His parents reinforced teaching efforts with fishing junkets to the High Sierras, and lessons on baseball's finer points. They also attended hundreds of his games from Little League through the bigs.

"I just learned all that very important stuff," he remembers, "at a really early age and it became a part of me."

His dad taught him how to look through the cold, crystal clear waters, quietly searching for trout beds, and how to spot hitters' weaknesses.

"My parents and I called our great adventures, 'See-Worlds,'" Chuck laughed. "And it worked out so great. My job, whether fishing or facing a hitter, very simply turned out to be beat nature when I fished or beat the bat when I pitched."

Outstanding Little Leaguer, youth, and high schooler, Crim also showed excellence at shortstop. Playing mostly shortstop as a junior, three no-hitters his senior year aroused MLB scouts. The Cubs drafted him out of Thousand Oaks High School in 1979.

"My dad's messages of focus literally made my senior year," Chuck beamed. "He taught me a slider, and how to spot it, and heck, I'd throw that thing with a 2-0 count, or 3-1, I believed in it that much."

Chuck turned down the Cubs offer, instead attending the University of Hawaii.

"I'm glad I went to Hawaii," Chuck grinned. "And what a year my freshman season was."

Chuck and two other freshman pitchers led the Rainbow Warriors with fifty-seven wins combined. In fifty-eight seasons of University of Hawaii baseball, Chuck's team became the first to play in the College World Series. He became an All-American with a 15-0 record, topping it off by making the USA All-Star team.

"I only weighed 160 when I went to Hawaii," Chuck laughed. "Once there, I picked up strength and solid weight and as I did my velocity really improved. I just needed to grow up."

Milwaukee's seventeenth-round pick in 1982, Chuck remained a starter in rookie and low A ball, setting a Midwest

League record with eleven complete games. Ticketed in 1984 for the Brewers Double-A rotation in El Paso, he morphed from starter to dominating closer. Paralyzing Texas League hitters with a 1.13 WHIP, he won seven games, saving seventeen in fifty-five appearances and becoming a Texas League All-Star.

"It all came together," grinned Crim. "I had new life and new energy for making it to the big leagues as a reliever."

Following so-so Triple-A campaigns the next two seasons, Chuck debuted in the Milwaukee bullpen in 1987. The road from that spring training to The Show wasn't easy, but new Brewer's Manager Tom Trebelhorn and pitching coach Chuck Hartenstein knew Crim's minor-league pedigree, grit, and tenacity.

"I just decided I wasn't going to allow anyone to take me off that team," Crim insisted. "I was having success in spring training; they couldn't ignore me."

He broke in with a team of stars.

"Great teams my first three years," he grinned. "And in my rookie year we went on a 13-0 run, and I won two of those games. Then we reeled off wins in twenty-one of twenty-four. I also saw Paul Molitor's thrity-nine-game hitting streak and Juan Nieves' no-hitter that year. What a rookie season!"

Crim spent two of his five Milwaukee seasons as a top-flight set-up man. Those campaigns 1988 and 1989 yielded a whopping 146 appearances, and two "Top Set-Up Man" awards from *The Sporting News*. His workload over his entire five-year Brewers stint led all of Major League Baseball, appearing in 332 games.

"He was Mr. Reliable," said Chuck Hartenstein, who was Crim's pitching coach with the Brewers. "We had a set schedule if we were ahead. Crim pitched the seventh and eighth, then we turned it over to closer Dan Plesac. Chuck had such great command sometimes he was unhittable, and he bounced back quickly."

Crim's arm and verve did not surprise Hartenstein.

"The first time I saw him was at the University of Hawaii when I was pitching coach for the Padres Triple-A team in Honolulu," Hartenstein said. "He threw over two hundred pitches and I said, 'Holy smokes, they're killin' this kid!' But boy he was relentless!!"

Heavy work year after year led to shoulder problems along with an above average ERA in 1991. Unable to compete with big market money, Brewers General Manager Sal Bando traded Crim to the Angels.

"I wanted to be a Milwaukee lifer," Chuck said. "Harty [Chuck Hartenstein] gave me the opportunity to set up Dan Plesac for those Brewers years and Tom Trebelhorn managed me in both Triple A and in the big leagues. I just didn't want to leave."

Crim moved back to his native Southern California, and once in the Angels locker room he found a true hero in Nolan Ryan, but he noticed a marked change in the game. Players no longer hung out together after games, staying to themselves, wearing headsets to drown out clubhouse noise.

"That, and I still had some shoulder issues," he remembers, "and my slider wasn't as sharp, my body didn't perform like it did before, but I still continued to give it all I had."

Crim's persistent shoulder problems forced the Angels to release him in 1993. He spent the second half of that season rehabbing his shoulder.

"I told Alan Hendricks, my agent," Crim said, "that I didn't want to go through with another team what I went through with the Angels. I made that clear."

Before spring training 1994, after tryouts with Oakland and the Chicago Cubs, the team that originally drafted Chuck signed him up.

"I had a good session with Cubs pitching coach Moe Drabowski, and I loved him," grinned the veteran reliever. "Going to the Cubs also meant a reunion with my former Brewers Manager Tom Trebelhorn, now Cubs' manager. I was thrilled to pitch in Wrigley Field, loved going to the park every day and I really loved the fans."

Drawing a uniform excited him.

"Rehabbing the second half of '93," Crim recalled, "I kept thinking, 'I cannot believe I get to go back. I had some struggles but one month I gave up zero earnies [earned runs]."

Chuck went 5-4 in 1994 with an ERA above four and didn't return to Chicago. Strike talked loomed in the off season before 1995. Still, he pushed forward looking for a place to pitch, finding himself a day away from a Dodgers contract.

"The Players Union nixed the signing," Crim grimaced, "and in fact issued an edict saying in essence no negotiations at all leading into spring training '95."

By that time, with a strike on the horizon, Chuck grew weary of being away from his family, and truth to tell the 1995 baseball strike ended his playing career.

"So often," he said with regret, "I thought I should have just ground it out and signed again. I always believed I could've pitched until I was forty-five."

Throughout his other career Crim never lost his love for fishing. Off seasons, Chuck disappeared to peace and solitude, fishing for bass in southern California or Arizona lakes.

"During baseball season, I used to practice casting at night in my room," he laughed. To test his precision, he would flip a jig—a fishing lure consisting of a lead sinker with an embedded hook covered with soft molding, used for fishing near the bottom—into a paper cup.

With his career ended, Chuck and his family moved to Missouri and an idyllic home near Table Rock Lake on the Missouri-Arkansas border. Just like that, an outstanding Major League Baseball reliever turned outstanding professional tournament bass fisherman.

"I especially love the professional ranks because it's so competitive," Chuck insists. "That target game I had going in baseball worked the same way in professional bass fishing."

Crim's occasional fishing buddy and friend Ron Cervenka, a writer for ThinkBlueLA.com., asked Chuck to name his best professional bass fishing adventure. He picked a two-day stint at Bull Shoals, a lake also on the Missouri-Arkansas border.

"Nobody was catching any fish when we got there," Crim told Cervenka. "I had talked to a guy who lived on Bull Shoals, and he hadn't had a bite in eight days."

The Challenge and Challenger hooked up in a knock-down, drag-out, battle royal, the intrepid yet patient Chuck Crim versus Bull Shoal lunker bass, in a wintertime festival and battle royal.

After a thorough site survey, Chuck headed for the end of a bluff point where he thought fish would "winter up"

"I caught a fish on every cast," he grinned.

Chuck limited out for a second time, winning the professional tournament.

"That tournament was against local guys," he beamed, "which made the win more special."

Fishing or no fishing, baseball lingered in Crim's heart.

"My son wanted a baseball life again," he said. "So, we moved back to Southern California."

Crim became head baseball coach at a Southern California high school, coaching his son. The ultimate dream? A professional baseball pitching coach's gig. After a handful of years as a Dodgers scout the dream came true.

"After the 2009 draft," he smiled, "I went out to Short Season A ball in Ogden, Utah, with manager Damon Berryhill, coaching rookie pitchers. Next to the Midwest League, then to Double A Chattanooga."

Dodgers GM Ned Colletti asked him to return to Chattanooga for one more season, then join the Dodgers as their major-league bullpen coach.

"The Dodgers' talent amazed me," Chuck grinned. "We went to the playoffs three straight years, and I thought it was the start of the Dodgers' latest dynasty."

After Dodgers' losses in two straight National League Division Series to the Cardinals and Mets in 2014 and 2015, Dodgers President Andrew Friedman cleaned house. Manager Don Mattingly, dozens of scouts, front office personnel, and coaches including Crim received walking papers.

"It hurt," Crim said, "I mean that was the team I'd grown up on. And it didn't have to end the way it did. Sometimes life just sucks."

But then there's fishing and disappearing to the peaceful stillness of lakes and streams. An expert hitting spots while fishing or in baseball, Chuck Crim's legacy in both, the friends he made, the people he helped in both sports, far surpasses impetuous front office decisions.

TRAVIS DRISKILL

"I've been everywhere, man...."

FOR FIFTEEN professional seasons and parts of six in Major League Baseball, Texas native Travis Driskill, entered games to Johnny Cash's Country hit. From the U.S. to Mexico, Venezuela, and Japan, he plied his trade through 494 professional games, fifty-seven of them in the major leagues with Baltimore, Colorado, and Houston.

"You name the minor-league, or major-league venue," Driskill laughed. "I made the treks, the three a.m. wake up calls, and bumpy bus rides. Yep, 'I've Been Everywhere,' tells my tale."

The road, and its baseball characters, immersed Driskill in his own piece of heaven.

"The guys I loved in the minor leagues were the veterans, no matter what level," he said. "Then again, I lived 'em myself. By the time I got to Triple A Buffalo and a team full of vets like Jeff Manto, Torey Lovullo, Casey Candele, and Trinidad Hubbard, all had time to talk and teach."

Those Driskill mentions mixed physical talent and plain old baseball smarts.

Travis Driskill with the Corpus Christi Hooks.
(Photo courtesy of the Corpus Christi Hooks Baseball Club)

"Our manager in Buffalo, Brian Graham, insisted we use veterans as mentors," Driskill said. "He told us they'd competed and succeeded against big stars because they knew the tricks of the baseball trade. They'd all had big league time and it was so much fun picking their brains."

Now out of the game for more than a decade, Driskill wonders if that important link between veteran players and youngsters coming into Triple A still exists. He fears Major League Baseball's avalanche of analytical data may be substituting numbers for much needed veteran clubhouse presence.

"I'm afraid we're moving toward teams made up of superstars and young kids," he says. "Seems to me they are hurrying youngsters along too quickly before they've had a chance to fully develop, never having a chance to learn from veterans who know exactly what it takes to recover from slumps, or pressured situations. It's the business of baseball behavior and should be taught by veterans who have been there countless times and learned from failures and successes."

Driskill first made it to the bigs with Baltimore as a starter/ reliever in 2002, winning a career high eight games. Back with the Orioles in 2003 as a reliever, the big-league adventure took him to the Colorado Rockies, and three separate stints with the Houston Astros.

"Travis Driskill is a guy who to me represents the epitome of 'grinder'—always working very, very hard to improve, and the more work he did the better he became," said former Astros General Manager Tim Purpura.

A star from his Little League days in Northwest Austin, Travis learned to love and appreciate the game from his dad, a retired Air Force lieutenant colonel who served as league president.

"Baseball was the family sport," Driskill said. "My dad's Air Force background gave him an impeccable work ethic, and I learned so much about hard work and never giving in from him and my mom."

From Austin's Anderson High to Blinn Junior College in Brenham, Texas, and two stints at Texas Tech, major-league scouts really liked what they saw.

"In high school, I had coaches who challenged me," said Driskill. "And [scouts] began noticing."

The Astros drafted Driskill out of high school in the now non-existent seventy-sixth round. He turned them down for a Texas Tech scholarship. Leaving Tech after a year, Travis transferred to Blinn Junior College, improving his grades, and regaining draft eligibility.

"Blinn was where I got it going," Travis notes. "Coach Kyle Van Hook, one of the greatest people I ever knew, and a great coach, pitched me in important games. In a playoff game, after walking a lot of guys, Kyle came out and challenged me to make something happen."

Van Hook's passionate challenge triggered a huge upswing in Driskill's velocity. Unleashing a fastball at ninety-four miles an hour, rather than the eighty-eight he'd been serving up changed Travis' baseball life.

"I struck out the side, and ultimately we went to the Junior College World Series," Driskill laughed. "That's when I really got on scouts' radar."

During that JUCO World Series, Angels GM Whitey Herzog, later a Hall of Famer, watched Driskill work. Extremely impressed, the Angels immediately drafted him.

"We couldn't reach a number that satisfied both my family and the Angels, and that was unfortunate," Travis said.

So, back to Texas Tech he went, and on his third trip through MLB's draft, Driskill signed a contract as the Cleveland Indians fourth rounder in 1993.

"I thought I threw pretty hard when I got into pro ball," noted Driskill, "but heading upward through the ranks, I knew I had to have another pitch, a real out pitch, to survive."

Travis developed a split-fingered fastball, delivered with fore-finger and middle digit wide apart (Pirates reliever Roy Face called it a "fork ball"). When thrown with a fastball motion, "the split" became the Driskill calling card.

"Yeah," Driskill said, "the ball appears to be a fastball until it dives into the dirt at the last instant. When it works, it's a beautiful thing, and when it doesn't? Well let's just say that it's a [batting practice] fastball that most professional hitters can hit a long, long way."

Some certainly did.

During a game against Omaha, Travis gave up three homers in a row, pitching for his hometown Round Rock Express, the Astros Triple-A affiliate back in 2006.

"Ugh," the always self-effacing Driskill droned, "Who could forget that? But I think the longest bomb anyone ever hit off me came from Calvin Pickering, the huge Omaha first baseman who played a little in the bigs. That shot might have been the hardest ball ever hit at Dell Diamond [Round Rock's home park]. It sailed over the swimming pool and picnic area beyond right field, cleared the back fence and into a parking lot. I hate to say it but that one seriously needed a flight attendant on it."

At that point Travis already pitched in parts of five major-league seasons—first with Baltimore, then with Colorado, which later sold his contract to Japan, then back to the states for an off-and-on run with the Houston Astros. Like so many, he credits wife Natalie. "She kept it all going, made all the moves, every single one from Double A to Triple A and back and forth to the big leagues, and I thank God for her courage and tenacity," Driskill said.

The first trip to the major leagues was special, coming in 2002 coming up from the Orioles, Triple A Rochester club.

"What a thrill," he remembers. "I pitched the day before the call up. The next day, an off day, Natalie and I took our sons to Cooperstown. As we headed back, the Orioles called my cell to tell me I'd need to head to Camden Yards as soon as possible. Wow!"

At that point in his life nothing could have meant more.

"The kids already knew the sacrifices their parents made to make it to the big leagues, they knew the lifestyle, and they were ecstatic." he beamed. "Then came the call to my folks."

Always deeply invested in their son's baseball life, Travis' parents were overjoyed.

"They sacrificed for me and there I am trying to be the cool one and they were more excited than I was," he said.

His first walk onto major-league turf took place in Kansas City. With his parents and a cousin flying in from Austin proudly watching, Driskill made his initial MLB appearance, relieving another Orioles rookie.

"That guy went two and a third that didn't go very well," Driskill said. "He'd left a couple on, then I faced Royals' catcher Mike Sweeny. I immediately served up the first of two straight doubles and I thought 'oh, my, my—this big-league stuff is really hard!"

After that rude awakening, and the second double, the third hitter up also provided more proof that Major League Baseball was, indeed, H-A-R-D.

"Carlos Beltran ripped a rocket up the middle, almost tearing off my foot, then ricocheting toward third. The third baseman fortunately tagged out the runner," Driskill remembers his first out recorded. Then he thought, "My god, *don't these guys miss anything?*"

Despite two runs and massive consternation, Driskill somehow dug his way out of potential disaster.

"Heck yeah," he laughed. "They even let me go out for two more innings and I put up two scoreless [innings] to finish. Once I found a rhythm, I was okay."

The next five games Driskill found his backside pinned to the bullpen bench. In the midst of those days, Baltimore's traveling secretary distributed flight and hotel instructions to players and staff for the upcoming Yankee Stadium road trip. Driskill received none.

"I thought, aw, God, no. I'm outta here. They're sending me down," he said.

Less than two hours later, with Baltimore's starting pitcher leaving the game with a pulled hamstring, the manager called in Driskill.

"As I pushed open the bullpen door believing this could be my last-ever big-league appearance," Travis recalled, "I thought, well damn it, I'm going down fighting!"

Travis Driskill's go-to word for any great baseball or life achievement fits what happened next. "Awesome!" Five shutout innings, and he lived to pitch another big-league day, and for many days, in fact. In his first lengthy MLB stint he sported eight Orioles wins.

"We had our eyes on him all along," noted the Astros' Purpura. "He really pitched well in Baltimore, and I've always said those were some pretty great days for Travis Driskill."

Along the way, Driskill absorbed knowledge from every pitcher, manager, and pitching coach he worked with. More big-league stops came in Colorado in 2004, the Astros in 2005, and his last MLB and minor-league pitches came in Houston and Triple A Round Rock in 2007, pitching in his third straight season for Express skipper Jackie Moore.

"Travis was just *so* reliable," Moore vividly remembers. "Whatever the role, he committed completely. Need him to work the bullpen two days after a start? No problem. Close a game? No sweat. His attitude remained, 'gimme the ball and I'll get it done, no fanfare, no complaints.'"

When Moore approached Driskill about the 2007 season, the reply came, "Skip, I'm done."

"My boys were really growing up," Travis remembered, "And I needed to be home to help Natalie make that happen."

The ever-persistent Jackie Moore won out.

"The more I thought about it," Travis said, "the more sense Jackie made. Plus, living in Round Rock wasn't like having to play halfway across the country. So, I said yes to one more season, and I am glad I did."

"If I had to have any player staying in the game, relaying to young players all the information he's learned," Moore summarized, "I'm talking the ups and downs he's experienced and how to rejoice and how to step over the bad and stay resilient, it's Travis Driskill."

So, in 2007, the "I Been Everywhere" man came full circle, back to his Austin-area roots. Travis' happiest professional baseball days happened when he brought his sons to the park

"They not only learned how to play the game the right way," Travis said proudly, "but they learned how clubhouses work, how guys from different parts of the country and different countries worldwide learned to get along in pretty tight quarters, day after day."

Oldest son, Tanner, took lessons and learned from his dad all the way to professional ball as a pitcher in the Washington Nationals system.

"I could see the finish line in '07," Driskill remembers. "And gosh, how great it was. I made the Pacific Coast League All-Star team, pitching in the All-Star Game. I had a fifty-two-pitch, five-inning relief outing against the Iowa Cubs at the end of August. Honestly looking back over fifteen professional seasons, that Iowa outing was the best I ever had in the big or minor leagues."

And for the third straight year Driskill made more than fifty relief appearances for the Triple-A Astros affiliate. What he thought was his last game, really wasn't.

"I had a little time with the Astros in August, then came back down," Driskill remembers. "And wouldn't you know we played my old team New Orleans in the final four games."

Driskill relished what he thought was his last game. After one perfect inning, striking out the side against New Orleans, in the next-to-last game that season, he believed in his heart that was it.

"How could you end it any better? I tell ya, I had tears in my eyes," Driskill said. "What a way to leave!"

Manager Jackie Moore, pitching coach Burt Hooton, Travis' family, and Round Rock Express staffers had other ideas.

"Knowing who Travis was as a baseball player, so entrenched in the game, so involved and in love with his family and the community, we decided this man needed an even greater send off than he could have had after leaving Major League Baseball," Moore remembers. "You couldn't stage this kind of celebration in the big leagues!"

"I truly thought my career was done," Driskill laughed, "Then Burt Hooton sent me down to the bullpen, in game four against New Orleans telling me, 'Hey Trav, you got the eighth!' I said, 'Come on Burt, you used me last night, why tonight? You're kidding me, you used me last night, I cannot be better than that!'"

The rare complaint uttered, and as Travis had done half a thousand times, following pitching coach and manager's orders, away he trudged, readying for his "last" inning. What happened next, even the happy-go-lucky Travis could never have guessed.

"I came into the game," said Driskill, choking back tears as he remembered that special night. "'I've Been Everywhere,' blared on Dell Diamond's PA system with a crowd of about ten thousand, standing, cheering their backsides off. As the bullpen door swung open, away I went on my last trip, I thought, to the top of the hill, and the crowd got louder!"

A successful, scoreless eighth sent Driskill to the dugout with an overwhelmingly raucous crowd standing, cheering goodbye, and greetings and handshakes and hugs from fellow players, coaches, and manager Jackie Moore.

"Then, as I'm sitting down, thinking 'Thank God that's over,' Burt Hooton says to me, 'Hey Trav, we got no one else, I gotta have you in the ninth!'"

"Come on Burt, forget it. I don't have it in me," Driskill battled his coach. "I'm emotional as hell, I tell ya I just don't have it in me, Burt."

Shaking his head in disagreement, Hooton remained adamant.

"Gotta have you," he insisted, "Gotta have you."

Never completely realizing what was next, not knowing the working conspiracy involving his family, manager, coaches, and Express staff, Driskill knew one thing for sure. This time, for certain, was his last.

"No sooner did I race up the dugout steps and onto the field headed toward the mound, the public address announcer cranked up "I Been Everywhere," one more time, even louder than before," remembers Driskill tears rolling down his cheeks.

"I looked into the dugout and out came Jackie Moore, my wife Natalie, and both my sons," Driskill said, tears continuing. "Looking up, there's the loudest standing ovation you can imagine. Ten thousand fans thunderously screaming at the top of their lungs, PA music making it louder. Pandemonium. Delirium. Believe me, I was stunned. I looked over at the New Orleans dugout, and to a player, they raced out, stood, clapped, and cheered. Me, I'm crying my eyes out."

"Sure, the New Orleans team was cheering," said Moore. "A lot of their guys traveled similar roads, they knew Travis, had faced him, and knew very well what he'd been through, and of course they gave him a well-deserved standing O. I'd never seen a night like this one in fifty plus years in the game."

Overcome, Travis never attempted composure.

"No one, major leagues or minor leagues ever got a reception like that on his last day," Driskill said. "No one in the minor leagues ever left with such a wild, emotional ceremony. I'm crying again as I tell this tale, and every time I think about it or tell someone about it and even though it's years behind me, I cry like a baby, every single time!"

No one inside Dell Diamond's gates had dry eyes.

"Surely not in our dugout, and looking at the fans, they were all crying as they cheered," Jackie Moore said. "But I tell you, no one deserved that celebration of a baseball life well lived more than Travis Driskill."

Travis became a pitching coach in the Astros organization in Rookie Ball, High A and Double A. Those days past at least for now, he and Natalie live in Plano, north of Dallas, where Travis coaches select teams and teaches youngsters the pitching arts. In the depths of his soul, he'd love another shot inside the arena coaching young, promising future big league pitchers. Maybe that day will come. Maybe some wise major-league organization welcomes him back, teaching the correct way to pitch as well as impeccable professional conduct. When an organization finally does that, the game improves immediately.

KELLY WUNSCH

"First rounder, side-armer, home builder..."

L EFTHANDERS IN BASEBALL have always had the reputation as "different," zany, or just plain nuts.

"When I was in Stockton," Kelly Wunsch laughs, "I took over the role of mascot, ultimately to ask my girlfriend to marry me in front of a big home crowd."

The left-hander profile fits like a glove. Instead of signing with the Cardinals out of high school, Wunsch attended Texas A&M, studying engineering. That move worked well. Kelly later became a hugely successful, environmentally friendly Austin home builder. So much more than an educated jock at six-feet, five inches and two hundred pounds, Wunsch was blessed with a lean, swarthy, movie star face, and singing voice rivaling Jon Bon Jovi or John Mellencamp. He could've easily made a living on stage with guitar in hand, and song from his lips.

"Ah, I don't know," he laughed. "I'm not bad at karaoke, but making a living at it, aaahhh, nah."

Kelly Wunsch on the mound for Texas A&M.
(Photo courtesy of Texas A&M Athletics)

Baseball ultimately won out, although the road to success at times moved uphill seemingly all the way.

"Heck, I loved the game the first time I walked on the field," he remembers. "And while I was by no means exceptional. Playing and not bench sitting is all I wanted."

As a youngster, tall for his age at age eight, he also tried basketball with, politely said, a perfect physical profile and less than average success.

"I was a horrible YMCA kid basketball player," he laughed. "Look, I played three seasons, made no points the first season, and precious little after that. Truthfully, my basketball game as a kid was all about fouls. It's really all I had!"

Kelly had no "dad-and-son-play-catch-in-the-yard" moment. His dad never played the game but loved his sons and learned to coach after Houston's Willow Creek Little League officials provided prospective coaches with rules manuals and ways to teach.

"Yeah, he coached our teams starting out," Wunsch recalls, "but I was a left-handed catcher... yes, I said lefty catcher, but the coaches said, 'well you can't catch as a lefty,' so they made me a first baseman."

Not just any first baseman, but an overly eager one racing after balls hit to other infielders or outfielders. Then, as a nine-year old, an older friend taught him to throw a curveball, much to the angst of league coaches.

"I am talking about a real *yakker*," he said. "And by the time I was twelve, I was a pitcher and I had one heck of a hammer, and no one could hit it."

The young curveballer had command, learning to throw it hard as well as slow, slower, slowest.

"In a game against one of my friends," Kelly grinned, "I threw him the slowest of slow curves. He violently swung his bat backward, then forward swinging again wildly, and as he did, it looked like a real Bugs Bunny swing. Problem for him: he missed on both swings!"

Covering his mouth with his glove, Kelly tried to stop laughing. After his victim violently shook his head in utter disbelief, pulling his cap over his eyes, Kelly's teammates and coaches lost it.

"My first baseman also had his glove over his mouth," Wunsch said, "but then I saw his shoulders shaking as he was fighting off laughing out loud. Couldn't do it. No one could."

A freshman at Houston-area Bellaire High's powerhouse baseball program, Wunsch described himself as "a scrawny, no-muscle kid who played on the B squad and almost got cut." A fellow pitcher's injury gave him a chance.

"Even then I had no realization," he recalled. "In fact, I was a third of the way through my senior year in high school when I realized scouts in the stands were there for me. My velocity rose from 85-86 to a solid 90-92, and apparently that helped."

Drafted by the St. Louis Cardinals in late rounds, Kelly uttered in disbelief, "Why would I ever play pro ball? I was more focused on playing in college and becoming an engineer. Interested in both USC and Texas A&M because both had great engineering schools, I had other offers but chose A&M."

Losing his weekend starter status at A&M awakened him to baseball reality. Trying to pick off runners and instead throwing balls into the stands three times stood as the death knell.

"Finally, [A&M Coach] Mark Johnson came out to get me," Wunsch remembered. "And he said, 'well, they finally figured you out.'"

Lacking confidence and questioning the future, Kelly pitched for the Orleans Cardinals in the prestigious Cape Cod (Collegiate) League for coach Rolando Casanova. Pitching for Casanova changed Kelly's approach.

"So much mechanically changed," he said. "Rolando helped me adopt a fast-with-everything approach. Fast hands out of the glove, fast feet, fast arm. I stopped trying to muscle up, and wouldn't ya know it, the ball just jumped out of my hand."

Casanova also preached relaxation and concentration.

"He told me, 'Kelly, pitch like the count has three balls for a walk, and you'll throw fewer pitches," Wunsch remembered. "And facing hitters with wooden bats taught me to jam hitters, break their bats and allowed my stuff to play so much better."

Returning to A&M, pitching coach Jim Lawler further refined Kelly's mechanics.

"Rolando got me to relax and concentrate," Wunsch said, "His two suggestions built my confidence, then Jim Lawler fixed me and my delivery."

As a junior, Wunsch dominated Big 12 hitters. A Brewers first rounder in 1993, then pitching a half season for Low A Beloit in the Midwest League, he averaged twelve strikeouts per nine innings. Opening 1994 in Beloit in the snow and freezing cold, he struggled. The following season, back in Beloit again, Wunsch's world changed forever.

"I got off to an 0-3 start my third season in Beloit," he laughed. "Our closer Chris Burt took me to a bar after a game and introduced me to his niece Jessica. We hit it off."

So much so, Jessica attended his next start.

"Looking back, I probably was showing off for her," he laughed. "I was perfect through eight innings, but in the ninth, I hit a batter, the next hitter doubled and out I went. In comes Jessica's uncle, my teammate and our closer, who got himself shellacked and we lost five to three."

Inseparable before Wunsch's call to High A Stockton, Jessica joined Kelly when college studies allowed. During the 1997 season the two began marriage talk.

"Rings and stuff like that," Kelly grinned.

Those get-hitched thoughts launched a plan designed to work only in the wild, wacky world of minor-league baseball—and a left-hander's mind. Knowing Jessica's favorite engagement ring, Kelly immediately ran to the jeweler and bought the "I will" diamond. Strolling into a meeting with Stockton's front office, he asked if he could play the team's mascot, Splash, for one night. (He wasn't scheduled to pitch that night.)

"Stockton had an on-field contest sorta like *Let's Make a Deal*," Kelly laughed. "A staff member hides prizes under three different papier mache boots, then a contestant picks. Jessica would be one of the contestants that night. He hid the ring in one of the boots.

His plan: Jessica would discover the engagement ring, then Kelly/Splash moves in for the big moment. He hoped. And prayed.

"First thing, Jessica picked a bouquet of flowers from me, second a bottle of champagne from me, and the third, the ring. As she spotted the ring, there I was dressed as Splash, down on one knee in front of her and the cheering, laughing crowd. I pulled off Splash's head and she gasped when she saw me. So, there in front of all those people, I proposed, and thank the Good Lord she said yes."

Domestic situation handled, back to baseball. Kelly made more changes.

"I hit a ton of batters throwing overhand," Wunsch admitted. "So, the Brewers pitching coordinator Bill Campbell, who'd seen me throwing from three-quarters motion in the bullpen, said 'why don't you try [throwing] it from the side.'"

Wunsch's first start as a three-fourths, side-arm hurler yielded five hit batters. So, El Paso pitching coach Dwight

Evans suggested, "See how low you can take it...see how far down you can go."

The lower motion worked beautifully.

"The ball had velocity, it had sink," Wunsch said with relief, "I was soooo comfortable with it and I pitched a complete game shutout against Midland."

After a few low three-quarters starts, Wunsch found the command and control that ultimately took him to the big leagues. His Brewers bosses were ambivalent.

"They hemmed and hawed, 'Well, you know, you cannot be a starter, that's just a one time through the lineup trick,' yak, yak, yak," Wunsch remarked. "I finally said, 'look I'm staying with the lower delivery slot.'"

After an outstanding 1998 campaign, and after joining a team in the Arizona Fall League, Kelly and Jessica married.

"The Brewers gave me two days off," he laughed. "They said, 'go get married and get your ass back to the team,' and that's what I did."

Despite a successful Fall League season, no spring training invitation came from Milwaukee. While the Brewers snub hurt, Kelly's wife, in a very quiet way, served notice the baseball dream might not work.

"Jessica began a master's degree at Texas A&M," Kelly remembered. "When I got home that night, she had left A&M admission papers on my nightstand as a reminder that baseball was not going well and that I might be at the end of the road. The message, accurate but hurtful, carried a deeper meaning: Get a degree! More importantly, it reminded me that I wanted to pitch in MLB more than anything. Truthfully? All boiled down to this—my wife Jessica is hot, and I didn't want to lose her!"

The marital politician went back for one more shot. In 1999, the Brewers rotated him between a spot starter's role and back-end bullpen work, first at Double A El Paso and then at Triple A in Louisville.

"Mixed success," Kelly moaned.

At the end of 1999 with no Brewers offer, Kelly became a free agent. Signing on with the Chicago White Sox, receiving an invitation to major-league spring training, he readied himself by pitching in both Venezuela and Puerto Rico.

"From having pitched competitively for almost the entire winter, I was in playing shape the day I arrived at White Sox camp," he vividly recalls. "I topped out at ninety-three from my low arm angle."

Initially pitching extremely well beginning spring training, Wunsch struggled, and worry began. That was until two days before the season opener, scheduled for The Ballpark in Arlington against the Rangers.

"Oh God," Wunsch winced, "the clubbie came into the clubhouse after I'd lifted weights that day saying 'Schu [Sox GM at the time Ron Schueler] wants to see you.' I'm thinking, 'aw God, they sent me down.' But there was Ron standing in the parking lot with my wife and as I walked up, he said, 'Jessica and I were just wondering if you have any Opening Day plans?' And I gulped, 'uh naw,' and he said, 'well fine. You're going with us to Arlington.'"

"Top of the World feeling," he mused. "It's third in line with marriage, kids. I felt like I'd won the lottery. Jessica and I headed out to celebrate and of course our parents were deliriously happy."

Coming back home to Texas and facing the Rangers made it all extra special. Parents arrived from Houston, Kelly's brother and sister-in-law, who lived in the Dallas area, made it for the debut. Then, doubt set in.

"Wouldn't you know, all I could think about was," Wunsch laughed, "'Hey here I am, Mr. Big Shot, and then what if I don't get to pitch?'"

A needless worry. The Rangers rang up a ton of runs on an extremely frigid Opening Day. Temperatures topping out in the high thirties with howling, swirling winds created a day in Kelly Wunsch infamy.

"I had never been so cold in my life," he said. "Opening Day or not, it was miserable. Cold and windy as hell. We kept moving in the bullpen. Either that or freeze, and of course we were getting clobbered!"

Warming up for his maiden MLB voyage, Kelly heard nothing but catcalls as kids surrounding the White Sox bullpen constantly screamed their frigid lungs out.

"Aw, it was hilarious," he laughed. "They yelled 'Hey rag arm, you suck! Nice jersey Number 65, you're not up here long. Then I missed the bullpen catcher's mitt by five or six feet and away they went again. 'Hey, rag arm, you missed him by a mile, coach, coach, he's ready.'"

As the bullpen door swung open, Wunsch remembers the cold disappearing.

"Yeah, and no idiot kids yelling their heads off," he laughed, "but better than that there was a low din in the crowd and even better than that, I felt my body temperature flush upward by ten degrees. I had three guys to face: Rusty Greer, Raphael Palmeiro, and A-Rod. Got 'em all—one, two, three. Hah!"

What a way to open a MLB career.

That 2000 season Wunsch became the Sox' go-to bullpen lefty. Making a MLB-leading eighty-three appearances, the workload took a toll as the season raced on, including three more in the playoffs. Kelly pitched every other day for a two-week stretch, then threw in four of six games. Shoulder tightness and a dead arm remained his constant companions. Cortisone shots on a semi-regular basis kept the party going.

"You don't last long pitching like that," he says. "And truthfully, it is not sustainable."

After the heavy rookie season workload, Wunsch lost velocity in his second season. In a June game against the Cardinals after pitching several days in succession, Wunsch served up two critical homers. The first, a two-run shot to Kerry Robinson, and the second a day later. Racing into a game, using five warmup pitches, then facing slugger Bobby Bonilla, Wunsch gave up a grand slam.

"After the slam, I said to the trainer, hey, something's really wrong with my shoulder," Wunsch winced at the memory. "And his response was, 'well, I've been waiting for you to tell me.'"

Wunsch overcame labrum and rotator cuff surgery, pitching through pain over his next five seasons with the White Sox. Some 212 appearances over that stretch and a 10-5 record and 3.76ERA brought on more surgery in 2004 as he moved to the Dodgers.

"I loved it there," he said enthusiastically. "Everything about it. The stadium, the weather, the crowds. Everything."

Forty-five appearances for the Dodgers in 2005, and a 1-1 mark, Kelly Wunsch was done. Achieving a dream he never thought existed, he came through his career with a host of injuries and a shoulder causing intermittent trouble. Looking back, he feels fortunate.

"Fortunate and blessed to have achieved what I did," he said. "I don't feel unfulfilled, I don't have, like some I know, a mid-life crisis from not achieving this dream or that dream or the other."

Wunsch works hard continually improving his home construction business in the hot Austin housing market. His athletic competitiveness fires his homebuilding passion.

"I'm not a former major-league player to most people buying houses from me," he said. "I work hard continually educating myself on the craft, providing people with homes they'll love. The hard work and the finished product, that's what drives me."

As it does most, achieving huge success.

CHAPTER 5

CHRIS GIMENEZ

"The pitcher is the catcher, and no one finer than niner!"

L ook, I don't think I ever pitched in high school, well maybe…." grinned veteran MLB catcher turned emergency pitcher Chris Gimenez. "Heck I probably pitched in Little League, or maybe not."

But there in the Texas Rangers bullpen on July 10, 2014, stood sturdy Chris Gimenez, a rock of a catcher, answering the bullpen call from Rangers pitching coach Mike Maddux as Texas found its doors blown off 15-4 by the Los Angeles Angels late in the game.

"Gimmie, you ever pitch before?" Maddux asked.

"Oh, hell yeah, I have," came the earnest, yet not completely accurate, reply.

"Well, you got the ninth then," Maddux said.

Those words stunned the veteran catcher, still wearing his gear. The bullpen coach overheard the Maddux call, and said, "Hey you need to get out of that gear, and start loosening, we're in the middle of the eighth."

Grabbing a fielder's glove, Gimenez went to work.

"I'm looking around, out of my catcher's gear now, the bullpen catcher's squatting down, and I ask myself, 'Holy shit, what did I just agree to?'"

Well, what he agreed to was nothing more than entering a

Chris Giminez rounds the bases as a catcher for the Round Rock Express.
(Photo courtesy of the Round Rock Express Baseball Club)

major-league game for the first time as a pitcher. With his hitter's walkup music blaring on the Ballpark at Arlington's public address system, Chris Gimenez made his debut as a reliever.

"Yeah, but I was locked in," he laughed. "There goes the first pitch, a seventy-mile-an-hour heater. Sttteeeerrriiiikkke one!"

Next pitch? Angels infielder David Freese grounded out.

"This is easy," Chris thought to himself.

Gimenez then struck out C.J. Cron swinging and induced a fly ball from Hank Conger for a merciful third out. A perfect one-two-three inning.

"I threw a couple at eighty-seven," Gimenez told a post-game news conference. "And when I did, the fingers on my pitching hand tingled and I kept telling myself, 'Don't blow out, oh God don't blow out.'"

A couple of days later he told reporters, "I tried to be a pitcher, I really did, but I feel like I'm gonna need Tommy John surgery, and two shoulder surgeries. Pitching is tough. I will never throw that hard again. From now on, if they need me to pitch, I'm going slow, slower, slowest."

A nineteenth-round pick by Cleveland in 2004 from the University of Nevada-Reno, Chris Gimenez ground through, literally, a career taking him through parts of ten MLB seasons. Mostly a catcher, he also found spot duty at third and the corner outfield slots. Like most backups, versatility helped. After bouncing through Cleveland, Seattle, and Tampa Bay, he hit .412 down the stretch for the Rays in 2012. After that nice run he spent 2013 between Triple A Durham and Tampa Bay, Gimenez came to a conclusion.

"I wasn't having as much fun as I needed to in Triple A," he remembered. "In 2014 I had a call from my alma mater, University of Nevada-Reno, asking if I was interested in coaching. When my wife asked me if I was interested, I said no. But knowing I'd thought about leaving professional ball, she told me, 'Make sure you're done before you leave pro ball.'"

Kellie Burton met Chris when the two attended the University of Nevada-Reno. USA Today named Kellie, who starred in basketball and volleyball in high school, their Nevada basketball player of the year. Playing volleyball in college, she attracted Chris' attention during a Wolf Pack game.

"Baseball players came to watch us all the time," she told Nevada Sports Network. "I guess they had nothing better to do. We passed out white rally towels and encouraged fans to write their favorite player's number on them and then wave 'em; my number was nine."

Obviously overwhelmed by Kellie, Chris used a magic marker to write the words, "NO ONE FINER THAN NINER," on his towel. Later the two met at a party.

"He was nervous," Kellie remembered, "All he said to me was, 'no one finer than niner,' and then walked away."

Later the two sat together at a Wolf Pack basketball game and hit it off. As Chris moved up the ranks to Triple A, while Kellie returned from a vacation with a girlfriend, he called to tell her the Indians called him up and he was headed to Minnesota for a series with the Twins.

"I called my boss," she told Nevada Sports Network, "and told him, 'Hey, I know I'm just off vacation, but Chris got called up. 'Go, GO, you GO,'" he said.

His third game, with Kellie watching, Chris hit a home run.

"As he rounded third," Kellie said, "he pointed to the stands [at me]. We have the ball he hit, his jersey from that day, and my ticket from that game hanging in a downstairs hallway."

"From an athletic standpoint she understood the struggle," Chris said. "She understood the competition, the feeling slighted. She simply told me, 'We know how much it means to you and we will follow you until you are done. Make sure you are done.' That always stuck with me."

Most importantly Kellie watched the struggles, the releases, the removals from the forty-man roster, and the moves to fifty different cities during his career.

"We've lived in Arizona, Texas, North Carolina, Florida, Minnesota, Ohio, and Washington State," she remembers nobly. "We took the kids with us, we never knew what tomorrow would bring, and I made friends with other ball wives, and really poured myself into my online master's degree."

Besides the nomadic lifestyle, Chris' career included serious injuries. Most humans do not survive:

♦ Two different staph infection battles; the first, a right knee infection hampered his Short Season A, 2005 season.

♦ Another staph infection, in the 2016 season while catching for the Rangers, almost cost him his left leg. "A foul tip created a lot of swelling and my leg felt on fire," he said. The spreading infection led doctors to tell Chris they might have to remove the infected leg. Two surgeries and massive antibiotics doses saved the leg, Gimenez' life and career.

♦ While catching, the recoil from a bat knocked him senseless, at Triple A Columbus in 2009.

♦ Perhaps more deadly than the rest, Chris cheated death according to the Reno Gazette-Journal when, on a snowy, icy day, he found himself stuck in traffic in Reno just before spring training 2016. A snowplow clipped a thirty-six-pound steel drain gate, propelling it 150 feet through his truck's cab. "Instinctively, I ducked," Gimenez told the newspaper. "What if I'd gone out that way? That wouldn't have been cool."

Gimenez also traveled a dizzying road back and forth between the Texas Rangers and Cleveland Indians. After making his first MLB relief appearance in 2014, the Rangers traded him to Cleveland in late August. Back to Texas on a minor-league deal in 2015 set a grand stage.

"Well, for the most fun I ever had as a player," he smiled. "We came back from twelve down to the Astros to win the division, and for the first time I made a playoff roster."

Despite roster problems and near-death experiences, Gimenez always looked for the perfect long-term place to play. He thought he'd found it as Yu Darvish's personal catcher with the Texas Rangers in 2016. That dream didn't last long. As he was coming back from his second staph infection bout General Manager Jon Daniels called Gimenez into a meeting.

"I thought he was going to ask how Yu and I were adapting," Chris remembered. "And then he told me 'We're trading you back to Cleveland.'"

Stunned again, off to Cleveland for the third time went Gimenez.

"That move was particularly rough," he said in Cleveland. com, "because Kellie and the kids were coming to Arlington to spend time with me, and the trade created some chaos for my family. But the other thing is, just when you think you found the right place, the Baseball Gods say, "oh no, just kidding!"

The backup catcher and veteran always assumed a role of a quiet yet humorous clubhouse leader.

"Chris is as cerebral a catcher as there is," said former Rangers Triple-A Pitching Coach Brad Holman. "He's funny, he's a character, but when it's time to strap it on, he's ready."

Later signed by the Minnesota Twins as a free agent before the 2017 campaign, he made sure Twins management knew if they needed catching or relief help, he was ready.

"I just thought why not," he said. "When my team's in a blowout situation and we don't want to go deeper in our bullpen, I was always happy to help."

Chris Gimenez turned out to be a record setter as a catcher/pitcher. Making six relief appearances for the Minnesota Twins in 2017, he accomplished a feat that had not been accomplished in Major League Baseball since the 1870's.

"Tell you something else that happened that year," he laughed. "Our bullpen coach Eddie Guardado taught me a knuckleball to develop a put-away pitch!"

Onto the Cubs he went. Not making Chicago's Opening Day roster in 2018 frustrated him and prompted Windy City sportswriters to infer that Chris' signing came about because he was brought in to become Yu Darvish's personal catcher.

"[During spring training, the Cubs] used me as a resource for familiarity with Yu," said Chris. "Then they sent me down, telling me to go down to Iowa. I was going to play, then I'd be called back in a month."

Gimenez played in sixty-eight games at Iowa before the Cubs called him up in late May. By then Darvish suffered elbow problems and Gimenez never caught him.

"I was pissed at the whole thing," Chris noted. "But the good news was, I got traded back to the Twins and I hit .300 the rest of the way."

In a Twins late-season relief appearance that season, facing his former team the Rangers, Gimenez ironically smoked a home run in an 18-4 loss to Texas. The 2018 season ended his playing career, and he became Game Planning Coach for the Los Angeles Dodgers, developing scouting reports for the manager and coaches.

By the end of the 2021 season, the Gimenezes decided Chris would come home. But he didn't leave the game entirely.

"I got a phone call after I retired from a Sirius XM-MLB Radio producer asking me if I could come on and talk about the Dodgers' Trevor Bauer," he said. "I said, 'Look, I don't work there anymore. I'm retired.' And the guy just shoots out, 'do you want a job here?'"

Starting at once a week on Sirius XM, his role has now expanded to twice a week, and a prejudicial judgment concludes he's among the top broadcasters among an exceptional former MLB player roster on that network.

"I had to scramble at first," he laughed. "But [SiriusXM] is outstanding. I get my baseball fix and now I'm working from home, with my family nearby."

With a bow to his wife "Niner," Chris Gimenez also followed her words, "Make Sure You Are Done," and found nirvana.

ALAN ZINTER

"I never surrender...."

THROUGHOUT THE AGES young men who battled to play and succeed in baseball also dreamed and fantasized their sons would follow. Alan Zinter's dad, also Alan, remains to this day, one of those.

"I never had to push," smiled the elder Zinter.

Finding himself awash in the game, playing college ball at the University of Minnesota, a few short years later, while holding his baby son, the dream grew wings.

"I felt in my heart," he remembered, "he'd love it as much as I did."

At age three young Zinter could swing a small plastic bat, shooting plastic ball liners all over his parents' living room. When he was still in diapers, the baseball dye was cast.

Alan Zinter with the Round Rock Express in 2006.
(Photo courtesy of the Round Rock Express Baseball Club)

"He always had that bat and ball with him," the older Alan beamed. "Later he wanted to practice every day when I got home from work."

"He's been there for me every single step of the way," the younger Alan smiled.

Any casual fan reading Cincinnati Reds hitting coach Alan Zinter's player biography might conclude his playing career didn't work out. Not true.

"I was a first-round pick who fought for his professional life," Zinter said.

Alan Zinter knows the extremes, the failures and successes of a nineteen-year playing career. Achieving his MLB dream took fourteen seasons, giving Zinter a different appreciation, love, and passion for the game.

"He represents one of those guys who loved it so much, all of it, he ultimately was going to succeed no matter what," said former MLB player, manager, and bench coach Jackie Moore.

Zinter's first big-league call came from Houston in 2002. His second, two years later was with the Arizona Diamondbacks. A total of seventy games made up the whole of Zinter's MLB career. It all began in El Paso, Texas, his youthful baseball exploits thrilling fans and exciting scouts.

"It was all willed, and planned," Zinter said.

At age five, his dad took him to Candlestick Park for a Giants game. Visiting with former teammate University of Arizona head coach Jerry Kindall, Alan's dad predicted, "Hey Jerry, (pointing to his son) I'm gonna have one for you in about thirteen years."

At six, Alan "could throw hard and accurately," his dad said. At age seven, his dad gave him a set of catcher's gear and taught him, with his mother purposely swinging and missing, how to catch with a batter at the plate.

"Alan couldn't wait until Little League began at age eight," his dad smiled.

"I played against kids older and much bigger than me," Zinter said. "The ten-year-olds were huge."

While owning older pitchers that year, Zinter took over catching duties when his team's ten-year old backstop suddenly couldn't throw or catch. Little League opponents quickly learned not to run.

"Boy, oh boy," Zinter recalled, "I could see myself in the big leagues."

Alan dominated each age group. Beginning his freshman season at newly opened Hanks High, his dad ordered, "You have to try out for the varsity baseball team."

So, the shy yet intrepid freshman located Head Varsity baseball coach Mike Williams.

"I said, 'excuse me, coach. I *have* to try out for the varsity baseball team."

"You have to what?" Williams asked.

"I have to try out for the varsity baseball team," young Zinter repeated.

"We don't allow freshmen to try out," Williams responded. "But you are the only young man who has ever told me he *has* to try out for varsity."

Fortunately, Williams not only understood, but he also appreciated freshman Zinter's chutzpah. "Okay," Williams said. "Show me what ya got."

Switch hitting, Zinter lined an RBI double to left, from the right side. Then from the left, two line drives scorched to right.

"I also ran as hard as I could," Zinter said proudly. "I wanted the coach to know how much I wanted it."

Williams smiled, loudly proclaiming, "Catch, run, switch hit a ton, yessir son, you made the varsity."

A year later, the chance of a lifetime. At a Milwaukee Brewers tryout at El Paso's Dudley Dome, home of the Double-A Diablos, the fifteen-year-old Zinter's mitt and bat acumen impressed Diablos manager Terry Bevington. Later an MLB manager, Bevington made an offer.

"Why don't you become our bullpen catcher after your season ends?" offered the Diablos skipper. "You can show up here every afternoon at one p.m. and work with our pitchers and pitching coach in the bullpen, and you can see how this professional game works."

"Wow!" exclaimed Zinter. "But there was just one catch. Because of state high school rules, we had to make sure I wasn't paid and wouldn't take trips with the Diablos. I didn't need to get paid for the education I got!"

Working with Bevington and future major-league star hurlers Juan Nieves and Dan Plesac, and surrounded by the entire Double A Diablos team, the fifteen-year-old also took batting practice and infield practice with the catchers.

"I got a great taste and feel," Zinter said. "For the way big leaguers-to-be went about their business."

After high school, Zinter turned down a 1986 Padres draft selection for a University of Arizona scholarship. Success followed. NCAA First team All-America, and All-American honors came from Baseball America, The Sporting News, and The American Baseball Coaches Association.

"Jerry Kindall was the best," said Zinter. "We didn't simply learn baseball. We learned respect for people, performed community service work, and learned how to be responsible men. Jerry taught baseball and important life lessons."

The Mets chose Zinter with their first-round pick, the twenty-fourth player taken overall in the 1989 draft.

"They flew my family and me to New York," he remembered. "I appeared on live TV, rubbed elbows with Mets' Gary Carter, Dwight Gooden, and Keith Hernandez as well as their GM Joe McIlvane. Then the New York City vibe, wow, what a thrill!"

His live TV interview represented anything but a typical first round draft choice chat with the hair-sprayed, fast-talking, New York sports guy. In fact, it was, well...different.

"Every time I answered a question, he looked at me like I was crazy," Alan laughed. "He only asked one or two questions and the interview lasted no more than one minute. He looked at me and asked, 'are you nuts?'"

"What do you mean?"

"Well," the interviewer responded, "I had to shut it off because every time I asked you something, you talked about the Yankees instead of the Mets. You're with the Mets, ya know!"

"Oh," responded a red-faced first-rounder.

At rookie ball in Pittsfield, Massachusetts, Zinter tore it up, crushing the baseball and performing well behind the plate. Then a big jump to High A brought first time failure.

"My dad taught me well and I always hit naturally," he recalled. "When coaches began fooling with my swing, making changes, I really was lost."

Brief peaks and extremely long valleys resulted.

"Failure became very real," Zinter recalled. "I had no idea how to handle it."

Seasons rolled by as players drafted later than Zinter passed him. At that point many become terribly disillusioned and give up. Alan refused.

"I loved it so much," Zinter said. "Loved the playing, clubhouse camaraderie, and constant, intense competition. I just embraced it."

Four years into his career Zinter played in the Arizona Fall League, postseason league, populated by the best pro prospects. He made the All-Star team and became the league's Most Valuable Player.

"For the first time," Zinter noted. "I really felt like a potential big leaguer."

Being traded from the Mets to Detroit shook his confidence at first, but Tigers spring training opened his eyes.

"Cecil Fielder, Alan Trammel, and Kirk Gibson came to the clubhouse early every morning, way ahead of everyone else," Zinter marveled. "They stayed late working on every aspect of their games. Their workloads astonished me."

The other lesson from the Tigers: using failure as a learning tool. After two seasons at Detroit's Triple A Toledo, Zinter moved to Boston's Triple-A club, Pawtucket, then Triple A Tacoma, and in 1998, in his t enth professional season, to the Triple A Iowa Cubs.

"Was I disappointed I wasn't in the big leagues? Yes," Zinter said. "Yet I kept fighting."

During batting practice in his first Iowa season Zinter discussed hitting with a younger player. Afterward, I-Cubs pitching coach Marty DeMerritt approached him.

"You're gonna make one hell of a coach," DeMerritt beamed.

"I'm not done playing," Zinter snapped back.

"I'm not saying *now,* Z," DeMerritt responded, "I'm saying when you're done."

Badly disappointed not making the Chicago Cubs opening day roster in 1999, Zinter briefly went back to Iowa, then onto Japan for "a bittersweet run" with the Seibu Lions.

"Marty DeMerritt's words," Zinter laughed, "stuck firmly in my head."

Returning to the states in 2000 at Triple A Tucson, veteran hitting coach Mike Barnett approached Zinter during batting practice.

"You get yourself out a lot," Barnett said. "I like your swing, but I want you to spread out in the box."

Barnett's words made sense. The changes worked.

"I hit .380 the rest of the way," Zinter grinned. "At age thirty-three and thanks to Mike Barnett, I finally got it."

In 2001 at the Astros' Triple-A affiliate New Orleans, Zinter banged out nineteen homers, driving in sixty-five. "Killing it," in spring training 2002, then, during an impressive season, New Orleans travelled to Colorado Springs for a Father's Day weekend series. Joined by his dad, Zinter experienced a life moment.

"Seeing my father in the stands, I found peace," Zinter remembered. "I said a little prayer, 'I'm grateful, God, for this journey,' and then I teared up."

The best stood ahead. Upset by manager Chris Maloney's removing him from a tight game that day in the eighth inning, suddenly New Orleans Trainer Mike "Otis" Freer's cell phone rang. Handing it to Maloney, Freer took a step back.

"Yes, yes," grinned Maloney, talking unbeknownst to Zinter, to the Astros front office.

"Otis," yelled Maloney to the trainer, "Can we tell him?" Freer nodded yes. The seven New Orleans players standing in the dugout screamed and yelled as Zinter looked on.

"Hey, Z," Maloney screamed, "Z, Z, you're going to the big leagues!"

"After a thirteen-year battle," Zinter remembers, "finally, I'm going up. I was stunned, but quickly found my dad and told him, 'Let's fly to Milwaukee and watch the Brewers play,' can you go?"

"Absolutely," came the fatherly reply.

Once in the visitors' clubhouse in Milwaukee, the wide-eyed veteran met with manager Jimy Williams who told him he should, "feel proud of this callup, and Z, I am going to use you."

Zinter homered against Cincinnati in his first MLB game. In thirty-nine Astros games in 2002, Zinter homered twice in forty-four plate appearances. His second callup came after signing in 2004 with the Diamondbacks' Triple-A club in Tucson. Twenty-eight Arizona games, forty at bats and a solo homer later, his MLB run ended. Saying no to an Astros coaching job in 2006, instead playing that season at Triple A, then in 2007 at Independent Somerset, his playing career ground to a halt.

"It was time to go," he said quietly.

From playing, yes. Arizona hired Zinter to coach rookie hitters in Missoula, Montana. Then on to High A Visalia, and then in 2012 he changed organizations. Cleveland hired him as its minor-league hitting coordinator, a critical portion of his development.

"I organized like never before," Zinter recalled. "I wrote down nineteen seasons of thoughts and experiences, simplified the club's hitting manual, and made it better."

Just as he had as a young player, making step by step adjustments to each level, Zinter found similarities in his coaching development.

"It's not about me anymore," he said. "It's all about the young players, and it's about explaining analytics and the hitting craft to a generation insisting on knowing 'why,' not just how."

After Cleveland, Zinter went back to Houston where he debuted in MLB, becoming the Astros assistant hitting coach.

"Leaving Cleveland was difficult," he says. "I watched their offensive future, Francisco Lindor, Roberto Perez, and Jose Ramirez, grow up as professionals and hated leaving them behind."

When Zinter arrived, the Astros had experienced a series of hundred-loss seasons but had an impressive offensive cavalry on the way in Carlos Correa and Alex Bregman.

"No one gave us any credit," Zinter smiled. "But we won the Wild Card game against the Yankees and our lefty Dallas Keuchel shoved it up their butts. It was really intense, but it was cool going back to Houston where I was first called up."

His first MLB hitting coach job in San Diego led to disappointment.

"Andy Greene was the manager, one of the smartest people in the world," Alan remembered. "They were rebuilding, but with a month left in my second season they let me go. I was shaken, then came the 'am I not good enough' questions again."

Longtime friend Blue Jays GM Ross Atkins, earlier involved in hiring Zinter as Cleveland's minor-league coordinator, called asking for recommendations for his open hitting coordinator job. Reeling from his Padres dismissal, needing financial security, Alan replied, "I'm available."

In the midst of discussions with the Blue Jays, former MLB infielder David Bell, just named director of player development for the San Francisco Giants, called. After an initial rebuff, Alan's wife told him, "Look, you need to call David Bell."

"We talked for three or four hours—really serious discussions," Zinter remembered. "David hired me as his assistant for the 2018 season. When David left for the Reds Manager's job, Cincinnati already had a hitting coach, so I stayed in San Francisco. Then after the 2019 season, the Reds made some changes, I interviewed for the hitting coach job, got it, and here I am."

In 2021, Zinter coached National League Rookie of the Year Jonathan India.

"What an unbelievable talent," Zinter said admiringly. "Jonathan owns great intensity, and an uncanny ability to adjust and he's calm and confident yet not cocky, in his skin"

Alan and the Reds also benefit from watching veteran first baseman Joey Votto.

"His teammates watch his meticulous work ethic," Zinter marveled. "They know he embraced changes, and now at age thirty-eight, looks and plays like he did a decade ago."

Alan Zinter and his wife have a son playing junior college baseball, and a daughter attending the same junior college in Arizona.

"Our message to them almost mirrors the one to young players," Zinter said. "I want them to love the journey, embrace the 'suck' and know how hard life is sometimes. Yes, they'll face disappointment, but don't turn it into discouragement. Finally, can you after getting knocked down, get up and fight for what you love? Feel good, fighting that fight."

CHRIS TREMIE

"A leadership rock..."

TRUE GRINDERS understand each other. They appreciate the different skill sets they're blessed with, and they honor those, like themselves, who've battled to reach the major leagues.

"Whenever I think of grinders," said former MLB and Japanese Major League righty Travis Driskill, "I think of Chris Tremie."

Driskill first knew Chris when both faced each other in the old Southwest Conference—Driskill at Texas Tech and Tremie at the University of Houston.

Chris Tremie catching for the Round Rock Express in 2004.
(Photo courtesy of the Round Rock Express Baseball Club)

"He was great in college at handling pitchers, seeing the whole field, and I got to know him better when he caught me in the Astros system at both New Orleans and Round Rock," Driskill said.

"His brain power, ability to communicate knowledge to us pitchers, and his retention of that knowledge was second to none," Driskill continued. "Plus, his leadership ability was off the charts and with those skill sets he earned his teammates' ultimate respect.

"And there's one other thing that drives Tremie over the top in my book," Driskill continued. "Like most grinders, he's always been all about passing the game along to the next generation. Whether it was taking young guys aside and teaching them the ways of the clubhouse, on field behavior, or whether it was bringing his son to the park with him each day, I related, because I was a grinder and I brought my two sons with me, just to pass the game along."

Wow what an endorsement.

Let's back up to where it all began for Chris Tremie—in Houston as a very young kid, working with his dad.

"My dad gave me this game," said Tremie proudly. "I could barely walk, and he already had me holding a bat, or a glove and either throwing or hitting a ball."

Nothing, Tremie says, was ever forced on him by his dad, but the early lessons stuck. And Chris loved every minute of it.

"Heck, he was with me all the way," remarked the stocky Tremie, "and I loved being with my dad in a situation we both obviously loved."

Tremie's coaches in Little League, PONY, and teen ball set the stage for the place where Chris Tremie really found his niche—at South Houston High School, where Coach Mike Gardner moved him from mound work and shortstop to the catcher's spot.

"I jumped at the chance," Tremie said, "to start learning everything from correct footwork, to receiving the ball, to the main challenges Coach Gardner issued—setting the team's competitive tone, controlling the game while knowing all the positioning for defenders, and literally becoming the quarter-back or coach on the field."

"When you think about catchers, and when you think about guys who 'got it,' and more or less knew instinctively what was needed, you think of Chris," remarked fifty-year major-league skipper and bench coach Jackie Moore, who managed Tremie in the Double-A and Triple-A ranks. "He simply needed one set of instructions, and he took it from there."

From high school to the University of Houston and instruction from coaches Bragg Stockton and Rayner Noble, Tremie became a sponge, absorbing all the knowledge he could. Then between his sophomore and junior seasons at UH, he caught for a team in the collegiate Jayhawk League against top college players from across the U.S.

"That's when I found out for myself that I could compete and succeed against these guys, that I could actually get better playing in that atmosphere, and I knew then in my heart I could play professionally," Tremie said.

The Chicago White Sox drafted him in 1992, and by 1994 he'd made it into the Double-A ranks for the Sox at Birmingham, where he had the opportunity to play alongside an NBA Hall of Famer, trying to prove he could play baseball at the professional level.

"The NBA legend Michael Jordan, trying to play my sport, what a thrill," said Tremie. "I had to pick his brain about competing and dealing with success and failure, what an absolute thrill."

Tremie played in parts of four seasons with the White Sox, Rangers, Pirates, and Astros. His major-league debut came with the Sox in 1995, when he received the call to catch up with the Chicago club in Minneapolis at the Metrodome.

"Walked into that clubhouse, and the feeling of being there blew me away," he mused. "That day, I had to move fast, grabbing my gear, and then catching an early morning plane, flying cross country, and making it to the park by six that evening, well that was a test. But I made it in plenty of time."

Walking onto a major-league field, readying for his debut, Tremie took it all in.

"Well, of course I was in a dome, but I'd been in the Astrodome before, and then I kept thinking, 'I'm a big-leaguer, I'm a *big-leaguer*,' and then I looked up at that Metrodome roof, and it was white and I thought, 'hey, that roof might make it hard to find a fly ball here,' that's funny, right?"

Chris' first starting call came several nights later against the Kansas City Royals, who loved playing the speed game, and one of their best, Vince Coleman, immediately got on base, and therefore became a Tremie target.

"When Coleman got on," Tremie remembered with a smile, "I thought, wow, my first base runner, well, I'm gonna throw him out."

And immediately, as everyone in the park knew he would, Coleman broke for second base, testing the rookie catcher.

"Hah," grinned Tremie, "the pitcher gave me a good pitch, and I made a good throw to get Coleman, and I have to tell you, I was pretty pumped."

After that initial major-league foray, Tremie, in mid-2000, found himself without a job after he asked for and received his release from the Marlins. But it didn't take him long to find a short-term home.

"I needed to work, needed to keep playing," he said, "so I signed on with Newark in the Independent Atlantic League, just to keep in shape. Then, because I had kept myself in shape by playing, I had the chance to sign back with the Marlins and finish with their Triple-A team in Calgary."

For the next five seasons, Tremie caught at the Double A, Triple A, and briefly the major-league level for the Houston Astros. At both levels with Houston, Chris found himself alongside Jackie Moore, former MLB catcher Mark Bailey, and former MLB pitchers Burt Hooton and Mike Maddux, both of whom went onto major-league pitching coach careers.

"Those guys were great," Tremie smiled. "I was an older player helping younger ones, but Jackie Moore and his staff shared stories with me and introduced me to people. More importantly than that, they communicated with me better than anyone during my entire career. Those interactions immensely helped me set the stage for my coaching and managing career."

"A very cerebral catcher," said former Astros General Manager Tim Purpura. "Chris saw the whole picture on the field, he put young pitchers at ease, settling them when they needed it, quietly correcting them when that was called for, and he knew how to run a clubhouse. Every minor-league organization, run the correct way, needs a force like Chris Tremie at all levels, if they want success."

Purpura also played an integral role in what turned out to be Tremie's final call to the major leagues, late in the 2004 season, after Chris had completed his minor-league work.

"I hadn't been in the big leagues since 1999," marveled Tremie. "A couple weeks went by since my season ended, and while I lived only about half an hour from Minute Maid Park in Houston, I didn't always watch all the games.

"And," he continued, "I hadn't seen the game where Astros catcher Brad Ausmus was run over and injured on a play at the plate in mid-September."

When there's a need, find Chris Tremie.

"Tim [Purpura] called and said, 'Hi Chris, where are you today?'"

"Right here at home, Tim," I responded, "a thirty-minute drive away from where you are!"

"We need you," he said.

Chris grabbed his gear and his car keys and raced to Minute Maid Park.

At the end of his playing career, Chris transitioned to twelve successful seasons as a minor-league manager from short season Single A ball to Triple A, winning at every level and developing scores of talent.

"I worked," he said proudly, "with great coaches, other managers, and great, great players."

Look at Cleveland's 2019 lineup, and if they came through the Indians system, Chris Tremie played a huge role in their development.

Now, however, this baseball lifer finished his first year in a completely different role as the Cincinnati Reds' minor-league field coordinator.

"I loved my years managing, but ultimately realized I needed to broaden my experiences and benefit even more people along the way," he said. "I am extremely fortunate to have this new opportunity and provide a positive impact for the Reds future players and the organization in general."

Tremie took the Cincinnati job remembering a few of the things his former manager Jackie Moore told him"

- ◆ "Every time you think you got this game figured out, it's about to bring you right back."

- ◆ "If you think you know everything, it's time to look in the mirror!"

- ◆ "Always stay on an even keel, because while roller coasters are always a lot of fun, the rides don't last very long."

Sage wisdom provided from catcher to catcher, grinder to grinder, generation to generation.

CHAPTER 6

★

BILL LUCAS

"He was the first black GM."

"Bill Lucas and I first met at Milwaukee Braves spring training in 1961," noted former Braves Scouting Director Paul Snyder. "We played together, and I loved the man."

A whippet-thin middle infielder, Florida native Bill Lucas profiled as a backup in MLB. But to Bill, an extremely intelligent student, and his parents, education and a degree from Florida A&M University and military service came first. Lucas loved the game immensely and after signing with the Milwaukee Braves in the late 1950s, his big-league dreams began.

"He just carried himself like a big-leaguer," Snyder said. "He was extremely smart and intuitive and heads-up all the time. One other thing; he read books that didn't have pictures. His teammates and I thought that was pretty amazing."

Snyder and Lucas played together at Double A Austin in the Texas League and Triple A Denver in the old American Association, as well as at lower minor-league levels.

"Those were the '60s, Jim Crow laws dominated the South," Snyder remembers. "Many times, Bill couldn't stay at the team hotel or eat at the same places we did, and that had to hurt him. We always brought food to him wherever we went. And you know what? Bill Lucas never said a cross word or got upset. He simply kept moving forward."

Turning a double play for the Austin Senators in 1964, an opposing base runner slid wickedly into Lucas' knees, taking him out of the play and ending his playing career. The ruined dreams and torn ligaments, however, opened new and more important doors for Bill and baseball. As the Milwaukee Braves moved South, Lucas became the club's liaison to Atlanta's black community. Five years later, he switched to player development. Then in 1976, Braves owner Ted Turner named Bill vice president for player personnel.

"They called him that," Snyder said, "and while Ted Turner gave himself the title of GM, Bill did everything an MLB GM does. So, on September 19, 1976, Bill Lucas became the first black General Manager in major-league history!"

Bill's wife and lifetime companion, Rubye, later a Turner Broadcasting System Board Member, told Atlantic Magazine in 2017 about the impact of her husband's new job.

"Because now it became, perhaps, his purpose in life," insisted Rubye, "to show that African Americans could be in higher positions in sports, especially in baseball."

Intelligent, intrepid, and instinctive, Lucas went to work. On one of his first stops, Greenwood, North Carolina, Lucas, looking for a special assistant, arrived at the ballpark twenty minutes before game time for a visit with Manager Paul Snyder.

"He came to offer me the assistant's job," Snyder laughed. "I said, 'Hey Bill, I'm twenty minutes away from starting a game, can we talk about this afterward?'

Meeting later, the question surfaced from Lucas, "Paul, will you move up and become my assistant?" The response from Snyder? "With all the baseball brains you have in Atlanta, why do you need me?"

"The quick answer from Bill was, 'Yeah, we got a lot of baseball brains there, but you're the only one who is color blind,'" Snyder said.

Snyder took the job of Director of Scouting and lasted more than two decades as one of the best in the game.

"Bill and I knew each other in high school in Jacksonville, Florida, and at Florida A&M," smiled Dr. Raleigh Washington, college baseball teammate and fellow Army ROTC friend of Lucas. "Bill had a heart for people, the heart to help."

Dr. Washington later became a lieutenant colonel in the Army, in charge of recruiting in Puerto Rico. As a means of amping up his recruitment numbers, he asked Lucas, by then the Braves general manager, if he could ask future Hall of Famer Hank Aaron to come to Puerto Rico and help his recruiting effort.

"I'm not going to ask Hank to recruit for you," Lucas told Dr. Washington. "I will set up a two-hour lunch so you can meet him and ask him yourself."

The lunch went extremely well. Aaron went to Puerto Rico and helped Dr. Washington's recruiting detail rise from twenty-eighth in the Army to number one.

"It didn't hurt a thing," Dr. Washington laughed, "that one of Hank's children was born in Caguas, and that Puerto Ricans in general loved Hank and those folks went wild when he was with us."

In his far-too-short general manager's tenure, Bill Lucas faced down sticky racial issues. He also found himself caught in contentious contract squabbles between tempestuous owner Ted Turner, first-round draft pick Bob Hoerner, and Hall of Fame knuckleballer Phil Niekro. Bill didn't mind standing up to Turner, especially when Ted named himself Atlanta's manager in 1977. Ted the manager lasted only one day.

"Dad stood up to Ted, when no one else would," Bill's daughter, Wonya, now president and CEO of Crown Media Family Networks, told Atlantic Magazine in 2017. "He didn't care if they fired him, he was all about doing the right thing."

Tragically, after watching Niekro win his 200th game, Lucas suffered cardiac arrest and a massive cerebral hemorrhage, three years after taking over the Braves. He died at age forty-three.

When the Braves opened their shiny new park in 2017, club officials named the new baseball operations room, "The Bill Lucas Conference Room." During the same ceremony, they renamed the street players and staff use as a park entrance, "Bill Lucas Way." In addition, the Braves began "The Bill Lucas Apprenticeship," aimed at young minority baseball aspirants.

"It's about reaching back," daughter Wonya told the Atlanta Journal-Constitution, "And helping others and paying it forward."

Atlanta's All-Star outfielder Dale Murphy weighed in on what Bill Lucas meant to him, and the Braves organization, calling Lucas a father figure.

"Bill wanted this organization to become a success," Murphy told viewers on WSB-TV, "and it's our sacred honor to fulfill that dream."

Lucas pushed the dream further by hiring future Hall of Fame Manager Bobby Cox who later, in a second stint with Atlanta, took the Braves from worst to first, then into the World Series in 1991, losing to the Minnesota Twins, another worst-to-first club. Many give Lucas credit for building what turned out to be a Braves powerhouse in the early 1990s.

KEVIN MILLAR

"From indy ball to world's champ,
there aren't many of him around."

"LADIES AND GENTLEMEN, *please,* please turn your attention to me…" the circus-tent, loud, clattering musical opening for *Intentional Talk*, MLB-TV's afternoon baseball show extraordinaire. IT's ringmaster, twelve-year veteran MLB infielder Kevin Millar, lip-syncs the words, directing the surreal scene. The former opening represents a metaphor for the ringleader Millar ultimately became in clubhouses from high school to the world champion Red Sox.

"He's the coolest guy in any room," beams Millar's Lamar University coach Jim Gilligan. "Teammates loved and gravitated toward him because he gets it, and everyone's role in it. He's blessed with a concrete understanding that this game is all about: T-E-A-M!"

Millar's *Intentional Talk* combines intense baseball talk and discussion of Kevin's adventures such as: appearances at the Country Music Awards or celebrity golf outings or hijinks-laced visits with former teammates and MLB friends. It's all served up in heavy doses for an uber male, baseball-centric audience. The underlying message to any guest? If you cannot take a verbal rip and return one, you'll find yourself under the bus.

Kevin Millar at Lamar University
(Photo courtesy of Lamar University Media Relations)

"That's one hundred percent true," Kevin grinned. "If you're not into self-deprecation, you don't belong on the show!"

Veteran college baseball coaches like Lamar's Jim Gilligan constantly search for the best talent available. Gilligan ranks as one of the all-time great collegiate coaches as his record in thirty-eight seasons attests. His Lamar Cardinals won almost 1,400 games, eleven conference championships, and thirteen NCAA regional appearances, supplying MLB with eleven players.

"I came back to Lamar in the early '90s after working as an agent supplying professional players to Taiwan," Gillian remembers. "A friend of mine, Barry Moss, told me about a player at Los Angeles Community College, so we worked him out."

Fellow named Millar he's talking about.

"We hit him fifteen grounders and he wore 'em all," Gilligan said. "We knew we could fix the fielding issues. He didn't run well, but boy could he swing the bat!"

Gilligan went the extra recruiting mile, playing golf with Kevin, his dad, and granddad.

"We pretty much knew he'd come after that," Gilligan smiled. "He took instruction and we never, ever had to explain things twice to Kevin. Tell him once, that was it."

On the field and in the clubhouse, Millar shined at Lamar and later in his baseball life.

"Whatever Kevin said in the clubhouse, that was how it went," Gilligan said. "He set the tone for those two teams, and we won because of it.

Millar played at Lamar in 1992 and 1993, the latter team winning forty-four games. In the midst of the 1993 season, well known Texas Rangers scout Doug Gassaway sidled up to Gilligan, "tell me about Number Fifteen. Can he run?"

"He can't run a lick, but he can hit with power," came Gilligan's straightforward retort. "And he will lead your clubhouse from A-ball to the big leagues. He will be the leader!"

Gilligan's assistant, forty-two-year veteran MLB player and coach Al Vincent, took Lamar's two future major-league hitters (Millar and Bruce Aven) aside, telling them they had potential big-league power. Their confidence grew markedly but shortly before the 1993 MLB draft, the Rangers called asking Millar to attend a pre-draft workout in Arlington. Gilligan warned against it.

"First off, you won't run well enough to suit them," Gilligan cautioned, "and that could come back to haunt you."

Gassaway initially told Gilligan he'd be drafting Millar, then called back the day before the draft reneging.

"So, I went to work," Gilligan said, "contacting my friends in independent ball, recommending Kevin."

Having managed the independent Salt Lake Gulls to an unbelievable record of twenty-nine wins in a row in 1987, Gilligan rang the St. Paul Saints, the organization leading independent baseball's resurgence in the early 1990s.

"I gave [Saints owners] Mike Veeck and Marv Goldklang the exact message I gave the Rangers," Gilligan said. "He'll hit a ton, fans will absolutely love him, and he'll take over your clubhouse. He's the real deal, plus an organization will take him off your hands at the end of the season."

Millar fulfilled every Gilligan promise.

"The Northern League is a hundred percent more than I expected," Millar told the Saints TV pregame host. "It's given me a chance I wouldn't have had otherwise."

"Once he settled into the lineup, he proved he could really hit," remembers Tom Whaley, the Saints assistant general manager in 1993 and now team president. "One other thing stands out. Kevin Millar loved our fans, they loved him, and still do."

At the end of the 1993 Northern League campaign, fledgling Florida Marlins scouting director Gary Hughes signed Millar. Before he left St. Paul, Kevin talked again with the St. Paul Saints TV Pregame Show about his opportunity.

"I'm getting to go to an organization that's just starting," he grinned. "I'm getting an opportunity I never had coming out of college. Now, if I hit .190 and have to hang up my cleats, at least I had that opportunity."

Over a handful of minor-league seasons, Millar took advantage, tearing through the Marlins system—two seasons each in

Single A and Double A, a season in Triple A before making his MLB debut with the Marlins in 1998.

Five seasons in Miami led to three with the Red Sox. Three seasons, three playoff teams, and everywhere he went teammates followed Kevin's lead. Former Red Sox All-Star shortstop Rico Petrocelli watched Millar intently during Kevin's Boston stay. Rico played in two World Series for the Sox, and once held the all-time MLB record with forty shortstop home runs. He now co-hosts MLB Radio's "Remember When," on Saturday mornings on SiriusXM with Ed Randall.

"First, every team should have a Kevin Millar," Petrocelli marveled. "He kept those Sox teams together. Showing great character, he kept his teammates loose, was one of the guys, and most importantly, he led 'em, had a lot of big hits, big homers. Plus, he was blue collar. The fans loved him because they thought, 'he's one of us.'"

"And don't forget," says former Boston Red Sox play-by-play broadcaster Jerry Trupiano, "Kevin drew a critical walk that led to the winning run in that American League Championship Series against the Yanks in 2004."

The Red Sox clubhouse those three Millar seasons stood firmly united.

"Our guys just loved each other," Millar told Dan Patrick's national radio audience. "There were the Yankees, who were Greek gods, Adonises, great bodies, All-Stars—Jeter and ARod, and all those guys, and there we were a bunch of bad bodies, but we loved each other and because of that we finally got 'em."

Kevin played a key role in 2003, his first Boston season. While the Yankees won the American League Championship Series that year, Kevin pounded out career highs in homers (twenty-five) and RBIs (ninety-six). Breaking a spell of no Boston World's Championships, the Red Sox won it all in 2004 behind "Big Papi" David Ortiz's forty-one homers, Manny Ramirez' team-leading forty-three, and a combined 269 runs driven in by the pair. Along with Millar's .297 batting average, eighteen homers and seventy-nine RBIs, great pitching from Pedro Martinez, Curt Schilling, and closer Keith Foulke, the Red Sox and their fans celebrated for days.

"Former ABC News Correspondent Morton Dean tells a great Boston World's Championship celebration story," laughs former Sox voice Jerry Trupiano. "He'd seen a female bartender yawning, obviously worn out [from] serving celebrants until dawn. As she tried to sleep, her husband created a racket grabbing three Boston newspapers, a bottle of Scotch, and two glasses from a cabinet, telling his wife 'I'm heading to the cemetery to celebrate with Dad.'" He wasn't by himself.

All over city cemeteries, Red Sox caps appeared on tombstones and graves. During the World's Champions parade, hundreds of thousands lined the streets and climbed light poles for a better look at their heroes.

"Wild, wild, unforgettable times," Trupiano remembered. "And well deserved."

Discussing the subject of Red Sox World Series rings, also on Dan Patrick's radio show, Millar told the host he didn't always wear his ring from 2004. Patrick quizzed further. "Why not?"

"Didn't do it, didn't think about it," came Millar's sincere reply. "But one guy told me once that I should wear it for the fans, for those who might not ever get close enough to see a real World Series ring. That made sense and I started wearing it after that."

Three seasons in Baltimore, one in Toronto, then back to the Northern League and six games for his old team, the St. Paul Saints, finished Millar's professional career—almost. A second return to the Saints came twenty years after he made his professional debut with the club and seven years after he retired as a major-league player. Saints President Tom Whaley picks up the story.

"There he was, at age forty-six in a Saints uniform," Whaley laughed. "Helping us celebrate our organization's twenty-fifth anniversary, hitting against the Winnipeg Goldeyes. And wouldn't you know it, he really, really got into one, a two-run bomb of a home run, at age forty-six! Can you believe that?

The story becomes even better, as Whaley picks up the ending.

"Our manager, George Tsamis, tried to sneak Kevin back out for one more at bat, but the Winnipeg manager said, 'the hell with that, we agreed on one at bat and one only!' But can you believe a guy like that, coming back to the independent league team where he started and hits a home run, a two-run homer to top it off? No one does that. No one. Well, Kevin Millar sure did."

Millar maintains a busier schedule than many U.S. presidents. Still hosting *Intentional Talk,* still professing honest takes, laughing and talking about what's good and what's not in his beloved game, still playing in celebrity golf tournaments all over the United States, Kevin Millar's become an iconic baseball face and voice. Although baseball experts once believed Millar couldn't, Kevin himself knew he could all along. And he proved it every season he drew a major-league uniform.

JEFF FRYE

"Bloody glove to big leagues to agent,
Jeff's hardball adventure."

"WHEN I DESCRIBE A GRINDER," smiled former Rangers and Mets Assistant General Manager Sandy Johnson, "Jeff Frye fits the definition perfectly. He *is* that guy!"

Frye was born in Panama, Oklahoma, a town "so small, I didn't even know Oklahoma had Double-A and Triple-A teams in the state," Jeff laughed. "Panama had one stop light. The town was tiny, I was tiny, the whole thing was small."

Tiny his hometown may have been, his first MLB call up was anything but. He vividly recalls July 9, 1992. "It was," Frye laughed, "the wildest of wild, almost unbelievable days."

"On the road with Oklahoma City [Rangers Triple A affiliate] and playing in Louisville," he remembers. "I got a phone call from Manager Tommy Thompson telling me, 'Grab your gear, jump on the first plane and be in Arlington for tonight's game against the Indians.' That started a great day!"

Jeff learned he'd lead off and play second base that night against Cleveland. Arriving at the airport, racing to Arlington Stadium, fielding a few ground balls, then heading back to the clubhouse, Jeff Frye donned MLB livery for the first time. Returning to the field to start the game, awed by the packed house, the once-scrawny kid from eastern Oklahoma achieved a dream millions crave.

"There I am throwing the ball around the infield," Frye grinned, "and there's Nolan Ryan warming up, as the public address system played George Strait's hit, "Gotta Have an Ace

Jeff Frye with the Tulsa Drillers.
(Photo courtesy of the Tulsa Drillers)

in the Hole," and I'm asking myself, 'how does it get any better than this?'"

Without batting practice, Jeff banged out two hits in three times at the plate, including a triple in his first MLB game. One week later, his first big league homer came in Baltimore against the Orioles flame-throwing lefty Arthur Lee Rhodes.

"And wouldn't you know, the next time up, Arthur Lee threw at me," Frye laughed. "He threw at me!"

Jeff's third time facing Rhodes, he hit a double. Years later at a golf tournament, he reminded Rhodes about his extra base knock.

"Arthur Lee said, 'hey, I threw at you,'" Frye grinned and said, "I know, but don't forget, I doubled off you the next time up!"

Frye's baseball beginnings trace back to his days as a three-sport high school athlete. As a five-foot, seven-inch, 145-pound phenom, Jeff accepted a basketball scholarship to Wilburton Junior College.

"One basketball scrimmage convinced me," he laughed, "I needed to play baseball."

Tearing up Oklahoma junior college pitching at Carl Albert College, then transferring to Southeastern Oklahoma University on the Texas-Oklahoma border, Frye continued to rake.

".388 my junior year, a school record .452 my senior year," Jeff remembered. "I swear to you I never once thought I had the juice to play pro ball."

Days later, Southeastern Oklahoma's star outfielder Benny Culver received invitations from the Reds and the Rangers, both tryouts on the same day. Benny went to the Reds, Frye grabbed Culver's Rangers invite.

"I took ground balls," he said, "then I faced a pitcher I'd seen in JUCO, and launched a homer off him. They handed me a wooden bat after I hit that homer, but it was uncomfortable. Once they taught me how to hold it correctly, I faced a big ole six-foot, ten-inch pitcher and I hit a rocket, thirty feet over the fence. One of the scouts pulled me aside and said, 'next tryout, two weeks from today at Arlington Stadium [then the Rangers' home park]. Be there.'"

While waiting for his chance, trouble developed. While water skiing on Lake Texoma, an errant ski sliced the ring finger of his left hand and the middle digit, leaving a bloody mess.

"I thought damnit," Frye winced. "One week 'til the tryout, how am I ever going to do it?"

Gamely wrapping gauze over the bloody wounds, dragging a rubber glove over the gauze, then jamming on his batting glove, Jeff went to work. Scouts noticed it as he ran sixty-yard dashes. They saw him wince taking a line shot into the pocket of his glove causing, as he put it, "hellacious misery." Swinging the bat with less force finally brought questions from Rangers scout Doug Gassaway.

"I told Gas, I had a skiing accident," Frye admitted. "He responded saying, 'you must really want to play very badly if you'd show up wounded and bleeding for a tryout!'"

Back at Southeastern Oklahoma, fearing he'd lost his professional baseball chance, Jeff's college coach brought great news.

"You've been drafted by the Rangers in the thirtieth round," beamed coach Mike Metheny.

"During the draft, our scouts Doug Gassaway and Jimmy Dryer fought hard for Jeff," Sandy Johnson said.

"All the tools might not impress," came words from Gassaway's report, "but the makeup and hard-nosed competitiveness certainly will!"

"Sheer makeup, one hundred percent correct," insisted former Rangers GM Tom Grieve. "I'd be willing to bet he said to himself, 'I might have a torn up, bloody hand, but this is my shot. Jeff Frye's one hundred percent the real deal!'"

That "real deal" began as a backup at his first Single-A stop. With the prospect ahead of him injured, Jeff played so well, the prospect never regained the job. Initially struggling at Double A, Frye adopted the high knee kick Rangers All-Star Ruben Sierra used as a power hitter. He ended Double A, leading the Texas League in ten offensive categories.

After his debut 1992 season, Jeff missed 1993, tearing his right ACL. In 1994 and 1995, he played a total of 147 Rangers games, pounding out a .327 average, and .403 on-base percentage.

"Jeff would've been starting at second base for us in '93," former Rangers Manager Kevin Kennedy said. "I loved him. Smart player, good speed, loved to hit and run."

"Kevin's a real player's manager," Frye responded. "And there's a crazy story involving how I came to play for him in Boston in '96."

In 1996 Texas removed Frye from its forty-man roster, sending him to Oklahoma City. He suffered a badly pulled quadriceps playing center field in Buffalo, New York, on a frigid night.

"My agent told me the Red Sox, managed by Kevin Kennedy, needed a second baseman," Frye said excitedly. "I jumped at the chance."

Rangers release done, showing up at Fenway Park, Jeff admitted the injury to his new manager, "I'm about sixty percent normal," he told Kennedy.

"Strap it up tight as you can," grinned Kennedy. "Because your sixty percent is better than anything I have right now at second base."

In just under five hundred plate appearances for the Sox, Jeff hit .286. In 1997 with Jimy Williams replacing Kennedy, Frye stole a career-high eighteen bases, banging out a .312 average. In 1998 another torn ACL, this one on the left, shut him down. Playing briefly in Boston during the 1999 season, trouble developed in 2000.

"Yeah, the GM and I got in it," Frye said. "I told Gordon Eads from the Boston Globe the most respected player in our locker room, catcher Mike Stanley, should have been treated better. They'd placed him on the disabled list, and he never should've been there. I was right but then they traded me."

Traded to the Rockies to finish the 2000 season, Jeff went on to Toronto in 2001 as an infield backup. In Toronto, he became the second Blue Jay in history to hit for the cycle against his former Rangers teammate, Darren Oliver.

"Before I went up for the fourth time needing only a single," Frye told the *Los Angeles Times*. "I asked Cito Gaston what I should do if I hit one into the gap. He said, 'stay at first.' I smoked one to the right center field gap and stopped at first. Some didn't like that."

"I didn't have any problems with it," veteran Toronto skipper Buck Martinez told the *Times*.

2002 changed Jeff's life completely.

"I called my agent asking a question. What did he have for me in '02, a simple question," Frye said quietly.

The agent's response?

"I'm really busy," the agent replied tersely. "You'll need to make calls for yourself."

So angry, refusing to believe an agent would behave that way, Frye swore he'd do things differently if he ever became one. Jeff made the calls, and found a job for himself, playing left field for the Reds' Triple A Louisville in 2002, wondering if he'd ever play in MLB again. Not hitting well, he made a life-altering decision. When his name wasn't on Louisville Manager Dave Miley's lineup, Frye went for a visit.

"Skip," he said to Miley, "I'm taking it to the house."

Telling Jeff he'd basically been given a night off, Frye responded, "Nah, I'm taking it to the house."

"Taking it to the house," simply expanded Jeff Frye's baseball world. Becoming an MLB player agent, Frye's first client was former teammate and veteran pitcher Darren Oliver.

"I told Jeff I didn't have a job and needed one in 2003," Oliver grinned. "Just like that, there I go to the Rockies."

"Rockies pitching coach Bob Apodaca helped Darren develop a cutter," Jeff said, "and he reinvented himself as a late innings reliever for the last nine years of his career. Amazing!"

Frye remains an agent, and now finds himself as a social media guru, challenging youth and professional coaches with far less experience.

"They try teaching all hitters to hit the same way," he winces. "Not every kid, or even a lot of professionals, should be taught to hit it in the air, yet they teach only one way."

In an interview with the Rangers flagship station, 105.3FM in Dallas-Fort Worth, Frye continued that discussion.

"We all should be taught to hit as individuals," he insists. "We have no real big-time rallies anymore. Everyone sits back and waits for the three-run homer. Hitters don't worry if they strike out. It's a hard game to watch now. Folks never having professional success shouldn't be telling major-league vets that we don't know what we're talking about."

FRED PATEK

"Boy did we miss on him!"

"FRED PATEK was an old school, all out on every play ballplayer, remembers Steve Busby, an All-Star former Kansas City Royals righthander. "Every single day he brought an aggressive, hard-nosed approach along with a lot of tools, a cannon arm, speed and quickness, and occasionally would hit one 450 feet!"

Veteran Texas scouts in the early 1960s—the late Red Murff, Al LaMacchia, Doug Gassaway, Billy Capps, and Jim Hughes—all possessed keen eyes for baseball talent. Murff, in fact, signed sixty-four players who made it to MLB, including Hall of Famer Nolan Ryan and three members of the 1969 World Champion New York Mets. But those scouts, every single one, took a big swing and a miss on Patek, future All-Star shortstop from Seguin, Texas.

"I apologized to him personally," Murff told me in a book we did together, *The Scout: Searching for the Best in Baseball.* "I dismissed him because of his size, and that was wrong on my part."

Freddie Joe Patek measured between five feet, four inches and five feet, six inches and weighed between 145 and 155 as a high schooler. Later, playing for the Randolph Air Force Base team in San Antonio, Patek's size became an issue to everyone but Fred himself. The main argument? Veteran baseball men refused to believe a player that small could hold up physically over a full major-league season. With full blinders on, they discounted Patek's rocket arm, blinding speed, and occasional power. They also disqualified a Texas-sized heart and a chip on his shoulder as big as the state itself.

"Every time I was told by coaches or scouts I couldn't do something," Patek noted proudly, "I broke my backside to prove them wrong."

The other factor scouts missed? Patek's inner fires. While playing catch, an uncle's throw hit the four-year-old Fred squarely on the nose, creating a bloody mess. Unfortunately for the uncle, he laughed at his nephew.

"I thought he made fun of me because of my size," said Patek with an edge to his voice, "so lying on my back, I fired that ball right back at him, catching him off guard, and it stung him. Not a lot was said after that, but he never made fun of me again, either."

One more thing scouts missed: A maniacal work ethic, proving true the old Texas saying, "I work from can to can't."

"In the summers from the time I was five or six," he remembered, "I worked with another uncle who owned a bread shop in Seguin. We met at the shop at four a.m. each day, loaded the truck four or five times, and dropped off the bread first, then jelly rolls and donuts, and twelve hours later we were done."

Young Fred monetarily made out like a bandit.

"I guess so," he laughed. "I made two bucks a day helping him load and unload, and that's how I earned money for my first real leather baseball glove."

Nothing kept young Patek from his glove and constantly practicing and perfecting his baseball skills. Patek played outside, using his family's garage back wall as a throwing target. When the intrepid youngster figured out how to take his parents car out of gear and push it out of the garage creating more room to play caroms off the walls, Fred really found himself in business.

"Heck, the only playing little kids did in Seguin," Fred laughed, "was small pick-up games, until you were old enough for Little League. So, besides those games, I used tennis balls and rubber balls, throwing them as hard as I could against those walls, chasing hard as I could, backhanding them, then turning around and racing to my left, and back and forth I went. I'd move out to the street and start all over, playing a game by making myself catch twenty in a row, and I couldn't quit until I did that."

Patek's resourceful nature aimed at playing Major League Baseball. In athletic infancy, he turned himself into a top-flight player from Little League to high school. His talents impressively stood out, playing better than those a half a foot to a foot taller, while leading his high school team to the playoffs as a junior. While taking batting practice before in a South Texas All-Star tournament in San Antonio after his senior year, he met Lou Carneseca, who later became one of the best college basketball coaches in the United States. But on this day, Carneseca, coaching baseball at St. John's University in New York, watched in disbelief as Patek torched pitch after pitch out of the ballpark, using a wooden bat. (High schools and colleges had not begun using metal bats.)

"I think he would've given me a scholarship," noted Patek, "but during the tournament my mom sent a message to call her immediately. I did and found out the military needed me."

To Freddie Joe Patek the military meant one thing: Baseball. In the 1950s through 1960s, the Army, Navy, and Air Force fielded excellent clubs, followed closely by major-league scouts. Patek signed up for the Air Force because he knew Randolph Air Force Base in San Antonio, near his home, fielded a team.

"They were fast and competitive, and we played more than a hundred games a year," he beamed, "and once or twice we played 140. More baseball the better, to me at least."

Two Pirates scouts, Larry DeHaven and Bob Zuk, had heard about the young phenom.

"They did," Fred laughed, "and lucky for me I always had great games when they came to see me."

By the time MLB staged its first-ever amateur draft in 1965, Patek was eligible. The Pirates took him in the twenty-second round and the diminutive Patek took off. Dominating Single A and Double A, by June of 1968, he made his major-league debut against the Dodgers' stylish lefthander Claude Osteen, who retired him four straight times. In fact, Patek went zero for twelve before picking up his first big-league hit against Houston's Denny Lemaster, six days after putting on a Pirates uniform for the first time. The next day, Fred hit his first big league homer off Houston's hard-throwing righty Don Wilson. Four days after that, the Dodgers Don Drysdale smoked Patek's left forearm with a fastball.

"I played through it initially," winced Patek, "but it kept on bothering me and finally they X-rayed it, and it was broken."

Shut down for the rest of 1968, but hale and hearty at spring training 1969, Patek took over the shortstop's job from All-Star and Gold Glove infielder Gene Alley. That same season, the Pirates installed artificial Tartan Turf on the Three Rivers Stadium floor, and after watching him play on the ersatz grass, Cardinals Manager Whitey Herzog insisted that Patek was the best shortstop he'd seen on artificial turf, including his own Ozzie Smith. Life between Patek and the Pirates however, turned incompatible.

"They never believed I could play every day," he said stoically, "I lost enthusiasm in them and they in me."

Traded to the Royals in 1971, Patek found an up-and-coming team headed for the playoffs and a fan base that loved and adored him. They should have, considering he put up the following numbers:

- ◆ Eight straight thirty-or-more stolen base seasons, including forty-nine stolen bases in his first year with the

Royals (1971) and a career high fifty-three in the playoff season of 1977.

- A career high eleven triples in 1971
- Hit for the cycle in July 1971
- Led the American League in double plays turned four straight seasons
- In a fourteen-season career, sported a better Wins Above Replacement (24.1) than any first-round draft choice in 1965 (his draft year) except the Dodgers Rick Monday.

The Royals, with Patek at shortstop, won American League West titles from 1976 to 1978, but lost to the Yankees in the American League Championship Aeries all three seasons. By the 1979 season, he'd been delegated to back up duty.

"Despite what they thought," Patek remembered, "I didn't think I was done by any stretch of the imagination."

Neither did the California Angels who signed Fred, at age thirty-four, to a three-year contract, and he immediately became a nemesis of the Boston Red Sox. Especially on the night of June 20, 1980.

"Yessir," he laughed, "I hit three homers at Fenway Park that night," he grinned, "and it could have been four, but the last shot missed going over the Green Monster by only about six inches!"

That feat represented only the second shortstop in MLB history to slug three in a game.

Finishing his career in California in 1981, Patek spent a brief stint as color analyst on NBC's *Game of the Week* telecasts, followed by coaching jobs in the Royals organization. In July 1992, Fred and wife Jerri's Christianity faced the severest of tests when their twenty-year-old daughter, Kimberlie, suffered a catastrophic injury, losing control of her car on Interstate 29 near St. Joseph, Missouri. The injury paralyzed her from the neck down, and later, specialists in Houston told the family Kimberlie would never breathe on her own again. While spending the rest of her life on a respirator in the lower level of the Patek's Missouri home, the Kansas City Royals, Kansas City Chiefs, and Baseball Assistance team staged several events with proceeds going to cover Kimberlie's medical costs.

"When I look back," Fred said, "this community and my friends with the professional sports teams here really came together to help and it was beautiful."

When Kimberlie passed away in 1994, Patek cut himself off from the world.

"It was awful," he said tearfully, "and I was hurt, angry, and sad. And I was dark."

Darkness became light again several months after Kimberlie's death when her sister gave birth to a baby girl.

"My first granddaughter," Fred smiled proudly, "and I will tell you this, God gave us that little girl to keep us going."

Telephone visits now with Patek stand as a joy and blessing. As he looks back remembering life and baseball's ups and downs and darkness, he remembers his Christianity helped him overcome all the darkness, especially from his doubters who always told him, "You cannot."

BILL MUELLER

"The nicest, greatest guy in baseball..."

"WHEN I DID IT, I really didn't know it was a record," said Bill Mueller, the switch-hitting 2003 American League Batting Champion and Silver Slugger Award winner.

The Mueller response to most reporters' questions: "just the facts, it's not about me." Never creating controversy, refusing to celebrate any personal achievement—that's Bill Mueller. His answer "I really didn't know I set a record," on July 29, 2003, comes as no surprise.

"Seriously I didn't know," Mueller laughed. "But holy cow what a night!"

That historic night, Bill became the first MLB hitter crushing grand slam home runs from both sides of the plate in the same game. He hit three homers that night against the Rangers, driving in nine total runs. But his postgame interview sounded routine.

"R.A. Dickey owned me when he learned that knuckleball," Bill laughed. "I mean I never hit him."

Well, he got Dickey that night. Righty Jay Powell

Bill Mueller at Missouri State
(Photo courtesy of Missouri State University Athletics)

and lefty Aaron Fultz surrendered the other two. An inadvertent comment by teammate Doug Mirabelli helped Mueller in his battle against Fultz.

"Before the game, Doug and I spied Fultz," Mueller said. "Mirabelli said to me, 'Fultzie loves to throw a 3-1 change.' Never thinking I might face him that night, there I was, facing Fultz with a 3-1 count. Here it comes, out it goes! I never had three homers in any league, Little to big. Three in The Show? Unbelievable!"

Mueller, only a bit excited, never flipped a bat, nor pumped a victory fist; nothing to pimp his home run.

"That's just not me," he grinned. "It's not who I am."

Raised in St. Louis suburb Maryland Heights, he learned the game from his dad, also Bill, who taught him to switch hit, and just as importantly, taught him focus and a competitive drive second to none.

"My dad was huge for me," he grinned. "He was like my main chess piece, always there."

Working at St. Louis-based McDonnell-Douglas, Bill's dad signed up for early shifts, allowing him early afternoons home. When the younger Mueller returned from school, backyard baseball schooling, Mueller to Mueller, began in earnest.

"We lived in a condo complex with plenty of room for baseball stuff in the backyard," Mueller said. "Our complex had a long driveway running to the clubhouse and pool, with a tennis court in the back."

With grounders aimed at the young Mueller, baseballs didn't hold up well, skidding across the complex's asphalt driveway. A twelve-foot-high chain link fence surrounding the club's tennis courts provided a great challenge for an irrepressible, high-energy kid.

"It took probably a whole year before I could hit the ball over that danged fence left-handed," Mueller laughed. "It really gave me an extra incentive to keep shooting for."

Yes, he said, "danged."

A Cardinals fan as a kid, Bill's dad came home with a pair of World Series tickets for the Cardinals-Brewers matchup in 1982. At age eleven, watching that series, Bill never dreamed that a couple of decades later he'd play a critical role in the World Series sweep of his hometown Cardinals.

"How about the chance I had to play with some great guys?" Mueller asked. "And great players they were: Big Papi, Manny Ramirez, Curt Schilling, and Pedro Martinez...what a great group."

Former Red Sox All-Star shortstop Rico Petrocelli counts Mueller among those "great guys and great players."

"What a clutch hitter," Petrocelli smiled. "A batting champion in 2003, sure. As, importantly Bill Mueller added real professionalism to the club."

A star player at St. Louis area's De Smet Jesuit High School, Bill went on to Missouri State (then Southwest Missouri State.) There he played for one of the top coaches in NCAA Division 1 history, Keith Gutin.

"Back yard, high school, American Legion, college or big leagues," coach Gutin said, "he never changed, always stayed the same great kid. I drove three plus hours to the St. Louis area to see him play shortstop. When I got there, he was in right field! I thought, 'uh-oh,' and then I saw him run, and play so hard in every phase of the game, I couldn't take my eyes off him."

Gutin watched Mueller at least a dozen times that summer.

"When I finally saw him play shortstop," Gutin laughed, "I was blown away!"

Gutin preached the "you belong at Southwest Missouri State" sermon to Mueller the rest of the summer. The message worked, but during his freshman year, Bill didn't play in the first six games, yet never complained.

"Bill's third base counterpart suffered an injury and we sorta had a 'Wally Pipp,' situation," Gutin remembered. "When I posted the lineup, Bill looked at it, then shook his head walking away. Returning for another look, he never said a word, stepped back, looked again, then smiled knowing he was in there."

Right then, Mueller became an All-American fixture at Southwest Missouri State.

"As a leader, it seemed he got better every game," grinned his coach, "I don't want to hurt anyone's feelings, but Bill Mueller's the best player I had in forty years coaching."

Umpires never threw him out of a game, ever.

"I kept my mouth shut, always tried to put the team first," Bill said stoically. "That's why consistency became my middle name."

Drafted in the fifteenth round by the Giants in 1995, Mueller, with a dogged work ethic, team-first spirit, quick, switch-hitting bat and solid glove made it to The Show three years later. In his MLB debut, Bill banged out the first of 1,229 hits, pinch-hitting against Cubs' righty Terry Adams. His third day with the Giants, he learned two important rookie lessons: The tentative nature of big-league rosters, and always expect the unexpected.

"Manager Dusty Baker said to me, 'hey, Bill, we're bringing [infielder] Robbie Thompson [the player Mueller replaced] off the disabled list and we want to make sure his groin injury is healed,'" Mueller remembered. "'How about hanging around in case something goes wrong?'"

So, Bill and his parents watched that night's game in Wrigley Field seats. Staying another day or two turned into a longer visit when the Giants asked him to fly back to San Francisco in case Thompson re-injured himself.

"I had to learn where to sit because I was a rookie," Mueller laughed. "But hey, the food was great, and they gave you all the Gatorade you could drink!"

The Giants called him back twice that year. In fifty-five games splitting time with popular Giants third-baseman Matt Williams, Mueller hit a solid .330, without much power. A controversial off-season trade sent Williams to Cleveland for up-and-coming second-baseman Jeff Kent.

"Jeff" remembers Mueller, "brought a third baseman's power numbers yet wanted to play second base. I, on the other hand, could play third, but without a third baseman's power, so it all worked out."

Over the next five Giants seasons, Mueller hit in the .290's, admitting he'd peaked with the bat. He made contact, but almost never hit homers or more than a couple dozen doubles in a season. While Bill sensed his swing wasn't right, the Giants traded him to the Cubs. Once in Chicago he found out Cubs hitting coach Jeff Pentland had been watching him with great interest.

"I had seen him many times and he was impressive," noted Pentland. Now he didn't have Barry Bonds' power or hitting gifts, but I admired his competitive fire, will power and he had a doggedly determined work ethic."

"What he saw," Mueller grinned, "was my dad's DNA and my Midwest upbringing. I drank the baseball Kool-Aid big time, never took what I had for granted and I knew I had to work and scratch for everything, then help my teammates."

"I really liked him a lot, Pentland remembers. "I thought I could help him, so we got after it."

As his new coach changed Mueller's whole approach to hitting, Bill bought in one hundred percent.

"I'd been spinning around on my back foot, never engaging my legs," Mueller said excitedly. "Jeff told me he could help me put ten to fifteen feet on each line drive by using my legs as a power source. That change kept my hands in the hitting zone longer, giving me pop I didn't have before."

Relentless work with Pentland unleashed more power, hitting in the middle of the Cubs lineup in 2001 ramped up Mueller's already electric intensity.

"With me hitting third," Mueller noted with glee, "Well, that was awesome, and having Mark Grace in the lineup, I was really looking forward to a big year, but then I got hurt."

In front of family and friends in St. Louis, in May 2001, Mueller broke his left kneecap chasing a foul pop up. In published reports, Cubs' Manager Don Baylor said losing Mueller hurt worse than the Cardinals' series sweep. Cubs hard-throwing righty Kerry Wood told *The Chicago Tribune* Mueller was irreplaceable.

"He's a Gold Glove third baseman, in my opinion," said Wood, "and that's the worst thing about this [bad road trip] and it will be tough for us to come back from that."

Chicago sportswriters made the case that up to the point of his injury Mueller had been the team's most valuable player, hitting .317 with five homers and fifteen RBIs. As impressive as that, Bill notched an on-base percentage better than .400.

"That injury broke my heart," Mueller said. "Jeff and I had done so much work, and I knew I was on the way to better power numbers."

Despite the injury the best for Bill Mueller remained ahead. Playing with the Cubs in 103 games, then traded back to San Francisco to end the 2002 season, the Boston Red Sox signed him as a free agent in 2003, supposedly as a platoon at third base with Shea Hillebrand.

"Boston moved Hillebrand to the Diamondbacks," said Mueller, "that set the stage for a great run for me in Boston."

Surrounded by Big Papi Ortiz, Kevin Millar, Manny Ramirez, and Cy Young Award winners Pedro Martinez and Curt Schilling, the Red Sox threatened the hated New York Yankees. In 2003, Mueller won the Silver Slugger Award and an American League Batting Championship with a .326 mark.

"It was all that work with Pentland," Mueller remarked. "Working with him turned around my career, it really did."

Finishing second to the Yankees in 2003 and losing to New York in the ALCS in 2004 the Red Sox, despite an uneven first half, leaped forward. Managed by Terry Francona, during a Sox-Yankees July meeting at Fenway Park, a brawl involving Red Sox catcher Jason Varitek and Yankees All-Star Alex Rodriguez emptied the benches.

"It was lightning," Mueller exclaimed. "That's all you can say about it, sheer lightning."

After the melee, Mueller faced future Hall of Famer Mariano Rivera, and (hitting .450 against the spectacular closer), slammed a game-winning home run. Boston won ninety-eight in 2004, finishing second to the Yankees. Fates changed dramatically in the ALCS. Bludgeoning their way to a three- games-to-none lead against Boston, the Yankees led Game 4 of the ALCS 4-3 into the bottom of the ninth. With closer Rivera on the hill, Red Sox magic continued. Sox first baseman Kevin Millar drew a walk, pinch-runner Dave Roberts stole second base with Mueller coming up. In the press box, writers bet on a Mueller sacrifice.

"Mueller was clutch," grinned Red Sox broadcaster Jerry Trupiano. "And in that ninth, he proved it."

Mueller singled up the middle, scoring Roberts, tying the game at four. Later, a Big Papi Ortiz solo homer sent Sox fans into a frenzy with a game-winning homer, keeping the ALCS alive, and setting the stage for the greatest playoff comeback in MLB history. The next three games, Boston rolled over the Yanks, winning the miracle series four games to three, then swept Mueller's hometown Cardinals in four straight games. The World Series win ended Boston's eighty-six-year world championship drought.

"That's all about grinding," Mueller beams as he remembers. "You must be relentless, you must never become content, you take nothing for granted and then you arrive. We arrived!"

In 2005, Boston lost to the White Sox in the first round of the playoffs. After a short Dodgers run in 2006, Mueller's injured knee needed a third surgery, so he stepped off the field into the Dodgers front office as a special assistant to General Manager Ned Colletti.

"I had always heard Bill Mueller was the nicest guy in baseball," mused Chicago Cubs Special Assistant to the General Manager Dave Klipstein, "And when I ran into him scouting at big-league parks, I found out those stories were true."

Bill became Dodgers hitting coach in 2007 under Manager Grady Little. Back he went to the Dodgers front office until the Cubs made him hitting coach for one season. In November of 2014, his hometown Cardinals named him assistant hitting coach, then fired him along with Manager Mike Matheny in mid-season 2018. Now, Mueller coaches younger players in Arizona.

"I tell all these guys,' you never, ever become content, or complacent or selfish,'" he said. "I tell them, 'You will not let your teammates down, and you can become a hero or goat in a short period of time. Prove yourself every single day and be relentless.'"

"Nice guys finish last," blathered the late MLB Manager Leo Durocher. Not a particularly nice guy himself, Durocher words of lunacy might never have left his mouth had he met Bill Mueller.

ADAM ROSALES

"Haz huelas...."

THROUGH FIFTEEN SEASONS, eight major-league teams, and eleven minor-league clubs, extremely versatile Chicago native Adam Rosales attacked the game, joyously filled with fire and abandon. A man MLB.com calls "an ultra-utility player" sprinted top speed around the bases on every homer, major or minor leagues. A youth league slow trot home run "that just wasn't me," fueled his mad dashes.

"From that moment on," he said, "it was game on when I hit a homer."

Reaffirming Adam's sprints later on during his Double-A season in Chattanooga, his dad said to him, "haz huelas." Translation? "Make footprints, make a mark!" So, Rosales' blistering sprints on every homer he hit made positive impressions everywhere he went.

Adam Rosales at the plate for the Round Rock Express.
(Photo courtesy of the Round Rock Express Baseball Club)

"And teammates loved it," he smiled. "After my dad's 'haz huelas' challenge, I clearly understood the importance of every step and breath we take, as well as every thought we think. The choices we make in life makes us who we are, and where we are supposed to be, at any given time in our walk on earth."

During the 2016 season, those words provided exceptional strength for Rosales. Playing in San Diego alongside Padres infielder Yangervis Solarte, tragedy struck. Cancer claimed Solarte's thirty-year-old wife, Yuliett.

"Anyone who homered that night against the Rockies gave Yangervis' signature home run hand clap above his head," remembered Rosales. "I got into one, drove it into light Colorado air, raced around the bases, stopped at home plate, raised my arms, and clapped loudly as I could. That was the least we could do honoring our teammate's loss."

Honor, friends, traditions, and family explain in vivid detail Adam Rosales' heart and soul—and his dad's.

"My dad and my mom have always been there for me," he said. "It was my dad that helped me see that I needed to give back."

Also in his Padres' days, Adam enlisted help from talented blogger Lora Michaels. Together they formed "Sandlot Nation," a non-profit giving kids across the United States a chance to play a sandlot game with Adam or one of a dozen of his MLB friends.

"We gave kids a chance to talk to big leaguers," Rosales continued beaming, "not only about the game, but the importance of education, developing both intelligence and athleticism."

Adam's dad stepped into a big role, giving Sandlot Nation parents a chance to visit with a major-leaguer's dad, learning how they helped their son's development as a student and athlete.

"It was a treat having dad along," beamed Rosales.

Of course, in any kid baseball venture, bruises and broken windows cause anxious moments.

"But anytime you have Jay Bruce meeting you outside Citi Field in New York, Vida Blue helping outside the Oakland ballpark, and a whole crew of former major-leaguers like John Buck and Vance Law in Utah," Rosales said, "that's pretty special."

His playing days dwindling, and scheduling events proving too time consuming, Adam gave up Sandlot Nation.

"Such excellent groups as RBI and Play Ball are doing the same things we were trying," Rosales said. "We just couldn't keep it up."

Adam bounced back and forth between Triple A and MLB with the Rangers and A's in 2013. In 2014 and 2015 with Texas, he ricocheted on and off major-league rosters three times in less than two weeks. Passing through San Diego in 2016, then a third Oakland stint in 2017, Adam finished that season in Arizona playing thirty-four regular season games and one playoff contest. To Cleveland in 2018, Adam believed the end was near.

"True," he remembered. "And I knew I needed to focus on ending my career with a flourish and I was nine days short, at age thirty-four, of reaching eight full years in the big leagues, and a much better pension."

Playing at Cleveland's top affiliate, Columbus, Manager Chris Tremie called Rosales into his office in September.

"You're going to Cleveland," the manager smiled. "And you're gonna get those nine days, my man."

For Rosales, pieces of a lengthy baseball life made sense.

"I thanked Chris profusely," Adam said quietly, "Then I realized my wife is a Cleveland girl, my first MLB callup had been to Cincinnati in '08, so we'd gone full circle with Ohio teams, and I thought that would be it."

But, in thirteen Cleveland games in 2018, Rosales hit his last MLB home run against the White Sox, then invited his parents on a "thank you" road trip for their sacrifices in giving him the game. Adam and wife Callie talked repeatedly about his next career step. After finishing his degree from Western Michigan University online, Rosales came up with a new plan: the healthcare industry.

"Adam, you need to think seriously before you jump into this," Callie counseled. "You have a Ph.D. in baseball, it's something you've loved your entire life, and I think you should keep playing."

Adam couldn't disagree.

"God, family, baseball, that's who I am," he said proudly, "My wife Callie recognized brilliantly that baseball is where my heart has always been."

An attempt to make the Minnesota Twins roster failed during spring training 2019. After fifty-nine games that season with Columbus, he said goodbye to his playing career. By August 2019, his former team, Oakland, expressed a different kind of interest.

"My former A's Manager Bob Melvin called," Rosales smiled, "After that the A's VP for Player Development Keith Lippmann rang me up."

The two told Adam a 2020 coaching opportunity existed within their organization. Always in love with the A's, Adam responded simply, "where do I interview and what time?" Lippmann cut right to the point.

"There is no interview," he said. "Everybody here loves you and wants you here."

Living in the Phoenix area near the A's spring training base in Mesa made it easy for Adam and his family. After two successful Rookie League coaching seasons, the A's named Rosales manager of the rookie team playing in Mesa in 2022.

"How great is that gig," he asked? "Wow, out the door, right to the park, work with great kids and coaches all day, then back to Callie and the kids and sleep at home at night. That's a huge break for a guy like me."

The A's brass simply recognized Adam's love and passion for their organization and responded in kind.

"I'm blessed to have a wife and family," he said proudly, "who understand my passion and endured the ups and down. I squeezed out every bit of talent and passion I had for this game when I played. Now, I'm giving back, heart and soul, to young professional players."

Dos haz huelas!

ELLIOT JOHNSON

"Small-town, tightly wound kid, afraid of nothing..."

THOSE PRAISE-FILLED WORDS made up a small portion of a scouting report about a high schooler from a tiny town in northeast Arizona. Craig Weissman, currently one of the San Francisco Giants' extremely gifted and experienced scouting operatives and superior talent evaluators, made the initial assessment of Elliot Johnson.

"I saw him at a tryout camp all-star game, after the 2002 baseball draft, while I was working for Tampa Bay," Weissman remembered. "I actually went to the camp to see Jason Pridie, another Arizona native we chose in the second round. But Elliot really caught my eye."

"What a break for me," Elliot grinned. "There was a scout who happened to be in the area and saw an ad in the paper for an all-star game from a tryout camp, and he came to watch."

The first thing Weissman noticed? Johnson could cover sixty yards in 6.4 seconds.

"He featured blazing speed, could switch-hit, and had a little pop," Weissman recalled. "But as we learned more about him, we worried about his lack of baseball experience because he came from such a small town up in the northeastern corner of Arizona."

A three-sport star athlete, Elliot Johnson at six feet and 170 pounds, featured a kangaroo-like forty-two-inch vertical jump. During his baseball career, Johnson wowed teammates by executing an impressive windmill dunk, which was videoed and played back on YouTube. Several disbelieving viewers demanded YouTube to take it down, insisting a man Johnson's

Elliot Johnson with the Oklahoma City Dodgers
(Photo courtesy of the Oklahoma City Dodgers)

size simply couldn't perform such a feat. The video remained.

"I knew I had athletic gifts," Elliot said, "but as far as baseball went, heck, at my high school we only had a short baseball season, then we were off to football, then basketball before baseball came around again. Plus, our football coach served as baseball coach, and despite hard work by our coaches, baseball in that part of Arizona simply wasn't as good as in other parts of the state."

Still, Tampa Bay's Weissman knew an exceptional athlete when he saw one, and Elliot's never-say-die attitude and passion convinced the scout that Elliot Johnson would play in the big leagues.

"He just left it all on the field," Weissman remembered. "And you simply do not see much of anymore."

Elliot learned a back breaking work ethic laboring in northeastern Arizona cotton fields as a youngster. The result? His path tracked more old school, more like players coming into professional baseball in the 1930s, 1940s and 1950s; photographs from that era mirroring young players' sunburned faces, sinewy bodies and calloused hands. Elliot Johnson fit that long-lost image perfectly.

"There he was," beamed Weissman, "taking nothing for granted, only looking for a chance."

Signing as an undrafted free agent, the most difficult road to achieve a big-league dream, Johnson made it happen. The overall dream began for Elliot and his three brothers, children of divorce, spending summers with their dad in Indiana.

"My dad was such a great influence for us," Johnson said. "He played catch with us every single day, helped get us into leagues in Indiana, and he was a huge Chicago Cubs fan."

Attending as many Cubs games as possible, Elliot and his brothers drank the Wrigley Field Kool-Aid.

"My grandfather actually started it," Elliot laughed. "He was a huge Ernie Banks and Ron Santo fan. My dad followed suit, and remember, those were the days of watching the Cubs on WGN and cheering Mark Grace and Shawon Dunstan and Craig Maddux."

Watching the Cubs in 1998 was magical.

"With Sammy Sosa hitting all those bombs, that was great," Elliot remembers. "We especially loved it when Mark McGuire came in from the Cardinals and the homer battles with Sosa began. They always hit it to the roof tops! We loved it."

The Johnson brothers and their dad built summer lives around each other. Ultimately all four brothers played professionally. One attended Harvard before the Rays drafted him, the others played in the Mariners, Phillies, and Cubs systems. Elliot himself played three seasons for the Rays, as well as two more campaigns for Kansas City, Atlanta, and Cleveland.

"No one really knew who I was when I started," he remembered. "But heck, if you look at the first round the year I came out [2002], I played in the big leagues longer than half of those guys."

His early minor-league days meant tons of personal adjustments, and baseball skills fine tuning. Being a speedster and switch hitter helped, but Johnson found himself far less experienced than most rookie league players.

"In those early days, the first couple of seasons, I never let a fastball get by me," Elliot grinned. "But when pitchers realized I had very little experience, I saw tons of breaking balls and trouble began."

Ultimately, Johnson learned to hit breaking pitches, and he also learned to live with players from all over the world.

"We had kids from all over, the Dominican, Venezuela, Puerto Rico, and uber prospects like Jason Pridie, and these guys were all different, but great players," Elliot remembered. "I thought listening to locker room conversations in English and Spanish was great."

Elliot's development received a huge boost when he met Jim Hoff, the Devil Rays' farm director and infield coordinator, and the Rays' minor-league base running guru.

"Jim watched me take batting practice, watched every ground ball I took," Johnson remembered. "And I became his project for the next few years. I was a blank slate for them to deal with. I had some talent but was very much not a professional at that point."

Additionally, the scout who signed Elliot, Craig Weissman, campaigned for him within the Rays organization, making sure the front office knew the name Elliot Johnson.

"Player development happens because scouts are there watching," Johnson said. "Craig Weissman, on his own dime, flew me all over the place so I could meet and visit with those who ran Rays' player development. After that, I had Charlie Montoyo, now the Blue Jays manager, as my skipper for a total of six years in Double A and Triple A. After my Double-A season he realized I was a stolen base threat. By the time I arrived at Triple A Durham, and [I'd stolen] twenty-plus bags, Charlie believed in me."

Then came the ups and downs. Top of the ride, until 2004 no one in professional baseball history homered in four straight at bats. Bottom of the ride, a sports hernia cost him the 2006 season, and 2007 stands as a washout except for the fact he married the love of his life, Nicole. But, in 2008, Elliot made 'em sit up and notice, bursting onto the Rays' radar with a doggedly determined spring training.

"I knew beyond a shadow of a doubt, I was going to make that opening day roster," Elliot remembered. "My game came together."

In the midst of his roster spot assault, a spring training performance against American League East rival Yankees, perhaps clinched Johnson's bid. Veteran Rays television voice Dewayne Staats picks up the story.

"So many believe in what turned out as a Tampa Bay World Series season," Staats said, "Elliot Johnson sent a message to the Yankees by running over their catcher Francisco Cervelli and scoring a run in a spring training game."

The play incensed the Yankees, and Manager Joe Girardi, but Johnson himself could have cared less.

"Elliot Johnson, to me," Staats continued, "was one hundred percent, stick his head in there and let's get it on guy. That crash into Cervelli sent a 'game on' message to New York."

"I am smiling as I tell you this," Johnson beamed. "Making that Opening Day roster and going to the big leagues for the first time was achieving my life's goal. There are only twenty thousand of us [major-leaguers] in the world! Excitement, you bet!!"

The first call went to his wife, the second to his mom, the third to his dad who didn't answer but who received the following message: "Hey, one of your sons just became a bigleaguer!" In his first game, matched up against the Yankees at Tropicana Field in St. Petersburg, dreams turned reality.

"Looking in that other dugout, I saw Jeter, I saw ARod, and there I am," he said, "in the lineup as the DH facing Andy Pettitte. Wow!"

His first time up, Johnson crushed a four-hundred-foot drive to center field, caught on the warning track. Second time, Elliot slapped a single to left for his MLB hit. Elliot's first MLB game yielded a knock in four times up.

"When you go up, there's elation and excitement," Johnson says. "It's always great making the bigger money in the bigs but going down after you've been there takes adjustments."

After seven MLB games, back to Triple A Durham Johnson went; back to the extremely frustrating roller coaster ride, playing extremely well and watching others receive calls up, while awaiting his turn for another call to The Show.

"The Rays didn't believe in September call ups, so I didn't go back, and because of that didn't qualify for a playoff or World Series roster," he remembered. "So, in 2009, I was playing pretty well, but in a scuffle with a teammate, broke my thumb."

More up and down loomed in 2010. Cut from the forty-man roster by Tampa Bay, Johnson went back to Durham putting up gaudy numbers. A .319 batting average and more than twenty stolen bases led to an appearance at the Triple-A All-Star game.

"Look," Johnson said forcefully. "I played well enough to deserve a call. I didn't get it, so what am I supposed to do? I wasn't a free agent, I basically was a pawn, and it angered me. I was trapped. It was like an abusive relationship. In a certain way, as angry as I was, it energized me."

Johnson used the energy well, forcing his way back on the Rays' roster for 2011. Still, more problems developed. While making the Rays Opening Day roster again and after slamming his first MLB homer against Baltimore's Jake Arrietta, the Rays ignored Johnson.

"I didn't play very well or very much," Johnson admitted. "Mostly I pinch hit, and I always seemed to be pinch hitting against the Aroldis Chapmans and Joe Nathans of the world. The best closers in baseball at that time."

The 2012 season had some upside. For a while, at least.

"After coming back from a pulled hamstring, I thought May and June were extremely productive," he remembered. "While I was hitting around .275, when we came back from the All-Star break, they benched me three straight days and I never really got it going after that."

During the winter meetings in 2012, the Rays, in a deal that created much controversy in Kansas City, shipped starting pitcher James Shields, reliever Wade Davis, and Elliot, for the Royals top prospect Wil Myers.

"Look," Johnson lamented. "I loved the Rays, loved my teammates, would've done anything to stay, but they made the deal in December, and didn't tell me until right before spring training in February of 2013, so I was pretty pissed off."

Johnson, however, turned his "piss-off," into a passionate dose of jet-charged adrenalin—especially when he played for the Royals against his former team the Rays.

"I felt disrespected by the way they treated me," Johnson said. "But every single time we played them when I was in Kansas City, I played great against the Rays. I had something like an OPS of 1.250. I even hit two homers against Jeremy Hellickson and so James Shields came up to me and said, 'hey Elliot, why don't you just imagine you're playing against the Rays, every time you get into a game?'

From the beginning, the great start for Kansas City, the trip headed downward. After seventy-nine games with the Royals, Kansas City removed Elliot from its forty-man roster, and two weeks later, in late August 2013, the Braves acquired him on a waiver claim.

"I hated to leave Kansas City," Johnson lamented. "I loved [General Manager] Dayton Moore and the organization and players, but overall, I didn't play well for them, and I regret that."

Finishing with Atlanta in 2013, Johnson played thirty-two games at second base, replacing Dan Uggla who'd had eye surgery. Elliot played alongside Braves up and coming prospect Andrelton Simmons, he hit .261 while making some highlight reel plays, but wasn't asked back.

"I really wanted to stay in Atlanta," Johnson said. "It is two hours from our home in Durham, and they were on their way to a ring. I truly believed with my skill set playing multiple positions, I would have been a better bench player in the National League. It just didn't happen."

A brief stay with Cleveland in 2014, ended Johnson's sixth MLB season. In 2015 after speaking with ex-teammate-turned Dodgers Manager Gabe Kaplan, Elliot signed a player-coach deal at Triple A Oklahoma City. The Dodgers needed the veteran Johnson alongside their up-and-coming future shortstop star, Corey Seager.

"I really enjoyed that," Johnson smiled, "because that guy has so much talent."

His last two hits in professional baseball came against the Memphis Redbirds and then in the Pacific Coast American Division Playoffs against Round Rock.

"I hit a ball a ton, off the top of the center field wall," Johnson remembers. "But after that game, I knew my time was up, so I called my family and I said, 'I've had it, I'm not going to do this anymore."

Johnson's best MLB season took place in 2012 playing for Tampa Bay. As a backup player, he hit .243 in 123 games with six home runs and thirty-three RBIs, using his blinding speed to steal eighteen bags.

His career still makes him smile, the business side of baseball does not. Elliot now uses his business degree to full advantage providing financial advice to up-and-coming professional players.

"I try to make it as simple for them as possible," he said with a smile, "I want them to have the knowledge I didn't have coming into professional ball, so they don't make the same mistakes I did."

CHAPTER 7

RON SWOBODA

"Renaissance man makes The Catch...."

As a young New York Mets outfielder, playing in the 1969 World Series against the Baltimore Orioles, making one of the best catches in Series history, Ron Swoboda well understood the adulation he received from "The Catch," was fleeting. We'll explain "The Catch" later, but in his earliest Mets days, Swoboda knew if he intended to stay in the major leagues, nothing would ever come easy.

"I didn't have superstar talent," Swoboda said. "Truth is, most MLB players don't. So, every single day I always knew I had to bust my ass just to stay on the same train with most of those guys. Fortunately, I learned that lesson at an early age and that's why I made it through nine big-league seasons."

Raised in the blue-collar city of Baltimore, Maryland, Ron Swoboda watched parents and family members grind out a

Ron Swoboda
(Photo courtesy of Kenny Morrison)

living in a variety of jobs. So, when the Mets signed him out of the University of Maryland in 1963, two years before the first major-league draft, for $35,000, the young outfielder aimed himself toward the big leagues.

"I only went to college for one reason," Swoboda laughs. "To play baseball."

Swoboda insists he didn't go to college to find a wife, but....

"Before class one day," he notes in his book, *Here's the Catch: A Memoir of the Miracle Mets and More,* "this burst of flaming red hair entered the room, and that was it for me. That red head just lit it up."

Cecilia Swoboda became the best baseball wife, organizing her family's spring training trips to Florida while raising two sons, and later beating Stage Four cancer.

"I am and was way out over my skis with Cecilia," Ron insists, "After more than fifty years together, I still think that with sunlight dancing in her hair, she's a Vision of Renoir!"

Playing only briefly in the minors, beginning at Double A and then a short stay at Triple A, Swoboda explains his time there.

"Yeah, two games, three for five in one with a homer, and I struck out four times in game two," he laughs heartily, "the story of my career!!"

Dismissing Swoboda simply as a ballplayer shortchanges a uniquely curious, abundantly open-minded intellect and Renaissance Man. As a published author himself, he's comfortably conversant on a myriad of subjects from Shakespeare to Somerset Maugham, Graham Greene, and Ford Maddox Ford, or the masters of easel, paint, and brush. There's one caveat: The abstract expressionism of William DeKooning and Jackson Pollack leaves him, let's say, a bit baffled.

"With Jackson Pollack's paint drizzling all over the place," Swoboda said in a baffled tone. "I don't know what's going on there, but some *thing* is going on!"

Ron's thoughts on U.S. politics offer passion and concern. He's a rabid history buff, especially dedicated to events, characters, and tales from his adopted home of New Orleans and its mystical, eclectic combination of Spanish, French, Creole, and African American culture. One of his favorite destinations? Ron treated us to a tour through Metairie Cemetery in New Orleans.

"It'll be a lot of fun and very informative," he energetically spoke in tightly-wound, school principal tones, "and you'll learn a lot."

"Sure, I will," whispered the cynic seated to Swoboda's right.

Here's a surface scratch of observations: Metairie Cemetery's stillness caresses hundreds of strikingly opulent tumuli and mausoleums, both simple and ornate, in a variety of colors. Deep green carefully manicured St. Augustine grass lines a system of smooth macadam paths, veiled by cypress and blooming magnolias. In its quiet stately beauty, the cemetery offers highlights of New Orleans' three-hundred-plus year history. The Civil War plays a huge role. French Creole New Orleans native and Confederate General P.G.T. Beauregard's body lies inside the tumulus of The Army of Tennessee.

"General Sidney Johnson sits atop the Tennessee structure," Swoboda informed. "During the bloody battle at Shiloh, Tennessee, Union gunfire killed the general, yet he stayed mounted, bleeding to death in his saddle."

As our chief tour guide eases his BMW further down cemetery paths, we learn that New Orleans native and baseball Hall of Famer Mel Ott occupies Metairie space, as does Andrew Higgins, New Orleans son and creator of World War II landing craft called the "Higgins Boat." The most entertaining Crescent City native at Metairie? Singer/Songwriter/Musician Louis Prima, whose hits include, "I'm Just a Gigolo." A portion of the lyrics remain forever etched into the door of Prima's quiet crypt: "Just a gigolo...life goes on without me."

"Lots of stories here," Swoboda said. "And I tell ya it's fascinating!"

So is Ron's Major League Baseball adventure. In *Here's the Catch*, an intense yet quick read, we find our hero on a mission, amid earthiness and raucous humor. In his early twenties Swoboda made his major-league debut playing for the legendary Casey Stengel during Stengel's last major-league manager's gig for the New York Mets. "Suh-bo'-da," as Stengel called his rookie outfielder, baffled his manager with the mistakes he made.

"Not so baffled," mused Swoboda. "I think I just flat pissed him off a lotta times. I really, really did."

Laughs abound at Stengel's ire over rookie players, specifically Swoboda himself. From his book, a classic Swoboda/Stengel soliloquy involves rookie Ron, playing in the outfield during a day game in St. Louis. With threatening skies at game time, the park turned brightly sunny. Of course, the rookie Ron forgot his flip-down sunglasses, and of course the Cardinals loaded the bases.

Infielder Dal Maxvill hit a blooper over second base, and Ron, in right field, lost it in the sun.

"Three runs scored, and it was all on me," Swoboda remembered. "I was livid, ashamed, and pissed, all in one swoop."

His next at bat, in the top of the tenth inning, Swoboda, still miffed, popped up, ending the inning. Even more miffed in the eleventh, he threw down his batting helmet stomping it literally to smithereens. Watching the rookie dancing a wicked two-step-stomp on the helmet, the grizzled, craggy-faced, bow-legged Stengel raced out of the dugout.

"YOU missed that fly ball," bellowed Casey, "but when YOU screwed up, I didn't go into the clubhouse and throw your wristwatch on the floor, so I don't want you busting up my equipment. You're out of the game!"

After that verbal dressing down, the rookie convinced himself he'd never play in the big leagues again, his career no doubt ruined because of his own immaturity and stupidity. Overreacting, of course, Swoboda sat out a couple games, but never forgot his mistake.

"I'm serious," Ron grinned, "I seriously thought I'd never play for him again."

He did, and by 1969 Ron Swoboda and the Mets had grown up. After three seasons as a baseball laughingstock, led by future Dodgers Hall of Famer and World War II combat vet Gil Hodges, the Mets came alive with a vengeance. They ran down and defeated a loaded Chicago Cubs team.

"They featured future Hall of Fame righthander Ferguson Jenkins, and lefty Ken Holtzman," Swoboda remembers clearly. "Then add to that, third baseman Ron Santo, shortstop Don Kessinger and second baseman Glenn Beckert and Hall of Fame outfielder Billy Williams and that bunch was loaded!"

So were the Mets.

"You bet we were," Ron insisted. "Think about it. Two future Hall of Fame Pitchers, Tom Seaver and Nolan Ryan, an All-Star lefty in Jerry Koosman, catcher Jerry Grote, infielders Ed Charles, Ed Kranepool, Bud Harrelson, and a late season add, power hitting Donn Clendenon, and an outfield of Tommie Agee, Cleon Jones and me—we could get things done."

Coming into Shea Stadium on September 8, 1969, the Cubs found themselves in turmoil, even though they led the Mets by two and a half games. Manager Leo Durocher failed to rest his starters down the stretch, consequently ace Ferguson Jenkins nursed a sore arm and Durocher himself created havoc with racial remarks made at his lefty All-Star Ken Holtzman.

"Topping that off," Swoboda remembered, "Leo ordered his pitchers to intimidate us, specifically aiming at Tommie Agee's head."

With Mets lefty All-Star Jerry Koosman facing Cubs third baseman Ron Santo after the attempt at Agee's head, Koosman zeroed in on the ear flap of Santo's helmet, in retribution.

"Yessir, Santo just got his elbow up to deflect that ninety-mile-an-hour heater," Swoboda grinned. "And [Santo] came away from that at bat a changed man. We won two straight."

That set the stage for a ten game Mets winning streak, blasting Chicago out of contention, winning the National League East for the first time in history. In roundhouse fashion, they clinched the division in late September, taking down Atlanta for the NL Pennant and in another first, making the Mets first trip to the World Series. Swoboda excitedly headed home to Baltimore, with his New York Mets teammates facing his boyhood favorite the Orioles.

"Exciting," he laughed. "And boy did I get a lot of requests for tickets!"

Orioles' brass built a juggernaut. Hall of Fame outfielder Frank Robinson won the Triple Crown in 1966 and became the only man to win Most Valuable Player awards in both the American and National Leagues. Brooks Robinson won the AL MVP in 1964, and in a Hall of Fame career won an astounding sixteen Gold Glove awards. Bolstered by second baseman Davey Johnson and slugging first baseman Boog Powell as well as speedy center fielder Paul Blair, and a pitching rotation rivaling any in MLB history, the Orioles were overloaded.

"Excellent starters like future Hall of Famer Jim Palmer, Dave McNally and lefty Mike Cuellar who won twenty-three games for the Orioles after coming over from Houston, were formidable," Swoboda remembered.

The Orioles took game one, but Mets skipper Gil Hodges soothed the upstart Mets with some postgame comments.

"Hodges said the most sobering and supportive thing he could say to a young team," remembered Swoboda. "You don't have to be anything more than what you got here."

With the pressure mitigated, Mets lefty Jerry Koosman matched up against Baltimore's twenty-game-winning lefty Dave McNally. The Mets' new teammate, Donn Clendenon, homered for the first run in Game Two. The Orioles tied it, but in the Mets' top of the ninth, an RBI single from shortstop Al Weis drove in the go-ahead run. Reliever Ron Taylor retired the final Baltimore hitter, resulting in a 2-1 Mets win and a series evened at one game apiece headed back to New York and Shea Stadium.

At the madhouse that was Shea Stadium, the Mets beat Orioles ace Jim Palmer, aided by center fielder Tommy Agee's two incredibly stupendous catches, one with the bases loaded. The Mets took game three and the Series lead with a 5-0 win. Game Four at Shea featured a second inning homer from first baseman Clendenon, as future Hall of Famer Tom Seaver shut down the Orioles early. With one out in the top of the ninth, back-to-back singles from the Orioles Frank Robinson and Boog Powell placed the tying and go ahead runs on, sending third baseman Brooks Robinson to the plate.

"At this point in the game," Swoboda, playing in right field that day remembered, "Robinson hadn't hit the ball out of the infield."

Seaver delivered a pitch down and away, and Robinson unloaded a screaming shot into right center as Swoboda picked up the flight of the baseball and the story.

"He squared it up, and nine times out of ten during the regular season that ball finds grass," Swoboda vividly recalled. "This time I saw the ball right off the bat and got a tremendous jump."

Never sure he'd make it in time, yet knowing he couldn't stop his sprint, Swoboda in what through the years turned out to be an ESPN and YouTube classic catch, launched an all-out, head-first dive.

"In free fall," he said, "I snagged that little bastard in the top of my [glove's] web, inches before it found grass. I'm rolling and skidding, I come up throwing and I hear a shriek and roar like you couldn't believe and made a catch that changed the game, changed that Series and changed my life."

Later Baltimore tied the game, as Seaver left. In the bottom of the tenth, pinch-hitting catcher J.C. Martin, with pinch runner Rod Gaspar on first, placed a perfect bunt toward first. Lefty Orioles reliever Pete Richert fielded it, threw it away, scoring Gaspar and giving the Mets the win. In the fifth and what turned out to be the deciding game of this miracle comeback season for the Mets, the Orioles took an early 3-0 lead, but World Series MVP Clendenon's two-run homer off Dave McNally and shortstop Al Weis solo homer tied the contest at three in the seventh. In the bottom of the eighth, with the go-ahead run on at second (Cleon Jones courtesy of a booming double-off reliever Eddie Watt), the defensive hero of Game Four, Swoboda came up to face the side-armer Watt.

"Watt threw a slider that didn't break and I one-handed it down the left field line," Swoboda remembered clearly. "I thought that ball should have been caught."

But it wasn't, and Swoboda scored a second run that inning on an error at first base to make it 5-3. The Mets held through the top of the ninth and for the first time in MLB history, the Miracle Mets, in perhaps the most improbable comeback ever took home a world championship.

The Mets stumbled the following season. They traded Swoboda to Montreal, and he battled a veteran outfield for playing time, but by late June, he'd been traded back to New York, this time to the Yankees. Never really finding traction with the Yanks, his final MLB hurrah came in 1974 with the Braves. Before Atlanta released Swoboda, his friend and baseball fan, Dave Marash, working as a reporter for CBS-owned Channel 2 in New York, came to the Braves spring training site in West Palm Beach, Florida, for a feature on the former Met and Yankee. Marash's boss saw the feature and asked if Ron would be interested in a job as weekend sportscaster for Channel 2.

"At that point I had no idea what I was going to do," Swoboda said.

So, off he went to a land he'd only seen from the front of his TV set. The intrepid Ron spent fifteen years as a sportscaster in New York, Milwaukee and then, in New Orleans, where he left the TV sports biz and began broadcasting Triple-A baseball with the New Orleans Zephyrs, later called the Baby Cakes.

"There's no one like him," said his long-time New Orleans radio partner, Tim Grubbs, speaking on an Austin, Texas radio program in February of 2020. "Not one person like him, and not only did he teach me so much baseball, in a certain sense he was a big brother and father figure rolled into one."

Part of the essence of having played Major League Baseball in New York, screenwriters remembered Swoboda in an early 2000s situation comedy Mad About You. He's also mentioned in the movie *Frequency* with Dennis Quaid, and *Righteous Kill* with Robert DeNiro, and perhaps most importantly by that eclectic genius himself Homer Simpson in a Simpsons episode.

"Homer's my kind of guy. He's not politically correct and that's why I love him," Swoboda laughs.

Now that his New Orleans ball club adopted another home, leaving the city without minor-league baseball, Ron plays golf religiously, he and Cecilia travel as much as possible and attend Mets events at spring training and in New York City. Most especially, as one might imagine the Miracle Mets, unlikely World Champions in 1969, hold a special place nearest Ron Swoboda's grinder's heart.

"We were black and white, conservative and liberal," he says, "in the case of the Mets, the bond was baseball and having that ultimate success heightened the bonds of respect we always paid each other."

Remembered in MLB history for his tremendously celebrated catch in the 1969 World Series, Swoboda received a gift that to this day remains a highlight of his career. He also insists that every MLB grinder should have the same gift he has.

"No one," he loudly proclaims, "whoever played in the big leagues should ever leave without at least ten seconds of high-light footage. That's what The Catch did for me, and it made my career."

BRIAN DOWNING

"Grinding from childhood..."

H OW DO ANY OF US come to love this game, grab it so pas-sionately, squeezing it to the depths of our souls? What gave us that subtle push, or maybe the light kick in the pants that started our baseball engines? Maybe a dad or mom introduces a

Brian Downing with the Iowa Oaks in 1973
(Photo courtesy of the Iowa Cubs)

son to baseball, maybe the youngster finds it with other young friends. In the case of an all-time grinder, Brian Downing, his grandmother gave him the game on a silver platter. But given the road he traveled, few would have endured long enough, few would have had the temerity, heart, and passion to achieve the baseball dream Brian Downing pictured for himself.

When we reached Brian's wife, Cheryl, asking if her husband would interview for our book, she wasn't optimistic.

"He doesn't talk about his career that much," she said. "I think a whole book devoted to him and his stories would really sell, but he just doesn't like to talk about it."

Eventually, Brian agreed to talk, but better than that, he put together on twelve pages of a legal pad, filled out on both sides, a handwritten account of his career. Downing purged his baseball soul, with vividly recalled stories and anecdotes, answering our twenty-question inquiry with a full-blown life history in baseball, packed with thoughts and insights. The man who'd rather not talk about his career provided one of the best, eloquent, and honest responses we've ever seen.

A young man no one wanted as a high school and junior college player, Brian could have cared less. He spent a twenty-plus-year career proving naysayers wrong. Baseball to him wasn't about self-aggrandizement. To Downing, the game meant life itself. And only one man in his life believed Downing could play in the major leagues. In an honest review of Downing's career, everything about the way he played the game screams "grinder." Downing showed baseball he could, indeed, succeed and handsomely at that. Retiring at age forty-one after playing for the White Sox, Angels, and Rangers, Brian played it, as he puts it, "the right way."

The story of where and how this game began for Downing remains one for the ages.

When the Brooklyn Dodgers moved west for the 1958 season, no seven-year-old in Los Angeles showed more excitement than Brian Downing. One year later, after watching Brian's immersion into his new love the Dodgers, his grandmother provided the youngster with perhaps the best gift of his life. Listening and watching on radio and television to the already legendary Vince Scully and riveted to the first World Series ever played on the West Coast, the wide-eyed youngster's world broadened in a flash when his grandmother spent some hard-earned money buying World Series tickets to Game Three of the 1959 Series played at the Los Angeles Coliseum. Little did his grandmother realize on the day of her purchase that not only did she light up her grandson's eyes, but she also launched what ultimately became an outstanding and lengthy major-league career.

"I couldn't get enough," said Downing. "We only got nine Dodgers games on television in Los Angeles in those days, and they were all against the Giants. A World Series game, to me, was an additional Christmas Day."

This World Series pitted the Dodgers, managed by Walter Alston and featuring Don Drysdale and Sandy Koufax, against the go-go Chicago White Sox, managed by Al Lopez and featuring future Hall of Famers Luis Aparicio at shortstop, pitcher Early Wynn, and second baseman Nellie Fox. Amidst all the nationwide attention on the Series and on the clubs themselves, plus the fact that the West Coast had never hosted a World Series game, young Brian Downing began his own personal quest to become a major-league player. Never did it dawn on the eight-year-old that he couldn't one day play like those guys he watched at the Coliseum. He carried that belief with him through the ups and downs this game brings to youngsters, and it ultimately paid off. Downing's heroes won the Series over the White Sox, four games to two. But that one Series game he saw, for all intents and purposes, set in motion for Brian, one of the most intense, lengthy, and eclectic careers in the history of the game. Downing remembers his first MLB game as vividly as if it were played yesterday.

"The game I saw, Game Three of the World Series, was attended by me, my grandmother and ninety thousand other people there at the L.A. Coliseum," he grinned. "What a great first MLB game to attend and that's when I was hooked on this wonderful game. But it's odd, isn't it? The White Sox became the first team that signed me, and I made it to the big leagues first with the White Sox. And, as the fates have it, Don Drysdale pitched Game Three of the 1959 series, and as it turns out, Drysdale was the first TV announcer for the Angels, when I was traded there from the White Sox."

In fairness, Downing faced a long and sometimes tough road before that MLB career broke out. A star in Little League, he still gives credit to his coach, Carl Koonce, for teaching him to play the game correctly.

"Carl Koonce gave me great teaching and guidance," Brian remembers almost reverently. "I never would have been able to achieve what I did without his early words of encouragement."

And that teaching carried Downing to extreme success leading up to high school. But once there, Brian slammed into some of baseball's brick walls. The story of Downing's high school days remains amazing at the least.

"I never got cut from a team in high school," he remembers, "but once there, until my senior year, I always played at the lower levels like "C," or "B," or junior varsity. My senior year I played center field and caught, but I only hit something like .231. After that 'stellar season,' I walked on at Cypress Junior College."

In the junior college ranks, life became even tougher.

"I went out for the team," he grinned, "but all I did was sit on the bench the entire season. Well, I did go 1-3, but seriously, my main job was to hang numbers on the scoreboard the entire game. I'm serious about that."

Disappointment from a junior college season yielding only three at bats most likely would've turned away most aspiring young players. Most, though, are not Brian Downing.

"My motivation to succeed in this game never was built on disappointment of being an underdog, feeling slighted, or being a heartbroken loser," Brian said sharply. "If that were so, I'd made it to the Hall of Fame from all the disappointments. I just never responded to disappointment with a chip on my shoulder. That's just not me. My absolute, true motivations were simply loving and playing this game as long as possible and playing in a World Series."

Although Downing came close to playing in a World Series in 1986, that dream never came true. And while the junior college disappointment didn't derail Downing, one man with Major League Baseball ties came to the rescue. A part-time Chicago White Sox scout, Bill Lentini, who had coached Brian in American Legion ball, saw something in Downing no one else had seen—a relentless fire and passion for the game.

"Bill told me when I was seventeen that if he had a chance he'd sign me," Downing said. "I never thought that would happen. But this was in the midst of the Vietnam era and MLB clubs were having trouble signing guys who were drafted into the military if they hadn't been involved in student programs."

Lentini sent a report on Downing to his White Sox bosses shortly before the 1970 draft. The report indicated Brian Downing could play multiple positions, could throw and hit well, and went on to report that Downing hit .333 in junior college which—technically—was true.

"Well, remember, I went 1-3 that season," Brian grinned. "Fortunately, Bill's bosses never found out about that! But it was Bill Lentini that believed in me and gave me my chance and fortunately he got to see me play in the big leagues before he died."

Signing with the White Sox surprised some of Downing's junior college teammates.

"In fact," he remembers, "a couple of them I ran into across the country during my big-league career couldn't believe it because they felt they were better than me."

Better junior college players, perhaps. That said, few players not targeted as high-level prospects by scouts, had the career Downing had. During his twenty MLB seasons, Brian hit at an almost .270 clip, homering 278 times. An All-Star in 1979, he ended that season as the third leading hitter in the American League, sporting a .326 average. With the Vietnam war still at full tilt, Downing's high draft number allowed him to spend his first spring training with the White Sox and not in the military.

"While I didn't hit much," Brian recalls, "they apparently loved my intangibles. They must have because when the White Sox called me up from the Triple A Iowa Oaks in '73, I had gone zero for my last six. I thought, 'I'm not ready,' but I kept my mouth shut and went on up."

Used mostly in right field and third base in the minors, Downing arrived for his major-league debut in the middle of a game between the White Sox and Detroit Tigers. Playing third base, on the first pitch of Downing's MLB career, Detroit shortstop Dick McAuliffe hit a high, checked-swing pop toward the third base dugout. The eager, aggressive Downing took off full speed after it.

"I took a dive and caught it about an inch off the ground," Downing remembers, "However, my knee was crushed, literally, and I'm carted off the field. All I could think was, 'what if I never make it back and I only had a one-pitch career?'"

That worry went away quickly, but the catastrophic MLB start for Brian Downing provided a lesson that became one of his mantras throughout his two decades in Major League Baseball.

"Truthfully, after that play," he said firmly, "I vowed to myself that I would play every play as if it were the last pitch or last play I would ever make in baseball."

The worst part of the Downing knee injury, which resulted in two months of recovery and rehabilitation, was that the White Sox were leaving Chicago after the game, headed for New York and the original Yankee Stadium.

"That was heartbreaking for me," he said quietly. "Because I'd always dreamed of playing there. After that season they renovated the original Yankee Stadium and that was a job that took two years."

Back to the White Sox after two months out and playing in front of a national audience on NBC TV's *Game of the Week*, facing tough Detroit Tigers lefty Mickey Lolich, rookie Brian Downing made his first MLB base hit, an indescribable doozy.

"My first big league at bat," Brian said proudly, "was an inside the park home run!"

And what a way for a rookie player to come back to the big leagues after a catastrophic knee injury.

"Think about it," he continued. "What a daily double I had in my first two major-league games. First pitch I see from my third base position is a pop-up when I badly injure my knee. Two months later when I came back from the knee injury, on the first pitch I see as a hitter, turned into an inside-the-park home run. What a way to start and that's pretty special. And to top it off, I felt no pressure from anyone in the organization, because I wasn't a top draft choice, or anyone known as a top prospect."

His second time to the big leagues that first season also expanded his value for the White Sox, demonstrating that he, Brian Downing could play not only third base but right field and fill in as a backup catcher.

"And that's despite the fact," he recalls, "that I had caught only one Triple-A game when I came to the big leagues. And to complicate the whole thing, the White Sox had a big, lefty knuckleballer, Wilbur Wood and I had to somehow master dealing with that."

After the 1977 season ended, Downing seriously considered retiring from baseball because he simply didn't enjoy the way that season ended. (He hit .284 in only sixty-nine games, but the best was yet to come.) Downing says he expected more from himself, but after the negative feelings ended, he decided to go to spring training in 1978 and give it one final shot. Then, that off-season, while lifting weights at a local gym near his California home, Downing heard on the radio he'd been traded home, to the California Angels.

"Obviously being a Southern California native," Downing said, "that news excited me, but in Anaheim the trade became very unpopular because the Angels sent a fan favorite, Bobby Bonds [Barry Bonds' dad] to the White Sox."

For the most part, Brian enjoyed playing in his home state, although initially in his baseball life, the Dodgers and not the Angels were his first love. He enjoyed the *Easy Rider* life, driving his Harleys up and down Los Angeles freeways. Brian

loved the life of a musician and still loves the blues. Always
the antithesis of self-promoter, Downing made an appearance
on television's *The Jeffersons*. He'd been told he'd be seen and
not heard. Instead, he found out he'd have to memorize and
deliver lines.

"I didn't like it at all," he said. "It was not what I expected or
told it would be and I was glad when it was over."

And there was the 1978 season when he only played part
time for the Angels.

"At that point in my career," Downing remembered, "I still
didn't feel that I had put it together as a player."

In 1979, baseball life changed not only for Brian Downing,
but for the Angels as well.

"In '79, pitchers Dave Frost, Chris Knapp, and I put it all
together, and we had a hell of a roster," Downing said. "Our
power guys were left fielder Don Baylor with thirty-six homers,
second baseman Bobby Grich [who] hit thirty, [and] DH Willie
Aikens and right fielder Dan Ford had twenty-one apiece. While
I was the lead-off batter [as catcher] and hadn't really developed power yet, I had twelve bombs. Frost and Nolan Ryan
won sixteen games each [Frost had twelve complete games,
Ryan seventeen] and the Angels won their first division title."

All the pieces came together for Downing.

"Certainly for me, that '79 season marked the first time I
really had any confidence in my baseball abilities," Downing
said. "Ultimately, the season we had and the division title made
fans forget about the trade that cost them their favorite Bobby
Bonds."

That year represented another landmark for Downing. He
began revolutionizing baseball's ideas about using weight

training for building functional strength in baseball players. Before Downing's exploits with the heavy iron, baseball trainers steered clear of weights, thinking they'd stiffen and tighten muscles and cause more injuries.

"I had been reading numerous bodybuilding magazines when I got to the big leagues in 1973," Downing remembered, "so weight training started as a hobby for me and something I really enjoyed, and really became good at. I started training on a Nautilus circuit—a system of machines, designed by a Louisiana native named Arthur Jones—that provided a very safe way to weight train and gain strength. Few if any players trained that way in those days, no weight training equipment existed in big league clubhouses in those days, and weight training was frowned upon. So, in the early days of training for me, I only did it in the off season."

Downing became a catcher fulltime in 1975, and had backed off weights a bit, feeling he needed to concentrate on learning to catch Angels pitchers Nolan Ryan and Frank Tanana.

"By then," he remembered, "I had switched from Nautilus to free weight training and I also came to the conclusion I really needed to train twelve months a year, in order to realize the strength benefits such training provides. As I said before, big-league clubhouses had no places to lift as they do now, so on the road I'd take cab rides up to twenty miles in order to find gyms where I could lift. Always finishing before eleven a.m. on game day before a night game, I never had any kind of bad side effects. Weight training always made me feel better, helped me in maintaining my body weight and strength during each season."

That same season also brought other changes to Brian's game. While his Angels team won big that season, Downing made a total change in his hitting approach.

"That all began during a game against Toronto and their righthander Dave Stieb," Downing remembers.

"Now Stieb had the best slider I ever saw, anywhere, and in one at-bat against him, I fouled off nine consecutive sliders and never connected solidly. So, the next morning in my batting cage at home, I came up with a wide-open stance allowing me to follow the pitch much better and allowed me to hit to all fields. That stance and approach change gave me a lot more confidence."

As good as 1979 was, 1980 left much to be desired.

"The 1980 season ended early for me, after I broke my ankle trying to tag out Rickey Henderson at home plate," Downing said. "Then when I came back the Angels moved me to the outfield because I'd been injured so much working behind the plate."

The Angels lack of communication in dealing with Downing disappointed him. No one from the club ever talked about the move with Brian himself.

"That's well and good, I guess, but here's how I found out about it," said a disappointed Downing. "I came to the park one day, looked at the lineup card and saw a seven [left field], instead of a two [catcher] beside my name. And I thought, 'what the hell?' I had played right field before and felt comfortable there, but I could never remember having played left field and in Anaheim I just never could see the ball well there."

The catcher's position always held Downing's heart and soul. So, he never truly enjoyed his time as an outfielder, even though he played well on the grass.

"I really liked catching," Downing professed. "Over the course of my career I played in probably 240 games in the outfield and my whole approach—purely and simply—was trying to knock in more runs than I allowed in."

Downing never allowed disappointment in playing outfield instead of catching spill over into a bad attitude.

I kept my mouth shut, didn't gripe about it and I approached the outfield with the same attitude adopted for every game I played," he said. "My attitude always was [to] find a way and go hard on every play as if it were my last."

Find a way he did, in the outfield. Downing reeled off an unbelievable stretch of 140 major-league games without an error in the outfield, an American League record. He also discovered an additional advantage in moving to the outfield from behind the plate.

"Because as a catcher, I developed a good feel for the other team's hitting tendencies," he said. "I carried that ability into left field. Knowing hitters' strengths and weaknesses I better knew how to set up, which gave me a tremendous advantage chasing fly balls. To be honest, though, I have to say that as I finished the last five years of my career as a designated hitter, that really made me happy."

With the move to the outfield in 1981, came a change in Downing's weightlifting passion.

"While catching, I believed that I needed to be quicker, looser, and more agile so I could reach pitches easier and help a pitcher avoid wild pitches, or me avoid passed balls. So, moving to the outfield, I adopted more of a powerlifting approach, using heavier weights to build strength. I did it because as a corner outfielder, I needed to supply more power in our lineup, and it worked."

As 1979 marked a year of change in Brian Downing's game, he added power and as he said, "put it all together in 1982." Need proof? By age thirty-six, when most power hitters either found themselves in decline or retired, Downing pounded out a whopping sixty-one extra base hits. He also fashioned an on-base percentage of better than .400 and remarkably did the same thing in his final season, at age forty-one playing for the Texas Rangers.

"After what I believed was seven seasons of trial-and-error training, and now being even stronger due to weight training, I became a lead-off hitter, crowding the plate more and going for extra base hits," Downing said, "I had twenty-eight homers in '82, and at that point in my career I knew what worked and what didn't, at the plate, on the outfield and in the weight room."

With his entire game coming together in 1982, and looking back over time, does Downing have any regrets?

"I do wish, at some point, I had been able to figure out in a timely manner, the missing link from the great rhythm approach I had during the 1979 season to a more powerful approach I had in the '82-'92 seasons," he said. "Oddly in a Texas Rangers fantasy camp game, ten years after I retired, I was hitting balls better than I hit twenty years before, and that made it extremely tough and frustrating wondering what could have been had I found the power earlier."

Outside of that mystery, was there a bigger disappointment?

"The Angels took on the Boston Red Sox in the 1986 AL Championship Series," Downing laments. "That Red Sox team ultimately lost to the Mets in the World Series [the Bill Bucker error costing the Red Sox an important game], but I thought we had the Red Sox well in hand."

Headed into Game Five of that series, the Angels led Boston three games to one and were playing in Anaheim with a chance to clinch the American League Championship. The Angels owned a three-run lead until the Red Sox' Dave Henderson tied it with a three-run homer in the top of the ninth, leaving the Angels with a chance to win it in the bottom of the ninth.

"Rob Wilfong, our third baseman, got on," Downing said. "Our ninth hitter in the lineup, Dick Schofield, standing on deck, listened to me—I was leadoff hitter—as I said to him, 'hey, why don't you try to inside-out one of his fastballs to right, that'll move Wilfong to third and we'll be in business.' Schofield was an outstanding veteran presence, handled the bat well, and he did just that."

At that point, Brian found himself with a chance to be a hero.

"So, here I come up with two on and the winning run at third with one out," he said. "I'm ready to go, this is my time, I thought. Then I looked up and Red Sox Manager John McNamara raised four fingers in the air to his pitcher and catcher, so they walked me, and then we proceeded to make two straight outs. The Red Sox won that game, the series switched to Boston, and they won two straight at Fenway and we were done."

Downing calls that series the biggest disappointment of his career, nothing else close, and he never won a ring.

"At the end of the day, I am proud I never used bad or negative things or thoughts throughout my life to motivate me to play this game," Downing said. "One of my motivations was the first game I ever attended (remember I mentioned it, the World Series Dodgers versus White Sox in 1959), when I fell in love with the game. The second was overcoming the first pitch injury I suffered in my first game in the big leagues, and the third, as I mentioned, never wearing that cherished ring.

Looking back at his career, Brian didn't like the way the Angels treated him, saying they discarded him two years early when they let him go to the Rangers to finish his career. Yet, fans chose him as an "All Time Angel," and later he entered the Angels Hall of Fame. Brian always thought he was capable of more. But when one looks at Brian's career in its totality, consider the following:

> "He was a gamer," said Brian's Angels battery mate and Hall of Fame pitcher Nolan Ryan. "Brian was quietly as intense as they came and a tough out and an outstanding player."

Downing's a man who realized from high school on that he'd have to battle his entire career, truly battle, to succeed. While he did just that, playing for the White Sox, Angels, and Rangers, he not only played extremely well, once making an All-Star team, but how many players can say they played twenty seasons, retiring at age forty-one? Only a handful. Downing's tale proves beyond a shadow of a doubt that scouts may be able to accurately judge a player's physical tools, but they cannot always judge just how much passion, heart, and determination a young player possesses.

DAVE CLARK

"Baseball's Rocky Balboa..."

CATCH DAVE CLARK coaching at first or third base for the Detroit Tigers and if you look closely, what stands out more than anything—more than his huge forearms and shoulders, more than his football-player neck, and more than his legs, still athletic at age fifty-eight—is the intensity, deeply ingrained in his facial expression.

"Man, the way he carried himself," remembers former Houston Astros player Mark Saccomanno, "reminded me of movies I'd seen that featured Marine Corps drill sergeants—rough and tough. That was an eye opener, but he surprised us."

The entire Dave Clark story represents surprise with its twists and turns.

"I was raised on a farm outside Tupelo, Mississippi," Clark said. "That's a pretty good way to grow up. There were fourteen of us and we always had lots to do tending crops and cattle, but it was a great childhood."

Dave's dad and his brothers found ways to make it even better for the youngster.

"I am so lucky because my dad and my brothers taught me how to play all sports," he said. One of his brothers, Louis, played wide receiver for the Seattle Seahawks for six years. Clark's father, using a portion of his farmland, built regulation-sized football and baseball fields and a basketball court for his sons and daughters—fourteen family members in all.

"Listen," Dave laughed, "if any parents in Tupelo, or from surrounding farms wanted to find their kids after school, or on

Sunday afternoon following church, they all knew where to go. You'd find all the kids at the Clark Farm because that's where we all learned to play and learned to compete."

Nine-year-old Dave's horizons stretched past most kids in Tupelo, however, because for parts of several summers he traveled to the Baltimore-Washington area to visit his favorite aunt, who by the way served as First Lady Pat Nixon's hairstylist. But young Dave's visits always included much more than a sightseeing trip and visits with an aunt and uncle.

"My uncle, Odie Pounds, took me to the Boys Club, where he volunteered as a boxing coach," Clark said. "And man, he knew his stuff. He sparred against Heavyweight Champion Sonny Liston and was a huge Muhammed Ali fan. So, he taught me how to box, and every time I went to his home back east and Ali was fighting on television, you better bet we were watching."

And maybe the boxing club marks the spot where Dave Clark's intensity began.

"Oh, I loved it," Clark remembers clearly. "Just the one on one, no one else to depend on, it was just me and my opponent. It was all up to me."

Clark also loved Joe Frazier's aggressive and intense, brawling boxing style. Dave's boxing acumen, his intensity, and his self-confidence resulted in a perfect 26-0 ring record with thirteen knockouts in his Golden Gloves career. Had President Jimmy Carter not boycotted the 1980 Summer Olympics in Moscow, Dave Clark, almost fully grown at six feet, two inches and 185 pounds, and tremendously strong, might well have been a member of the U.S. boxing team.

"Well, that's true," he remembered, "but one factor remained in that equation that has never been discussed very much when we talk about boxing. That hugely important factor was my mother. She had vowed she'd never let me go because she thought boxing was dangerous and more than that she thought Russia was even more dangerous. Me trying to talk her into allowing me to go to Russia never would have worked, and so let's just say I was really pretty good at boxing, and let it go at that."

From elementary to junior high then onto high school, while he loved boxing, Clark's heart truly belonged to baseball. While he only played two high school seasons in Tupelo, Clark never saw a scout and no college came calling with scholarship offers. Fortunately for Dave, however, he was always big and strong for his age. So, from age eleven through his high school years, Dave played for a fast, talented semi-pro team in Tupelo.

"Playing for six or seven years against grown men really pushed my baseball development," he said. "And right after I finished high school, I decided I'd go to the Marines, thinking that I'd develop more physically, and mentally, and have a leg up on making some money to attend college once I finished my hitch."

In Dave Clark's opinion, The Man Upstairs had plans for Dave other than going into the Marines.

After, a particularly spirited game against his semi-pro team's biggest rival, a game in which Clark hit two home runs, the opposing team's catcher sat the recently graduated seventeen-year-old down for a serious discussion about the future.

"Now you gotta remember, I was headed toward the military, to the Marines," Clark recalls, "but this guy asked me if I had a scholarship, and I said, 'no and no one's ever talked to me about one.' So, this catcher told me he'd played at Jackson [Mississippi] State, and he said I was good enough and I belonged there.

Better than that, he promised he'd have their coach contact me. He did, and in a whirlwind, I ended up at Jackson State."

So, the young man who had no scholarship turned his three extremely successful Jackson State seasons into a first-round draft selection, eleventh overall, in 1983 by the Cleveland Indians, and Dave Clark was on his way.

"Look," the rock-jawed Clark said intently, "I grew up in church, and I had been taught to love God and always do the right thing. Being at Jackson State and having that faith set the stage for some really great blessings to come."

Dave Clark adapted to life in professional baseball very well.

By his third year in pro ball, the young outfielder with the big bat, and bigger heart, found himself knocking at the major-league door while playing for the Triple A Maine Guides, Cleveland's top farm club. There, Clark pounded International League pitchers over a 109-game adventure, for nineteen homers and fifty-eight RBIs. The result? He received his first MLB callup late in the 1986 season. Playing in eighteen games, Clark ripped three homers and drove home nine runs. Not a bad showing. That season he met a player who helped him deepen his faith in God.

"Andre Thornton really had it together," Clark grinned. "He, like me, had been raised in church, and when he told me the story of God's master plan for his life, a light went off and so, like Andre, I began to take responsibility and take charge with God in the midst of my life."

Fortunately for Clark, he became closer to God and to his friend Andre Thornton. While the two played together in 1987, Dave himself became frustrated with baseball's roller coaster ride, from Triple-A ball to the big leagues.

"From then on," he remembers, "my life amounted to the up and down game. Seems like every time I got going good, down I would go, and you know that's frustrating for a young kid wanting to prove himself in the big leagues."

Clark played much better for the Indians beginning in 1988. In 1989, he played in 102 games for former Yankees catcher Doc Edwards. Edwards and Clark developed a friendly professional relationship and during a 1989 game, Texas Rangers future Hall of Famer Nolan Ryan struck out Clark three straight times.

"I really thought Doc might take me out for a pinch hitter because we had two on when it was my turn up again," Clark grinned. "But he left me in, and wouldn't you know, I hit a three-run homer and Doc and I grinned at each other when I came back into the dugout, and as I sat down, I thought, 'whew, thank you Doc and thank you God!'"

By 1990, Dave Clark left the Cleveland Indians and became a super utility player for the Chicago Cubs. More importantly, a fellow teammate on the Cubs that season, Lloyd McClendon, became a huge role model for Clark the player, and later for the coach and manager he became.

"You look at Lloyd McClendon's career," Dave marveled, "And you see that as a player he was a lot like me, a super utility role player. He really taught me how to pinch hit. Oh yeah, I had pinch hit a bunch by the time I got to the Cubs, but Lloyd took it a step further."

McClendon urged Clark to pay close attention to the box scores of upcoming opponents, and especially those bullpen pitchers he'd be facing late in games. Remember, no internet

GRINDERS

with complete day-by-day player rundowns existed in those days, but McClendon's advice helped immensely.

"I'd look at who had pitched, and how many innings each one had thrown over the last few days," Clark said. "And I began to pick up those little, tiny details—knowing how many times they'd thrown over the last few days—and having this new information really turned me into a much better, more alert pinch hitter when I came to the plate in late-game situations."

Then, after that year with the Cubs, and after a brief Clark stint in Kansas City, McLendon and Clark ended up with the Pittsburgh Pirates. Clark settled in for a five-year run in the steel city, and his best season in 1993 propelled him to a career high eleven homers off Pittsburgh's bench and ten the next season.

As McLendon's playing career wound down, he found himself back in Pittsburgh for the 2000 season as the first black manager or head coach of any of Pittsburgh's three major sports teams. Ironically, Clark had finished his playing career with a year with the Dodgers, another season in Chicago, and finally with the Houston Astros. Once he finished playing, Dave took the next step, coming back to the Pirates as their rookie-league hitting coach in 2000.

"Actually, the GM, Cam Bonifay, called me and asked me what I was doing," Clark remembered. "When I told him I was going to school, he said, 'oh no, come on back to us as a rookie-league hitting coach in the Gulf Coast League.' I was thrilled."

More thrills awaited Clark than he realized at the time.

"And what a privilege it was to be back in the same organization as Lloyd," beamed Clark. "A man's man [who] loved players, stood up to them with the umpires and loved helping players succeed, and he's still going at it. What an inspiration he was and still is to me."

Instead of becoming the rookie league coach for the Pirates, Clark became the hitting coach at Triple A Nashville. Then, the next two seasons, 2001 and 2002, McLendon hired Clark as his hitting coach.

"How about that," Clark laughed. "You start the season thinking you're going to be coaching the greenest of the green kids, and instead you're working with seasoned professionals in Triple A, earnestly battling to polish their skills for the big leagues. What a ride that first year was, and then the next two as *the* Pirates hitting coach...what a blessing!"

Always aspiring to manage, the Pirates offered Clark the manager's job at High A, with the Lynchburg Hillcats. Clark led the club to the Carolina League playoffs, and the next season won the South Atlantic League Championship with the Pirates Low A Hickory Crawdads, finishing a whopping thirty games over .500.

The Houston Astros knew Dave Clark from his career as a bench player, they followed his coaching and managing career with the Pirates, and before the 2005 season, Houston hired him to pilot their new Double-A Texas League team, the Corpus Christi Hooks.

"We had heard so much about Dave when he was with the Pirates," said former Astros General Manager Tim Purpura. "We knew him from his days playing in Houston, but we also knew his baseball IQ was off the charts and he knew how to relate it to young guys."

In the Hooks second season, 2006, they ran the Texas League table. Under the guidance of Clark, and led by future major-leaguers like Hunter Pence, Ben Zobrist, and Matt Albers, the Corpus Christi Hooks won the Texas League title against Wichita.

"Hunter Pence had a great, great season for us," Clark said. "I mean awesome. Something like twenty-eight bombs, close to one hundred RBIs, thirty-plus doubles, seventeen steals, but toward the end of that season, he'd been asked to play for Team USA, so he had a big decision to make."

Dave insists he did nothing to sway the young outfielder's decision about Team USA.

"I told him that was an outstanding opportunity for him and his career," Clark remembered. "And I told him to relax and do what you feel is best. I can say it now that secretly I wanted him to stay with us through the Hooks playoff run, but I never, ever told him how I felt personally."

After considering his options for a few days, Pence walked into Clark's office at the Corpus Christi ballpark and made his announcement.

"Hunter told me, 'Clarkie, I know Team USA's cool, but I gotta stay with my teammates here in Corpus for this championship run,'" Clark said. "I just told him, 'Well, I was cheering for you to do what you felt you needed to do, but I am happy for those guys in that locker room that you will be with them.'"

In mid-September 2006, the Hunter Pence-led, Dave Clark-managed Corpus Christi Hooks needed five hours and fourteen innings to win the Texas League title from the Wichita Wranglers, 8-7, taking the series three games to one. That win and that championship marked the first time since 1958 that a Corpus Christi team won a Texas League title. Dave Clark won

Texas League Manager of the Year accolades, and right-hander Matt Albers, who later pitched for the Astros and Brewers among other big-league clubs, won the Texas League Pitcher of the Year award.

Hunter Pence fashioned an outstanding MLB debut with the Houston Astros in 2007, hitting .322 over 105 games, homered seventeen times, drove in sixty-nine runs, hit thirty doubles, and stole eleven bases. Traded to the Phillies and then to the Giants, Pence became an iron man playing in all 162 games in San Francisco in back-to-back seasons of 2013 and 2014, with a career-high twenty-seven homers in 2013, and a career-high 650 at-bats in 2014. With the Giants through 2018, Pence spent 2019 in his home state of Texas, and then went back to San Francisco to the Giants for the pandemic-shortened 2020 season, which represents his eighteenth MLB season.

"We drafted him knowing he had what scouts called a strange way of running, throwing, and hitting," said Purpura, the former Astros GM. "But looking at this long term, Hunter's body worked for him, he's been outstanding in every phase of the game including leadership, and hey we're glad we didn't change a thing because he's proven it with the success he's had."

Dave Clark's work did not go unnoticed.

"Clarkie had that upfront tough guy approach to players," remembers Purpura. "But when he'd made his point and his players understood it, that's when the fun began for all of them. When players trust their managers and coaches, that's when improvement happens on the field."

Clark moved up from Corpus Christi to Triple A Round Rock in 2008, and then the Astros added him to their coaching staff at the end of Clark's Triple A season. Once Dave arrived in Houston, he began lobbying the Astros to bring up a young corner infielder Mark Saccomanno, a twenty-third-round draft pick from Baylor who had played for Dave at both Double A and Triple A. Finally, toward the season's end, Saccomanno came to the Astros.

"He deserved it," Clark remembered. "This kid played his backside off for me and he had some power and was a great kid."

In his first game, Saccomanno received the call to pinch-hit. Clark took him aside and asked if the newcomer had a plan of attack in his first major-league at-bat.

"He told me something like, 'well, I think I'll look at a couple and then get aggressive,'" Clark explained. "I told him, 'No don't do that, he's going to throw you a first-pitch fastball to test you, so look for it and swing your ass off.'"

First pitch swinging at the fastball Clark predicted, Saccomanno ripped it out of Minute Maid Park. That bomb was the only homer Mark Saccomanno hit in the big leagues, and Dave Clark's still excited about it.

"Well, yeah, I am," said Clark. "Think about it. This kid is from the Houston area, dreamed about being an Astro all his life, got his chance in front of his family and his friends and bang, out it went. A home run in his first at bat. What a great story!"

"And again, this proves a point about Dave Clark," grinned his former boss, Purpura. "There he was, knowing Saccomanno is making his first plate appearance, and Dave's thinking ahead, trying to have Mark focus, and what he told Mark about that first pitch fastball was a hundred percent correct."

In 2009, Clark became third base coach for the Astros. By late in the season, the Astros dismissed manager Cecil Cooper and named Dave Clark the interim skipper.

"Wow, what a ride," Clark said. "All that work and time and effort, I thought, had finally been recognized."

Clark felt he'd paid his dues, both as a big-league player and coach, as well as a minor-league manager. While he no doubt was ready for the challenge of becoming a major-league manager, it didn't happen.

"It certainly disappointed me that I wasn't chosen manager, but we move on," Clark, who remained an Astros coach, lamented. "After the 2013 season, I headed for Detroit."

First as third base coach, now as first base coach and outfield instructor, Clark loves his life and the four decades he's spent playing, managing, and coaching the game he loves. One of his pet projects—center fielder Jacoby Jones.

"This kid has five tools, and he wants to learn," Clark observed. "My baseball life is so much fun, and so great because of kids like this who love this game, and that's really what it's all about, bringing up the next generation the right way."

That final sentence, in a nutshell, explains why baseball people love this "tough guy" Dave Clark, and why Clarkie loves them back.

JASON LANE

"Major-leaguer, bat and mound..."

I N 2021, Northern California native Jason Lane held down a job coaching third base with the Milwaukee Brewers. And that, my friends, remains the simplest and easiest portion of his story to follow. Let's simplify further: Jason Lane knows the ups and downs, the highs and lows, the heartbreak and success of Major League Baseball and how difficult it is to play there day to day and to stay there better, perhaps, than most who ever played.

Lane's bullet-pointed resume looks like this:

- ◆ He had no offers from professional or college baseball when he left El Molino High in Forestville, California in 1995.

- ◆ He proved to himself he could, indeed, play this game, at Santa Rosa Junior College, and by the time he left in 1997, had indeed proven himself as the Northern California Junior College Player of the Year and conference MVP.

- ◆ At the University of Southern California, he began turning the heads of professional scouts, earning All-American status his senior year as a first baseman. He led the Trojans, along with fellow future Houston Astros third baseman Morgan Ensberg, to the 1998 College World Series, beating Arizona State with a three-for-six plate performance in the Series finale. That performance included a grand slam in the ninth inning while pounding out a College World Series record eleven hits and a .417 batting average. Hold on to the following

Jason Lane slides into home with the Round Rock Express in 2007.
(Photo courtesy of the Round Rock Express Baseball Club)

information for later—Lane also pitched two and two-thirds innings and picked up the win over Arizona State.

◆ The Houston Astros chose him in the 1999 major-league draft as a first baseman, then moved him to the outfield simply because Houston had an All-Star at first, Jeff Bagwell.

◆ Earning his professional spurs, Lane tore up the Midwest, Texas, and Pacific Coast Leagues before landing in Houston in time to play in the 2005 World Series loss to the Chicago White Sox.

"2005 was an incredible year in my life," Lane recalls. "I got to start and play every day and that was the only year I had a chance to play every day in the big leagues."

The Astros in 2005 featured a howitzer-style offense, and a pitching staff full of baseball royalty. Still, the veteran presence on that club made the difference. All-Star, "Killer Bees," Lance Berkman, future Hall of Famers Craig Biggio and Jeff Bagwell led the way. Former Yankees Roger Clemens and Andy Pettitte won fifty games between them, young righty Roy Oswalt put up his second twenty-win season, and closer Brad Lidge saved for-ty-two. Even so, the Houston club limped to a fifteen and thirty start in 2005. And then, almost out of nowhere, the club jelled.

"With that kind of offense, veteran leadership and great pitching," Lane says, "the team stuck together, the injuries healed, and we found ourselves in a tremendous run, fighting for our lives from the All-Star break to season's end. We were conditioned to win games that had to be won."

The dream season for the 2005 Astros continued, as they took care of the St. Louis Cardinals to win a slot in the World Series against the Chicago White Sox. But the fun ended in baseball's Big Show. Houston ran into a speedy Chicago White Sox club that swept the World Series in four games.

"I believe if we'd been able to win one of the first two games at home and a game in Chicago," Lane remembers, "we might have fared better. But the intensity of playing in the World Series is something I'll never forget."

World Series loss aside, Jason Lane found himself at a pin-nacle that most players never reach. But for Jason, and his highest of highs, his baseball passion, life, and career took a completely surprising and unwanted U-turn less than a year after playing on baseball's biggest stage.

"That started," he grimaced, "a run of the absolute worst years of my baseball life."

After a great power year at the plate, and an outstanding season playing the outfield, Lane struggled out of the gate in 2006. He struggled from the start, even though he put up some competitive at-bats.

"After forty games, I was taken out of the starting lineup," he laments, "My power numbers with homer runs and RBIs were okay, but I got caught up in a batting average slide, and when I went down [to Triple A Round Rock] and came back I platooned the rest of the way, and then I lost confidence which didn't help."

The next season, 2007, confidence problems plagued Jason the entire year, and he's convinced that's when his opportunities as a starting MLB player came to an end.

"I'd seem to go from organization to organization in Triple A," Lane laments, "and the story remained the same. I couldn't get a callup. This went on until the Marlins released me from Triple A New Orleans in May of 2010."

The only chance he found to keep playing came in the independent league ranks for the Southern Maryland Blue Crabs in the Atlantic League.

"I'm telling you now, I was at an all-time low," he recalled. "I just kept thinking about the fact that only a few short years ago, I was starting in right field for the National League Champion Houston Astros and playing in a World Series. Those were hard times, believe me."

The next year, 2011, Lane played in Las Vegas for the Toronto Blue Jays Triple-A affiliate. While the year changed, the story still remained—no regular playing time, no meaningful at bats, and a career all but stalled out.

"So, I found solace working some in the bullpen," Lane said, "And then the San Diego Padres GM Kevin Towers saw me pitch an inning one night in Reno. He came up to me the next day [and] said he didn't realize that it was me on the mound. He went on to say he thought the ball came out of my hand very easily and that I needed to think about pitching again and being left-handed would give me a shot to extend my career."

Convinced he'd never receive another shot at an everyday outfield job in the big leagues, at the end of his Triple-A season in 2011, Lane began a new path, with a newly found hope and passion—making it back to Major League Baseball as a pitcher.

"In the offseason after 2011, one week into the free agency season, Kevin Towers called me," Lane recalled, "and he offered to bring me to big league camp as a pitcher. Now, I gotta tell ya, I hadn't been to anyone's major-league camp in two years and so I said, 'you bet, let's do it!'"

Lane made the San Diego Padres Triple-A team in El Paso as a reliever, and he put up eight scoreless appearances for the El Paso Chihuahuas as a reliever, but he'd suffered a sore arm caused from pitching back-to-back days, and the Padres released him.

"I hit rock bottom again," he said painfully. "And I must say I was angry at the way that all worked out."

Right back to independent leagues went Lane. A call from Gary Gaetti, a former All-Star third baseman with the Minnesota Twins who was then managing the Atlantic League's team in Sugar Land, Texas, lured Jason back. Gaetti wanted Lane as a hitter. Lane told him he was pitching now. So, the two cut a deal.

"He said he'd start me on the mound every fifth day," Lane laughed, "if I would DH the other days I wasn't pitching. What a deal!"

Dutiful baseball soldier that he is, Lane loaded his car, left California headed for a new baseball life in Sugar Land, a stone's throw from Houston. Jason had a whale of a season. He pitched 110 innings for the Sugar Land Skeeters and hit at a .300 clip with twelve homers and signed in the off-season with the Minnesota Twins. The Twins cut him on the last day of spring training, so back to Sugar Land he went for the 2013 season.

"I was thirty-six years old that season," Lane said, "and truly wondering if I was done. I had a great first half for Sugar Land, but got no calls from anyone, and then my dad passed away unexpectedly of a heart attack, and I was crushed."

Rather than allow grief to take away his entire life, back to the game he went. And, once again, back to Sugar Land and independent baseball. Then a month or so later the call came. The Padres again. They needed a starter and a pinch hitter at Triple A El Paso. Lane ably fit both roles and went back to El Paso for the 2014 campaign.

"El Paso's manager, Pat Murphy, was so instrumental in my success," Lane fondly recalls. "He helped me regain confidence and believed in my ability. I needed that so badly."

"Thirty-seven years old, and a former starter in the World Series, a guy with legit ability as a hitter," Murphy laughed during a visit with us in 2014. "You just wonder, and you stand amazed at someone, Jason Lane, who simply would not believe he could not compete as a pitcher in the big leagues. You have to hand him all the credit in the world."

The road through Sugar Land, the time in El Paso with Pat Murphy and the Padres organization reenergized Jason Lane's love and passion for the game. On June 3, 2014, the San Diego club called Lane to the big leagues, this time as a pitcher. On July 28, he made his first MLB start, a 2-0 loss to the Atlanta Braves. Before returning to El Paso later that season, he'd thrown ten MLB innings, with six strikeouts, no walks, and an outstanding 0.87 ERA.

In 2015, former El Paso manager Pat Murphy, by then the bench coach with the Milwaukee Brewers, helped bring Lane to the Brewers as assistant hitting coach. In late 2019, Brewers manager Craig Counsell named Jason first base coach, then moved him to the third base coaching box in 2021. A perfect, experienced fit for any major-league club.

"I love Milwaukee, Craig Counsell, my fellow coaches and the organization itself," Lane grinned. "It's a friendly, down-home organization, first rate and I'm lucky to be here."

And they're lucky to have Jason Lane.

CHAPTER 8

THREE HAIRSTON GENERATIONS

*"Baseball's Biggest Family; working people.
No more, no less."*

HREE GENERATIONS. Five major-league players. Four minor-league players. One unbelievable legacy. Their mantra? Belief in God, self-respect, respect for the game, its people, its fans, and the day-to-day hard work aimed at improvement. Dealing with disappointments and failures, they rose again and again, refusing to surrender their dreams.

"The Hairston family not only were the biggest family in terms of numbers, but they are among the most important families from generation to generation to generation in this sport," said Bob Kendrick, president of the Negro League Hall of Fame.

Sam Hairston Sr. catching for the Indianapolis Clowns.
(Photo courtesy of the Hairston family)

The story begins with the late Sam Hairston, born in Alabama in 1921.

"Baseball gave Sam, and so many others, the opportunity to pursue their life's dream," Kendrick said. "Baseball in the Negro Leagues didn't always represent financial security, so many had to find off season jobs. But playing in the Negro Leagues gave Sam Hairston the start and ultimately the life he dreamed of."

Sam passed his love for the game and his iron-willed determination to succeed to his sons and grandsons.

"None of our baseball dreams would've materialized without my dad," said son Jerry Sr., a fourteen-year MLB vet.

Another son, Sam Jr., became a minor-league player, as did grandsons Johnny Jr., Jeff, and Jason Hairston. Jerry Hairston Sr.'s sons Jerry Jr. and Scott spent a combined twenty-seven seasons in The Show.

Oldest son John spent parts of two MLB seasons with the Chicago Cubs, then became a world class educator in the state of Oregon.

"He had parts of two seasons with the Cubs," Jerry Sr. noted. "Then in a spring training game with the bases loaded and Johnny Sr. catching, a tapper right back to the pitcher resulted in the runner [a teammate] intentionally coming out of the baseline, smoking my brother's knees, both of them. He needed major surgery and that was it."

Not to be denied and adamant about finishing his degree, John Hairston spent decades as a teacher, counselor and coach in Portland, Oregon. John now lives in Lacy, Washington.

Their matriarch, Sam Sr., one of fourteen children, left school in Birmingham after the eighth grade, then lied about his age so he could work for an iron pipe company in Birmingham.

"His family needed money," noted grandson Jerry Jr., now a TV analyst for the Dodgers. "The older I get the more I realize and appreciate how much older guys like my grandfather went through."

Sam Sr. caught a big break joining and playing for his company's powerhouse industrial league team that included future Negro League stars Arte Wilson, Double Duty Radcliffe, and Piper Davis. Signed first by the Negro League's Birmingham Black Barons, the Barons traded Sam Sr. to the Indianapolis Clowns.

"A rookie in Indianapolis, my grandfather moved from catcher to third base against the Homestead Grays and perhaps the greatest hitter in the Negro Leagues, Josh Gibson," says Jerry, Jr. "Double Duty Radcliffe caught for Indy that day and noticed my grandfather was playing even with the third base bag against the powerhouse Gibson. Radcliffe motioned him to move back, move back! As he did, Gibson crushed a shot past my grandfather. Had he stayed even with the bag, he'd been killed!"

Grandson Scott, an eleven-year MLB vet, modeled his baseball approach, the work ethic and passion, after Sam Sr.

"He told me once," Scott said, "that he wasn't the most talented, but he worked his backside off every day, no matter who he played for. His strongest delivered message remains, 'you bring it, every single day.' My attitude always was I'd be dishonoring him if I didn't go all out all the time."

Sam Sr. won the Negro League's Triple Crown in 1950; a .424, seventeen homers, seventy-one RBIs in seventy games.

"Everyone knew what a great player and devoted teammate Sam Sr. was," grinned Bob Kendrick. "But that Triple Crown, the batting average, RBIs and homers in such a short time woke up Major League Baseball to Sam Hairston."

The White Sox signed Sam Sr. and sent him to the minor leagues before bringing him to Chicago on July 21, 1951, for a four-game stay. Not one for self-aggrandizement, Sam Sr. didn't dwell on his big-league time. In fact, son Jerry Sr. was sixteen before he knew his father made it to The Show.

"My father didn't talk much about what he accomplished," Jerry Sr. said. "His attitude was, 'hey, today's game is over, so we work hard getting ready for tomorrow's game. Baseball's how we feed our families, live and survive. We are working people; no more, no less.'"

Jerry Sr. "was born a grinder, still a grinder, and being raised in the fifties and sixties he's old school, and he fought for everything," says son Scott.

Jerry had always played winter ball in Hermosillo, Mexico, but after a Pirates release in 1977, he spent the next four seasons playing summer ball there as well, for Durango. He won a batting championship, but as a player some conditions in Mexico proved problematic.

"When I think about places down there," he told the *Chicago Tribune* in 1983, "and all the time I had to fight flies for food, you had to love baseball to put up with it."

White Sox manager Tony La Russa and General Manager Roland Hemond rescued Jerry Sr. from Mexico summers, bringing him back to Chicago. But winters in Mexico turned his life around. Playing for Hermosillo, he met and fell in love with his bride of more than forty years, Esperanza Arellano. They married in 1974 at home plate inside Hector Espino Stadium in Hermosillo.

"My parents trained me with God's help, scriptural values, and the Bible," Jerry Sr. said. "If not, I'd never have found a woman as great as my wife. She's a teacher, extremely intelligent and says what needs to be said even if you don't want to hear them. But she knows smoothing words as well."

"She's our rock, period," said Scott.

Jerry Sr. and the rest of the Hairston family greatly admired Sam's Sr., his stories, and the love he had for them.

"When my dad wasn't playing, sometimes he tended bar," Jerry Sr. noted. "And he'd come home with corks from wine bottles...all kinds of corks. We used them for batting practice and let me tell you, corks thrown hard, well, they are tough to hit!"

The elder Hairston taped one end of each cork, then threw batting practice to his sons.

"He could do crazy things with those corks," Jerry Sr. remembered. "But it worked. If you could hit those corks, you could hit anything. It gave us a ton of confidence."

"He also wadded up newspapers," grandson Scott added. "He'd wad 'em up tight, then like he did with the corks, he'd tightly tape one side, and then throw batting practice. What a nightmare to hit. But it helped build confidence that we could hit anything."

Baseball life continues to permeate the Hairston family. Jerry Jr. still serves as color analyst for the Los Angeles Dodgers and has become an agent as well. Jerry Sr., along with Scott and the rest of the family still follow the game closely. Does any chance exist for a fourth Hairston generation of professional or major-league players?

"That might happen," grins Scott. "I have two teenage sons and Jerry Jr. has one teenage son, and they might be able to play, we shall see."

"We never had baseball forced on us," Jerry Jr. grinned. "Baseball was always what we wanted to do. We saw our grandfather and our dad heavily involved in the game, and we always wanted to be there at the ballpark. Look, our family didn't become big stars. But we always loved the game, and if the kids come on and we have four generations, so be it. My dad said it best, 'we are working people in this game, no more, no less.'"

MIKE JIRSCHELE AND SONS

"Connecting Generations..."

F ANS SEATED at Pittsburgh's PNC Park on a cool, wet, late September evening, wanted one last look at baseball in 2018. Unless these Pirates fans really knew the Kansas City Royals, they had no idea the circumstances bringing Royals third base coach Mike Jirschele to the coaching lines.

"Jirsch, no doubt, is one of a kind," insists Royals Special Assistant Gene Watson. "No one better."

Mike Jirschele ranks as one of Wisconsin's all-time great high school athletes. His father, Don, played football for legendary coach Bear Bryant at the University of Kentucky. Mike, however, turned down a chance to quarterback the Wisconsin Badgers and said no to college hoops offers as well.

"The love for the game of baseball," Jirschele insists, "simply won out."

Mike and his family overcame a life filled with disappointments, missing kids growing up and their athletic and school events. The mind-numbing wait of almost four decades provided mixed feelings of torture and roller coaster ride.

"Sheri and I sat and wondered if that call to the big leagues would ever really come," Mike remembered. "At one point I told her, 'I guess we're just going to have to be content to be Triple-A people.' And it hurt being passed over several times, especially after years of managing successfully at the Triple-A level. That was really tough."

March marked each season's beginning, leaving Sheri and their two sons and a daughter at home in Clintonville, while

Mike headed out for spring training and another minor-league season.

"People would ask my wife, especially when the kids were little, 'How in the world can he do that to you?'" Jirschele said.

Sheri Jirschele's husband has the answer.

"Sheri's a special woman," the baseball lifer continued. "The wives of players and coaches and everyone else associated with professional baseball teams must have an understanding spouse and believe me quite honestly some don't make it through this."

Oldest son Jeremy clearly remembers tearful goodbyes.

"That was definitely the hard part," he recalled. "He used to see us at the end of our football seasons and part of basketball season, but then he'd leave and never see any of our baseball games."

Mike and Sheri's daughter Jenn, a tremendous high school athlete, describes dreaded days her dad left for baseball.

"We always really missed him, and it wasn't the same, dissecting my volleyball game on the phone with him," Jenn remembers clearly. "One time before an extremely important high school game, he sent me flowers with a card on it that said, 'sorry I can't be at your big game tonight, but I love you, Dad.' That's pretty special."

For son Justin, dad leaving never got easier.

"Every spring training, I think about how sad I would get," he remembered. "Then my mom would take us down to spring training, or to wherever he was coaching or managing and that made up for all the sad goodbyes."

Jenn gives her mother loads of credit for keeping the Jirschele home well under control.

"She was the rock holding this family together," Jenn smiled. "She attended all of my athletic events and all of my two brothers as well."

Despite baseball's demands, both sons turned baseball into their life's work. Jeremy and Justin both played in the minor leagues. Jeremy draws raves as head baseball coach at the University of Wisconsin-Stevens Point. Justin's extremely sky-high baseball IQ stood out. He now manages in the Sox' system.

"He spent his life in clubhouses where his dad managed, he came into professional baseball, experienced in the ups and downs, ins and outs of the game," said White Sox scout Kirk Champion. "For Justin Jirschele, in the professional game, coaching or managing, the sky's the limit."

Champion continued piling on genetic praise.

"In 2018, Mike walked in the clubhouse after the South Atlantic League all-star game," Champion smiled. "Of course, he was there for Justin, but that was so impressive for a big-leaguer on his All-Star break spending time with us, drinking a cool one and shooting the baseball breeze."

Only once in thirteen seasons did Mike the player come close to the major leagues. He'd been drafted by the Texas Rangers out of high school as a shortstop in the fifth round in 1977. Late in his thirteenth minor-league season, things changed while playing in Triple A.

"I flew all over the infield making plays at shortstop," Jirschele remembers. "And I hit like I never hit before. My game truly came together."

Quiet talk surfaced that the Rangers would call him up soon. During a late-season game in Louisville, Jirschele describes how his dreams came crashing to a halt.

"One of their players hit a high foul pop up on the left field side," he remembered. "The third baseman and I chased it, we ran into each other, our legs tangled up, pain seared through my knee, and I knew I was in trouble."

The collision and an ACL tear wiped out any MLB playing chance.

"I laid it all out there for years, gave it everything I had," he lamented. "I was really worn out from the whole thing."

Back in Clintonville, Mike and Sheri opened a sports bar entertaining friends and former high school teammates. Mike couldn't compete in a sports bar. The main motivator in his life?

"Muscular Dystrophy," he quietly remembers, "ultimately took down my three brothers."

A hereditary condition normally affecting all brothers in a family, MD interferes with protein production, and the building of healthy muscles. Mike's brothers Jim, Doug, and Pete suffered from MD, but miraculously Mike dodged the disease's death sentence. Fully aware of his good fortune, he worked diligently helping his brothers.

"They couldn't take care of themselves at all, couldn't dress themselves, or go to the bathroom themselves," Mike remembered sadly. "Little mundane tasks I might have otherwise griped about like taking out the trash, heck they would've given anything to be able to take out that trash."

Back to the game, specifically the coaching ranks this time, he went. From low-A to Triple A in Omaha with the Royals. For twenty-three seasons, Mike flourished. He refined players skills, but more importantly, provided more than a baseball education.

"We could talk to him about anything," former Royals outfielder Jarod Dyson, who played for Jirschele in Triple A and the major leagues, told ESPN in 2013. "It wasn't just about baseball; it was about life."

After Omaha's 2013 Triple-A national championship came an initial postseason call from Kansas City General Manager Dayton Moore, telling Jirschele the Royals needed him in the big leagues. While on a family vacation at Disney World, a call came from Royals Manager Ned Yost.

"I was excited," Jirschele.

Closing a bedroom door, as family members tried to sneak a listen, he heard great news from Yost. A major-league coaching job with the Royals now belonged to Mike Jirschele.

"I really was more excited for my wife Sheri and my kids," Mike grinned. "They made a lot of sacrifices for me to stay in the minors that long. It's just special."

Buckets of happy, happy tears flowed that night as a seemingly impossible dream became very, very real.

"Now my dad and mom, grinders their whole lives have made it to the pinnacle of baseball," cried son Justin. "And because they sacrificed a lot to get to this point, it's incredibly special."

At the end of the 2019 season, Mike Jirschele completed his sixth campaign on the third base coaching lines for the Kansas City Royals. His sons continue their coaching careers, and a Jirschele grandson continues baseball lessons, joining his grandfather, dad and uncle in educating young, would-be players all over Wisconsin.

"Those are great times," Mike grins. "The fact all these guys embrace this game takes a little bit of the sting out of my absences through the years. I'm proud of my kids for who they are and what they are. They're a gift from above."

And so is their father, who laid it all out there, setting baseball examples, but more importantly, life's lessons.

JIM AND JIM ADDUCI

"World Class Talent..."

AS THE YEARS GO BY, father-son grinder tandems become less rare in this game, but perhaps none tell better stories about their experiences from top to bottom of their careers than Chicago-area native Jim Adduci and his son, also Jim.

"I have a ton of bus ride stories," laughs the younger Adduci. "I think I'll keep 'em to myself."

Not so his father. While playing for the Brewers, he was sent down late in spring training to a major-league camp to "play" the following day. Jim immediately changed plans to fly home before heading for his minor-league assignment. Cancelling the flight, and arriving in the clubhouse, Jim saw his name wasn't on the day's lineup card.

"I marched into the manager's office," he remembers, "and I said, 'I told you I would *play*, not sit for six or seven innings and then take someone's place. I'm not doing that."

Triumphantly ambling out of the clubhouse, never looking back, Jim boarded a plane home, satisfied he had called out his bosses for "falsified information."

Originally drafted in 1977 out of Southern Illinois University, the elder Jim played in seventy MLB games across four seasons with the Brewers and Phillies. A trade and nine minor-league seasons later, he made his MLB debut in Milwaukee.

"Well, when you were with the Brewers in those days, as an outfielder, I competed with the likes of Gorman Thomas and other All-Stars in that era," Adduci said. "That's some tough competition."

Younger Jim, taken by the Marlins in 2002 as a forty-second-round draft choice out of high school in the Chicago area, played professionally for eighteen seasons and now coaches for the Chicago Cubs. He spent parts of five major-league seasons with the Texas Rangers, Detroit Tigers, and the Cubs. He never remembers when baseball wasn't a big part of his life.

"I was born in 1985, when my dad was playing in Triple-A ball out in Vancouver, British Columbia, in the Phillies organization," said the younger Adduci. "So, my earliest memories involve following my dad into clubhouses in the minors and majors."

The elder Jim never pushed the younger toward the game. "I let him dictate the process," the father said, "and he was relentless about playing catch, about working on fundamentals and lifting in the off season. From the very beginning, I saw some pretty special athleticism carrying over to his mid-30s."

Young Jim, zipping around on ice skates at age three, gave his father the idea his son might turn into a hockey player. But by age six, he amazed his dad by competing against kids three years older.

"More amazing than that, to me at least," said his father, "this six-year-old had me hit him sky high and I mean *sky high* popups, and there he'd be, running them down. I just thought that was extremely unusual."

The elder Adduci also tells the tale of young Jim, at age nine, climbing out of the shower after baseball practice one day, still dripping wet, staggering his dad with a question.

"Dad, can I play in the big leagues some day?" young Jim inquired.

"That knocked me out," said the elder Adduci. "I handed him his towel, still shaking my head in amazement."

"Yessir, Jim," his dad smiled proudly. "Yessir, you sure can, and I mean every word of it!"

Throughout high school, the elder Jim encouraged his son to play other sports, and he excelled, especially at basketball. It wasn't all smooth sailing, of course. The elder Jim recalled one time in particular.

"I was on his ass about needing to lift weights more than he did," said Adduci. "He was playing basketball in the winter, running up and down the court, burning tons of calories and never could keep any muscle on his bones. Honestly, he needed to develop strength. I told him to take that basketball fierceness into the weight room and onto the baseball diamond, and that message ultimately got through."

Challenges remained for the elder Adduci.

"One time in his senior year his free throw game sorta went away," said the elder. "Before that, I had a neighbor install a hoop on the garage attached to the house, but Jim only used it when he was grounded, which wasn't that much. One morning, I was on him during a rare outside free throw shoot."

The younger Adduci stopped his free throw practice, set the ball on the ground, then almost knocked his father off his feet with a reply of, "I'm a player, not a *practicer!*"

"Fortunately," elder Jim laughed, "Jim loved baseball way more than basketball, and enjoyed working on baseball skills, most likely because he competitively craved success."

By the time Jim was eighteen, he became an all-regional baseball player in polls taken by the *Chicago Tribune* and *Sun-Times*. He committed to playing baseball at Northern Illinois University—until the Marlins showed interest in drafting him.

"I didn't know much about college baseball," said the younger Jim. "Where I come from in Chicago, it's just not as big as it is where I live now in College Station, Texas, or in other spots in the south. I knew a lot about professional baseball because I always followed my dad everywhere, so to me being drafted at eighteen was great, playing for money was great, and I had the chance to begin living my dream."

Did older Jim worry that his son would miss the college experience?

"No, I didn't because my horizons broadened so much after I signed to play pro ball," said Adduci. "When you play in the states, you're in clubhouses all over the country, and all over the world, really, with young guys from Venezuela, Puerto Rico, Panama, the Dominican Republic, Mexico, and of course in Japan."

"This game turned into a global business," Adduci said, "and a whole lot of knowledge about how the world works comes out of clubhouses filled with different cultures. My son and I both played overseas in Mexico, Korea, and Japan, and we found out how to get along with others who may have less than we do in the States, and conversely, with bonus babies who are filthy rich. That's quite an education in dealing with humanity."

The other education? Being traded from one organization to another. The move the younger Adduci made to the Cubs from the Marlins turned out to be huge, especially from a personal, family perspective.

"Jim's uncle, my wife's brother-in-law, passed away unexpectedly at age forty-nine that year. My son being traded to a Chicago team with our family located here turned out to be huge because the joy of his coming to the Cubs brought some sunshine in the midst of the death of a family member.

Constant moves challenged both Jims.

"Yep, we had that in common," said the elder Adduci, "and it was constant. Okay we're in Little Rock, gotta pack up and head to Triple A. We're in Triple A, gotta pack up and head to The Show. Go up for a while, oh no, back to Triple A, and on and on it went. We counted up the moves the other day, and for an eleven-year career we figured we moved fifty-six times! *Fifty-six!*"

That said, Jim's dad and mom followed their son's career all over the minor-league landscape.

"I loved having them there at my games," the younger said. "But my dad's lessons continued as positives and at the end it was always, 'you *must* have *fun!*'"

"We did relay that message," said the elder Adduci, "We went to see him in Double A and in Low A in Peoria, Illinois, playing for Hall of Famer Ryne Sandberg. In the midst of that season, I repeated a lesson I gave Jim earlier. I said, 'you make sure you contribute to every win in every game you play. The numbers stuff works itself out if and only if you contribute. And, maybe when Ryne manages in the big leagues, he will remember what you did for him here in Peoria.'"

The Cubs didn't promote Jim to the major leagues until they reacquired him in 2019. His first MLB callup came ten years into his minor-league career, in 2013. Playing in Triple A for the Rangers after a career-high sixteen homers and sixty-five RBIs over 127 games, son called father while holding an airline ticket to The Show.

"I couldn't believe it," the elder Adduci exclaimed. "Ten years in the minor leagues and the call came. I hyperventilated. I was so excited!"

Two generations of Adducis took similar paths and made it to The Show.

Younger Jim flew west out of Texas, to join the Rangers in Oakland. His parents watched his first start on television from Chicago before they joined their son in Arlington, Texas.

"He called me from Oakland," said Jim's dad, "and he said, 'Hey dad, I'm starting today, my first time.' And wouldn't you know, on the first pitch he saw, he lined a clean single to left. I just lost it again, I headed outside to cry, it was that overwhelming and that powerful, you cannot imagine the emotion!"

Back in the Rangers organization, the younger Adduci spent a brief amount of time in Triple A at Round Rock in 2014, then finished the season with the Rangers. Despite good numbers, back to the grind he went.

"Yessir, once you're on it, it's hard to get off," laughed the younger. "But this time, the grind included a trip overseas."

In two seasons in Korea with the Lotte Giants in 2015 and 2016, Adduci's best was a .384 average with twenty-eight homers, 106 RBIs and a .942 OPS his first season. Now a thirty-two-year-old vet, he headed home for more up and down time between Triple A and MLB in the Tigers organization. Then Mexican winter leagues entered the equation.

"I was playing against so many guys from the Dominican, Puerto Rico, Venezuela, and Mexico who played all year," said Adduci. "My family and I just decided that I needed to keep up by playing as many games as I could, so that's what I did."

In 2019, the younger Adduci spent a quick two-game stint in the major leagues for his hometown Cubs, but he spent the majority of 2019 in Des Moines with the Triple A Iowa Cubs. He led not only the team, but the entire Chicago minor-league system with a .301 batting average. The younger Adduci and his wife, Lauren, grasped the kindness of the Iowa Cubs and their fans.

"We've come full circle a few times, and this was another," he said after Chicago sent him down in June 2019.

"Jim Adduci knows this game, knows how to play it, plays it well, and he leads with quiet words and by example," Marty Peevey, his Triple-A skipper said while in the Des Moines airport as his club waited on an early morning flight for the second round of the 2019 PCL playoffs. "Being the son of an ex-big-leaguer, and him being one is extra special for all of us."

Approaching age thirty-five, younger Jim realized his playing days remained numbered.

"I want to play one more season, at least," he says, "and my dad taught me never to say no to any real baseball opportunity."

Jim made it one more year, becoming part of the Texas Rangers' sixty-man available player contingent during the Covid-shortened 2020 campaign. In December of 2020, shelving spikes for the final time, he signed on with his hometown Chicago Cubs as run production coordinator. The father-son, four decades long grinders' adventure, continues with both father and son fueling each other's competitive fires.

"A lot of work has gone into this for him," says his dad, who directs elite baseball at the Chicago White Sox/Chicago Bulls Academy. "I tell my campers participation entitles you to nothing, and it's about the intangibles, working hard, becoming and remaining a good teammate, and most importantly never giving up the dream.

That's a lesson son Jim learned long ago, along with the dad-driven mantra of "always have *fun*."

"Jim," his dad says, "has some sayings of his own about this game."

Such as:

> "Laugh off bumps in the road, that helps you relax and focus."

"Don't expect, you'll be disappointed."

"Nothing comes easy in this life, but this life is who I am."

And guess what else? There's another Adduci waiting in the wings, four-year-old Charlie, already a T-baller playing against five- and six-year-olds. Sound familiar?

So, Jim, what do you tell Charlie at this young age?

"I tell him, just like my father told me, to swing hard, throw hard, play hard, and not worry about the fundamentals so much as having fun right now...*fun*...have fun. The fundamentals we'll work on when you're older!"

JOHN AND RYAN LANGERHANS

"Pitch, hit and Buck Command..."

R AISED AROUND THE GAME of baseball by a Texas high school baseball coach, John Langerhans at an early age seemed destined to succeed at the game, whether as a pitcher, hitter, or later as one of the greatest high school baseball coaches in Texas history.

It follows that the son of one of the great coaches in Texas high school baseball history might also end up completely immersed, right? This story sounds as if it comes from baseball heaven, right? Well hold on, baseball fans. Some bumps existed.

"That's right," laughs John, "and it all came down to a disagreement between my son, Ryan, and me that happened before I actually coached him in high school."

Ryan Langerhans came to earth with tons of self-confidence, bordering on cockiness, even in junior high. He followed his dad everywhere—church, hunting, and Round Rock High's ballpark. But one day Ryan and his dad teed it up during a Round Rock High practice after John spotted Ryan throwing rocks at the outfield fence.

"Yessir, I brought him in, sat him down on the bench," John remembers clearly, "and I told him 'Listen, if you're gonna be on that field, then you're gonna pay attention to baseball and not rock throwing, son. You're gonna learn to do it the right way.'"

Ryan didn't take scolding well.

"I said if that's the way you want it," Ryan recalled, "I'll just go over to Westwood High School when I'm a freshman and we will beat your butts, that's what I'll do."

Cooler heads prevailed, Ryan finished junior high, then as a freshman pushed for a starting role on his dad's varsity.

"Matched against some juniors and seniors, he won a job," John grinned. "God blessed him with real talent, and he worked so dad-gummed hard and did everything right. He was first on the field, first in races, pitched well, hit well, that qualified him."

"I'd always been taught to love this game and to work hard at it," Ryan remembered. "I always did anything I could to learn the game. Whether it was keeping score or just being there learning from my dad."

Ryan Langerhans at bat for the Salt Lake Bees.
(Photo courtesy of Asay Photography and the Salt Lake Bees)

Ryan's dad, John, ranks as one of Texas' top high school players and coaches. An all-state pitcher and first baseman, Langerhans played both in high school and college for legendary University of Texas baseball coach Cliff Gustafson. Leading South San Antonio High to a state championship his senior season, he followed Gustafson to Austin. The Longhorns dominated Southwest Conference play, as Langerhans led his team to three College World Series appearances. As a senior he signed with Cleveland. But pro ball brought problems.

"I struggled at the Double-A level with serious shoulder issues," Langerhans remembered. "Nothing had ever hurt me so badly, and it kept me from pitching for a month. In what turned out to be my last start ever, with Cleveland GM Bob Quinn watching, I came off the mound in serious pain."

His message to Quinn? "I'm taking it to the house."

"Not so fast," replied Quinn, "You cannot simply quit."

"You can release me or whatever, but I'm done," Langerhans doggedly insisted. "And off I went, assuring them I'd never pitch or play professionally."

Back on the University of Texas campus, fully intent on following his father into the coaching profession, while working in the UT mailroom, Associate Athletics Director Bill Ellington stopped the young mailman with a question.

"Hey, John, I thought you wanted to coach, that's what you got a degree for, right?" asked the hard-nosed Ellington?

"Uh, yessir," replied Langerhans, "but at this time of the year, I'm sure I can't find a coaching job, they're already taken."

"Well, the hell with that," Ellington replied. "I've got a guy sitting in my office right now who'll hire you today!"

His first stop, Lamar Consolidated High in the Houston area. A year later the athletics director at newly opened San Antonio Madison High asked John to start a new baseball program. The year after that, he moved to Uvalde, Texas, where he helped develop an outstanding future lefty MLB reliever, Norm Charlton.

"Norm Charlton to me was so special," Langerhans remembers. "He didn't always throw hard, but I suggested he use a speed bag to develop hand speed and fast twitch muscles."

Rice University Coach David Hall loved Charlton.

"I promised David that Norm would throw ninety miles an hour," Langerhans said. "David was big-time excited when he called me on the phone telling me that scouts clocked Charlton at ninety-five!"

Later in his MLB career, Charlton told Langerhans he "still used your speed bag workout, because it works."

Uvalde became the last stop before a return to Central Texas.

"By then we had kids," Langerhans noted, "and my wife Sharon began telling me she really wanted to raise my son and daughter in Central Texas, so I started the search."

Gustafson told Langerhans about two Austin-area head-coaching vacancies. After interviewing with superintendents and athletics directors at both Anderson High in Austin and in Round Rock, he chose Round Rock. At an American Legion game, players who had heard about Langerhans' interview approached him.

"They had known who I was at UT," Langerhans grinned. "They said, 'please come be our coach,' so I went home to Uvalde and told Sharon we're going to Round Rock."

Meeting with players' families, Langerhans explained he would tolerate no interference from them, and would not be second guessed from the stands.

"It was my way or the highway," Langerhans said, "I just didn't want any interference and I wanted those folks to know that. I knew if they listened, we'd succeed."

Parents and sons bought into everything baseball-wise John Langerhans offered. He turned the Dragons into a high school baseball juggernaut, consistently winning their way to the Texas state baseball playoffs. In 1995, 1996, and 1997, led by future major-leaguers Brian Gordon, John and Jordan Danks, Travis Schlichting, and Langerhans' son, Ryan, the Dragons dominated.

"They knew each other well," Langerhans said. "[They] played like a team should with no jealousies. They were all about winning."

Team concept, yes. Individual talent, absolutely. Lefty John Danks spent ten seasons as a White Sox starting pitcher. John's brother, Jordan, spent parts of four seasons with the White Sox and Phillies. Reliever Travis Schlichting made appearances for the Dodgers in parts of two seasons. Brian Gordon started professional ball as an outfielder, switched to pitching, then made the big leagues as a reliever with the Rangers in 2008 before two starts with the New York Yankees in 2011. John's son, Ryan, played in parts of eleven MLB seasons.

"We looked at Ryan first as a lefty pitching prospect," notes former Atlanta Braves national cross checker John Flannery. "When our scouting director, Paul Snyder, came to see him in a workout, Ryan smoked line drives all over the place, and given the wooden bat power, we drafted him as an outfielder."

Once comfortable in the Braves organization, Ryan began meeting superb players like Andruw Jones, Gary Sheffield, Chipper Jones, and Brian Jordan.

"There was Chipper, who shared my love for the outdoors," Ryan recalled. "Gary Sheffield always stuck with me, and when I watched Brian Jordan toward the end of his career, working so hard at his craft, that made a positive difference in the way I worked."

By Ryan Langerhans' Double-A season in 2002, he'd made great strides. Playing in a game against the A's Double-A affiliate in Huntsville, Alabama, Ryan's mom and dad attended a Texas crawfish boil while watching an Atlanta Braves game on TV.

"The announcer said earlier in the game a Braves outfielder injured himself crashing into a wall," John recalled. "Folks said, 'well maybe Ryan will get called up.' We said, nah, not from Double A."

Mom and dad were wrong.

"The emotions were overwhelming," Ryan said. "Before I even packed, I called my folks. Then as I packed my bags, I thought about being a kid and telling my teachers I was going to be an MLB player and they told me, 'Pick something more realistic.' I just wouldn't give it up."

The reality of "how tough it is to stay once you get there" set in. Ryan had one at-bat in only one game. He received another call to Atlanta in September of 2003, but the Braves used him as a defensive replacement only. Frustration continued in 2004, playing for the Triple-A Richmond Braves, Ryan put up career-high numbers: A .298 average, twenty homers, seventy-two RBIs and thirty-four doubles. Disappointingly, no call to Atlanta.

"I begged to go to winter ball to prove myself," he said stoically, "but they said no. So, I talked with friend and scout, John Flannery, and he told me I could not become frustrated. I needed to develop a bulldog mentality and none of the other stuff, the disappointments, etc., matters. He said, 'Ryan, you have a team you have to make.'"

And make one he did. Two straight springs, 2005 and 2006, Langerhans won spots on Atlanta's Opening Day roster. As a regular in 2005 hitting a solid .267, the numbers came down a bit in 2006. After a slow 2007 start the Braves sent him to Oakland for two games, then onto Washington for two seasons. Hitting a composite .211 for the Nationals those two years disappointed Langerhans.

"I knew I could still play," Ryan said, "but then I was DFA'd in 2007, so that had me frustrated, and then my wife and I talked it over."

For years Shari Langerhans experienced the grind right along with Ryan. She'd seen the disappointments, yet she knew in her heart of hearts how much her husband loved the game and his camaraderie with teammates.

"She said, 'Go down there [to Columbus, Ohio, Triple A] play and have fun,'" Ryan remembered. "We had both seen bitter guys go down and never make it back. She said, 'have fun playing and when rosters expand in September, back you'll go,' and that's what happened."

From Washington to Seattle for parts of three seasons with minor-league stops in Tacoma and Syracuse, the Mariners sold Ryan to Arizona in July 2011, where he split the season between Tacoma and Reno. A free agent that fall, he signed a minor-league deal with the Los Angeles Angels and played briefly in L.A. in 2012 while spending most of his time at Triple A Salt Lake, hitting .250 in ninety-six games with eleven home runs. Amid ups and downs, Ryan enjoyed a nice career, so why keep going?

"I knew I could still play, and my wife was so great about all of it," Ryan said. "I just decided to hang with it."

The young Texan also spent parts of a couple of seasons in independent ball, playing for his home state Sugar Land Skeeters in the Atlantic League. Signed again as a minor-league free agent by Toronto, Langerhans started slowly in the cold weather at Triple A Buffalo, and the Blue Jays released him. So, he went back to Sugar Land, playing for former MLB All-Star Gary Gaetti.

"I loved playing for him," Ryan said. "Plus, the weather was warm, and I knew I would have never been called up by Toronto, so I played in Sugar Land through their playoffs that year—and played well."

During his MLB career, Langerhans made friends with several fellow major-leaguers who loved hunting and fishing. That ultimately led him to become a *Buck Commander* TV star, along with Willie Robertson, former major-leaguers Adam LaRoche and Tom Martin, as well as country music singers Jason Aldean and Luke Bryan. In the midst of loading up for a *Buck Commander* hunt in Missouri, Langerhans received a call from Toronto General Manager Alex Anthopoulos.

"Jose Bautista had been injured," Langerhans remembered, "and Alex wanted to know if I could get to Baltimore for the game that night. It was noon when he called, and I was more than an hour away from an airport. I raced home, surprised my wife, who assumed I was going to be hunting for six days. I packed clothes and gear and made it to Baltimore."

Langerhans went back to Sugar Land in 2013 and 2014. But an injured shoulder later chased away potential offers. The 2012 season became his last. Today, he and wife Shari live in Round Rock and are raising two sons. He and his dad coach the boys' Little League teams, and Ryan now makes his living selling Central Texas real estate. He still appears on *Buck Commander* episodes. Any regrets?

"I miss going to the locker room, miss my teammates, and wearing that uniform," he laments. "And I miss the competition and swinging that bat."

That summarizes the disease so many baseball lifers carry forever. And there's no vaccine powerful enough to end its hold on those who've played.

RAY CRONE–
SENIOR AND JUNIOR

"The strong, quiet history book..."

"BOY, I LOVED THE MOVIES as a kid in the 1930s," grinned ninety-year-old Ray Crone, Sr. "I loved Gary Cooper and John Wayne. You know the strong, silent types."

"Strong, silent types" perfectly describes professional baseball scouts working in Texas and other states for more than six decades beginning in the 1940s.

"Well, we never, ever shared personal thoughts on specific players," said the late Red Murff in *The Scout: Searching for the Best in Baseball*. "Eyes open, mouth shut, keep your opinions to yourself, that was our motto."

Count Ray Crone, Sr. as one of Murff's group of "keep it to yourself" baseball soldiers.

"I don't like to gab or talk a lot," Ray Sr. said stoically. "I'm just not the huggy type, and I never did jump off the mound or pound my glove if I did something well. I just walked off quietly."

Crone fell in love with baseball as a child in Memphis, Tennessee. Even though Hall of Fame Giants first baseman Bill Terry served as his freshman coach, Ray's dad, Gordon, who played on a Sunday men's over-thirty-five team, gave him the game.

"Every Sunday meant church, then to the ballpark to watch my dad and his team," he grinned. "We were a baseball family, always were. After games back home we went, got something to eat then headed back outside to play or go watch some semi-pro ball."

His days at Memphis' Christian Brothers High School and in American Legion baseball in Memphis were anything but quiet. Ray Sr. first attracted

Ray Crone Sr. and son, Ray Crone Jr.
(Photo courtesy of the Crone family)

attention from scouts, by winning a total of ninety games and throwing five no-hitters in high school and Legion play.

"I didn't really have anything in high school I wanted to study for or become," he said, "but I was good at baseball, and I went for it."

Signed in 1949 by the Boston Braves, Ray Crone moved step by step from Class D to B, to Single A to Double A, impeccably learning his craft. As a master craftsman, Ray won seventy-one games, while throwing 929 innings before his MLB debut in 1954.

"Remember, only sixteen major-league teams were in business in those days," Crone said, "so it was hard to move up, and there simply weren't that many jobs. But my generation did learn to play the game correctly before we made it to the big leagues. And don't forget, baseball got all the best athletes in those days. The NFL and NBA weren't much if anything, then."

One other factor that almost never happens in MLB now? In Ray Crone Sr.'s day, big-league starting pitchers were expected to finish what they started. Impressively Crone, who won twenty-five games with the Braves in parts of four seasons, threw six complete games among fifteen starts in 1955, and six complete in twenty-one starts the next season.

"I expected to pitch a complete game every time out," he grinned. "Managers and pitching coaches didn't use pitch counts, they trusted their eyes and ears. When a pitcher faltered, managers and pitching coaches could see it, and the crack of the bat, how loud it was, told them the pitcher was struggling."

Speaking of complete games, Crone picked up his first big-league win in his first MLB start, a ten-inning win at Wrigley Field against the Cubs. Ray himself drove in one of the Braves first two runs in the ninth, Ernie Banks tied it with a two-run homer in the bottom of the ninth. His teammates gave him a two-run cushion in the top of the tenth.

"No one asked me if I was tired," Crone remembered. "It was expected that I'd pitch the tenth."

A shutout tenth inning gave Ray the win. In September 1954, he threw nine shutout innings in a loss to the Cardinals. In May 1956, matched up against the Reds hard-throwing righty Johnny Klippstein, Klippstein had a no-hitter working through nine and two-thirds. The Reds took a 1-0 lead off Crone in the eleventh, but Ray's teammates worked a couple runs giving him a 2-1 win in an eleven-inning complete game.

"No one asked me if I was tired in that one, also," Ray grinned.

No situation nor hitter seemed to phase Crone. Hitters like Stan Musial, Roberto Clemente, Willie Mays, Hank Aaron, Ernie Banks, and Duke Snider didn't intimidate him.

"Heck no, I knew they were great," Crone laughed. "But I had been teammates with Aaron in the minor leagues and the Braves had invited me to spring trainings in 1953 and '54 before my MLB debut, so I had faced a lot of those guys and I was ready."

"Just think for a minute how many great players he either played with or against," said son Ray Jr. "Plus, he's a history book. Tris Speaker and Rogers Hornsby coached on teams my dad pitched for, and Charlie Root, the guy who allegedly gave up Babe Ruth's called shot homer in the 1932 World Series, was his pitching coach with the Braves."

"Yeah, well," Ray Sr. told *Ballnine,* "he said Babe never pointed."

Ray Sr. won thirty and lost thirty in five MLB seasons with Milwaukee and the Giants. He spent the last New York Giants season pitching at the Polo Grounds in 1956, moving to cold, windy San Francisco with the Giants in 1957. Two-plus seasons of minor-league ball in Toronto and Dallas-Fort Worth led to Crone's retirement and a move to his wife's hometown of Hartford, Connecticut.

"My dad played there in the Eastern League," Ray Jr. noted. "He met my mom there and he was out of baseball several years before the Orioles signed him to a scouting job."

In 1977, the elder Ray moved his family to Waxahachie, Texas, twenty-five miles south of Dallas. For the next twenty years he scouted Texas, Oklahoma, and New Mexico for the Baltimore Orioles.

"I missed playing hockey," Ray Jr. beamed, "but the move made me concentrate more on baseball and I got a chance to play for one of the best high school programs in Texas there in Waxahachie."

Ray Jr. played high school ball at Paul Richards Field, named for the Waxahachie native and former MLB player and general manager.

"I knew in high school that I could play at a higher level," Ray Jr. smiled, "but my dad and I never talked about colleges. He was away scouting, but I talked seriously to Coach Butch McBroom at the University of Texas at Arlington and Coach John Skeeters at Sam Houston State in Huntsville."

A talented middle infielder, Ray Jr. became a freshman starter for Sam Houston. He led the team in hitting and made all-conference his sophomore year. A knee injury limited him his junior year. Still, the Baltimore Orioles drafted him in the twenty-first round in 1985.

"My dad drafted me," Ray Jr. said, "then signed me and off I went."

As it turns out, minor-league baseball and Ray Crone Jr. didn't fit well.

"I just couldn't get comfortable with it," he said. "And in a certain sense, I kinda regret not going back to Sam Houston for my senior season."

Out of baseball, the thought of becoming a scout like his dad never dawned on the younger Crone. Enter Paul Robinson, son of legendary MLB player and General Manager Eddie Robinson. Paul attended Sam Houston State a few years ahead of Ray Jr., signed with the Phillies, and later became a scout with the Angels.

"I knew Paul," Ray Jr. remembered, "and after I was done with pro ball, ran into him at a Texas Rangers game in Arlington."

Robinson, scouting the Texas-Oklahoma-New Mexico area for the Angels, was about to be reassigned to a national cross-checker's role. Knowing the younger Crone was out of baseball, Robinson asked if a scouting job would interest him.

"Look, I've said this dozens of times," Crone said, "I really didn't know what I'd do once I quit playing. Paul Robinson helped put me on the right path. I told him I really would be interested in talking about becoming a scout."

Next, enter longtime baseball executive Bobby Fontaine, Jr., a second-generation scout and executive, then the Angels scouting director.

"Bobby took me out to dinner, and we talked baseball, of course," Crone said. "He told me about Paul's new job and that they'd like me to take over his scouting area."

Both Robinson and Fontaine planned to be in Texas for Crone's scouting debut. But a huge winter storm kept them away.

"And there I am," Crone laughed, "running around with no clue."

Fontaine mapped out scouting assignments in North Texas, Oklahoma, Kansas, and Nebraska for the brand-new scout. And he added an additional challenge.

"He sent me to Michigan," Ray smiled. "Knowing I needed to become accustomed to airline travel, renting cars, and seeing players out of my area. That really helped."

After three years with the Angels and ten years with the Boston Red Sox as an area scout, he became a national crosschecker—a much more important gig with bigger responsibilities.

"And boy, did I get to meet a load of great scouts," he said. "While I felt bad about leaving Bobby Fontaine and Paul Robinson, I met Red Sox scouts like former Twins manager Sam Mele, and former Red Sox legendary third baseman Frank Malzone. Both taught me so much, especially when I paired up with them to advance scout the playoffs."

Those scouting reports helped the Red Sox sweep the 2004 World Series against the St. Louis Cardinals.

"Yessir," said Crone, "we broke the 1918 curse of the Bambino with that Series win."

Moving on to the Detroit Tigers in 2006 while maintaining a rigorous schedule scouting the American League West, Ray Crone, Jr., appreciates his baseball life, the relationships with three generations of scouts, visits to Chicago while Chuck Tanner, his dad's former Braves roommate, managed the White Sox, and Sox players Dick Allen and Wilbur Wood.

"My dad and I didn't talk much about baseball through the years," Ray Jr. recalled. "But I admired him because nothing stressed him, he didn't worry and just maintained the attitude to 'get up and go.' Subconsciously, I did the same thing, so I understand."

If any distance ever appeared between the two, a question from son to father made the distance disappear.

"I asked him why he never asked me why I got into scouting," Ray Jr. grinned. "And my dad said, 'well, I knew you had it in you all the time!'"

CHRIS AND RUSSELL CHAMBLISS

"Make a joyful noise..."

C HRIS CHAMBLISS, his wife Audry, and son Russell make up one of baseball's most eclectic families.

Father—seventeen-year veteran MLB player, MLB Coach, minor-league manager, broadcaster.

Mother—An incredibly gifted professional singer.

Son—A three-year minor-league veteran, high school and college baseball coach, stockbroker, screenwriter, twice-published author, filmmaker and now electronic music producer and editor.

The family also maintains a strong Christian faith.

"I believe that God puts us on this earth to serve His purpose," insists Russell Chambliss.

At age one, held in Audry's arms watching his dad, Chris, the New York Yankees first baseman play the Kansas City Royals in the 1976 World Series, Russell Chambliss could not have known his life's direction was already taking shape. Nor could he know his father was a great husband, exceptional player, and power hitter, but more importantly a man driven by God.

"My dad was a licensed AME [African Methodist Episcopal] minister and a Navy chaplain," said Chris. "Audry's dad was a Baptist preacher, so religion and faith and God and spirituality is a big part of who we are as a family."

As Audry and her little son watched, the Yankees held the early lead against the Royals.

"George Brett tied it with a three-run homer that tied it in the ninth," Chambliss remembers vividly.

Firecrackers, bottles, cans, and other assorted trash thrown by beer-fueled fans, rained down on Yankee Stadium's turf into the bottom of the ninth. Diligent grounds crew workers removed the debris, as Chris and righthanded reliever Mark Littell both pawed the ground, anxious to battle. Trash cleared, the conflict ended quickly.

"The first pitch from Littell, I hit it well," Chambliss remembers. "It went out in deep right-center field. I thought the right fielder had a chance, but it was gone. I went into a home run trot, then looked up and what I saw was very scary."

Beer-fueled fans by the thousands poured onto the field as Chambliss' home run trot turned into a full-bore sprint. A chaotic riot devoured Yankee Stadium as Chambliss, now speeding toward second base, revived his college running back days, flattening a fan trying to steal his batting helmet. Plowing deeper through the crowd, another fan made the mistake of grabbing too hard.

"I hit him with a forearm shot," Chambliss recalled. "It was rock solid and down he went."

Chambliss found no third base bag (a fan had stolen it) as his broken-field run headed him toward home plate. With drunken fans surrounding home plate, he stampeded his way, with help of a security guard, to the dugout's safety.

"I went out later, at the urging of Craig Nettles, to touch home plate," he laughed. "Fans had gone, but so had home plate."

The Chambliss pennant-winning shot and resulting riot remains a significant part of Yankees lore. His homer gave the Yankees their first American League Pennant since 1964, sending New York to the World Series against the Cincinnati Reds who swept the Yankees in four straight. While Russell was too young to remember his dad's 1976 heroics, such moments seemed normal later on.

"I never saw my father as a celebrity," Russell said, "and when my family went out to dinner, people recognized my father and asked for autographs in the middle of our meals, and that was the norm."

As a youngster, Chris moved many times. His father, mother, and three brothers finally settled in Southern California. The Reverend Carroll Chambliss blessed his sons with extremely athletic, competitive genetics. Football, baseball, basketball, and track were huge. As a family bragging rite, father and sons played ping pong.

"My dad was a great ping pong player," Chris laughed. "It turns out that the game creates great hand eye coordination, especially for baseball players. But believe me, beating my dad at ping pong was a chore. I never beat him until I was seventeen."

The third of four brothers, and even as a small child, Chris found himself playing football, baseball, and basketball against older boys, sometimes as much as six years older that he was.

"Playing against them," he remembered, "held so many benefits, but the biggest, I think, was the fact they were all bigger and stronger than me as we grew up. I just had to work harder and harder, and I think that made me better."

Turning down two professional chances, Chambliss signed on with UCLA. In 1969 he homered fifteen times for the Bruins, then played in an extremely fast Alaskan Collegiate League. His Anchorage Glacier Pilots won the National Baseball Congress

Tournament in 1969, and officials chose Chris as the tournament's MVP.

"I hit over .500 in that tournament," Chambliss remembered. "I think scouts really became serious about me then."

Less than four months later, he became the first pick of the first round by the Cleveland Indians. For Chris, spring training in 1970 went so well, he was assigned to Triple A Wichita.

"The fact that I played at a tough junior college and at UCLA and then that extremely tough amateur tournament helped me handle the pressure," he said.

Tearing up Triple-A pitching at a .342 clip while sporting a league batting championship that first season, further opened the Indians' eyes. In the spring of 1971, with All-Star Ken Harrelson still at first base, Chambliss transitioned to Cleveland's outfield. Making his MLB debut, he earned AL Rookie of the Year accolades. In April 1974, the New York Yankees acquired him in a seven-player trade.

"We had really settled into Cleveland," Chris remembered. "And we really hated to leave."

Once in New York, he became one of volatile Yankees manager Billy Martin's favorites.

"I can put Chambliss anywhere in my lineup," Martin told reporters, "And he will drive in a hundred runs."

After six seasons playing in the tumultuous George Steinbrenner vs. Reggie Jackson vs. Billy Martin era, Chris found himself working for another "outside the box" owner, Ted Turner.

"George was always firing people, always tempestuous," Chambliss recalls, "Ted was unique, but he was more laid back and more comfortable in the clubhouse."

In seven Braves seasons, Atlanta provided a great baseball home for Chris and a perfect stage for Russell's first baseball memories. His playground? Fulton County Stadium surrounded by Braves players and their kids.

"I remember sitting in on my father's card games with Claudell Washington and Terry Harper," Russell grinned. "My father used to slap the cards down on the table when he knew he had a winning hand. I tried to mimic it, but never could—mine would fly off the table."

Trips to the ballpark for Russell also meant learning the game's nuances from his dad, who always insisted on being at the ballpark early.

"That was great for me," Russell laughed, "because I could hit with my dad in the batting cage. He was the best coach I ever had."

Russell's ultimate baseball experience came during extra batting practice before the starters manned the batting cage.

"I got to shag flies in center field," he grinned. "The players knew I could catch those fly balls and I wanted to show them my fielding skills."

For the son of a prominent MLB player, Little League meant a great adventure. Russell points to a summer league game he played in the family's then hometown of Upper Saddle River, New Jersey.

"My dad was actually there at a championship game," he grinned. "You have to understand how much of a treat that was because he was either playing or coaching at the major-league level himself during my childhood."

Russell put on a show for his father.

"I hit a homer on an inside pitch over the right field wall," he said excitedly. "That homer helped win the game in the last inning, and just the fact that my dad was able to see my little moment of success meant more to me than the game itself."

Russell Chambliss represents the best genetic traits from both parents. A star athlete in St. Louis in both high school and at Washington University, Russell showed speed and power. He also inherited his mother's love and appreciation for the arts.

"Boy, my mother could sing," Russell smiled. "I was blown away when she sang The Star-Spangled Banner at one of my dad's games. She did an awesome job and people really admired her performance."

Audry knew baseball and was eager to share opinions. She steadfastly believed her son should go to college.

"At the end of my senior year in high school, a Padres scout came to my home with an offer," Russell remembers. "It didn't include much money, but my mother insisted I finish my education and my dad agreed, saying I could get signed later."

At that point, Chris Chambliss had become the St. Louis Cardinals' hitting coach under Joe Torre. Chris, Audry, and Russell continually discussed the pros and cons of professional baseball versus the collegiate game.

"My dad understood how hard it was to play on Division 1 college teams," Russell said. "My stats in high school were good, but not enough to guarantee me a starting position on any collegiate team."

Russell initially chose Meramac Community College, close to his St. Louis home. There he met a former minor-league player, Ric Lessman, who had coached at Meramac but had since become head baseball coach at Washington University.

"Coach Lessman knew my background and my athletic ability," Russell said, "and he told me when I was ready, he wanted me to consider transferring to Washington University. I flourished there as a ballplayer and under Coach Lessman's guidance my baseball skills improved dramatically."

As a result, while his father worked as the New York Yankees hitting coach, the Yankees drafted Russell in 1996. But as he told Audrey Hall from Great Britain's All FM 96.9 in a September 2020 interview, the professional baseball life was not easy.

"I attended one of what I consider the top five colleges in the U.S., Washington University in St. Louis," Russell said. "I was responsible for my education and baseball future. MLB wants to sign young players in their late teens, preferably. Signing in my early twenties, I knew I wasn't good enough, and pretty much knew I wasn't going to make it."

So, Russell left his three-year professional baseball career for a completely different journey. Back to college he went. Receiving a political science degree, minoring in film at Washington University, Russell continued his education at Boston University with a master's degree in screenwriting.

"I'd written a lot in high school, but became serious about screenwriting at Washington University," he said.

At Boston University, Russell hit his artistic stride.

"I wrote, directed, acted, and edited half a dozen short films," he said, "and hosted screenings for actors and staff at BU. I shot all my short films digitally which was more efficient and economical."

Film editing challenged his artistic genes even further, and it aided a transition to producing electronic music.

"I'm able to structure a song without mimicking what I hear on radio," he grinned. "It's a God-given gift and I can usually hear something in my head and match what I hear on my computer software."

Through all Russell Chambliss' eclectic pursuits, one constant remains: Baseball.

"Sure it does," he laughs. "After I stopped playing in the minor leagues, I became a coach. I said before, my dad was always my best coach because he kept it simple, and so do I."

Two years as hitting coach with the St. Louis Cardinals' Single-A affiliate in Peoria, Illinois, went well the first season, not so well the second. Russell always taught private lessons, and now operates Chambliss Grandslam LLC, performing video analysis, helping young hitters' physical and mental approach. He also hosts a tremendous podcast called: *On-Deck: Analyzing the Hitter's State-of-Mind.*

"My folks always allowed me to pursue things I loved, allowed me to stretch boundaries," Chambliss noted. "Rather than coach me, my dad mainly gave me the experience allowing me to enjoy my environment and discover for myself the type of player I would become."

Russell's gifts could only come from a mother's love and beautiful songs, and from a father still known today as "The Gentleman of Baseball."

CHAPTER 9

★

T HE IDEA THAT Ivy League schools produce "grinders" might present a slight pause for baseball fans, and maybe even a quizzical disconnect. "Grinders" and "Ivy Leaguers" spoken in the same sentence?

Ah, yes, but....

If one is so blessed with the superior cerebral acumen allowing the gates of any Ivy League institution to open, and then so talented to earn the prestige degree, it makes complete sense that such gifts can also claim a spot of any kind at the top of the world of perspiring arts. All that said, the term Ivy League Grinders makes all the sense in the world.

Heart, passion, and fire for the game, with a huge dose of intellect added in for good measure, means one now holds a recipe for a very special brand of grinder and human being.

ROSS OHLENDORF, PRINCETON

"The Eclectic Cowboy..."

S INCE WE'RE DEALING with Ivy Leaguers, how about a question and some hypotheticals? From where you sit or stand, does it boggle the mind to find out that a big, handsome Texas cattle rancher could accomplish the following?

- ◆ Attain a Princeton degree in "operations research and financial engineering."

- ◆ Finish his prestigious degree while pitching in the Arizona Diamondbacks organization.

- ◆ While playing professional ball, finish his senior thesis entitled: "Investing in Prospects: A Look at the Financial Success of Major League Baseball Rule IV Drafts from 1989-1993."

- ◆ While pitching for the Pittsburgh Pirates on September 8, 2008, face off with fellow Princeton graduate Will Venable, the leadoff hitter for the San Diego Padres, the first time two former Princeton players faced each other in Major League Baseball history.

- ◆ Become the fortieth hurler in MLB history to strike out three hitters on nine consecutive pitches in his first full major-league season while pitching for the Pirates.

- ◆ Love playing in Japan for the Yakult Swallows, as much as those tiny birds love Capistrano.

Texas cattlemen take on an aura more than a century and a half old. It's a well-known look, a swagger, and attitude, especially if you're a fan of Western movies and John Wayne.

Ross Ohlendorf in action for the Round Rock Express in 2012.
(Photo courtesy of the Round Rock Express Baseball Club)

Embrace the scene of a long, tall, slow-talking, slow-walking dude, wearing jeans and a plaid shirt, topped off with a ten-gallon Stetson. Texas cowboys came to their mommas with an innate sensibility for judging beef and beef cattle.

"Raising cattle, well, it's second nature for me," Ross laughed. "My family has been in Texas agriculture since the 1830s."

Meet Ross Ohlendorf. Six feet, four inches tall, 225 pounds, possessor of a sturdy, handsome face, a killer smile, he loves people, and is as comfortable in boots, jeans, and plaid as he is in slacks and a polo. He loves his wife, Lex, and their three kids, and he adores baseball. In fact, he pitched fourteen seasons professionally, and ten in Major League Baseball with the Yankees, Pirates, Padres, Nationals, Rangers, and Reds. Throw in a season in Japan and that's a long time toeing the rubber. While he contemplates a return to baseball in analytics, that'll wait for now.

"Right now, family and cattle come first," he admits. "It's in my blood."

Ross and his dad run Rocking O Longhorns, a two-thousand-acre ranch near Lockhart, Texas, about forty miles south of Austin. The Ohlendorfs raise registered Texas Longhorn cattle. Yep, that's the same breed of steer (they call him Bevo) the Texas Longhorns trot out to the sidelines of UT football games. The Ohlendorfs cattle story's so good, they've drawn attention from publications like *AG Daily*, *The New York Times*, *Sports Illustrated* and several news organizations in Japan.

"I love these Longhorn cattle," Ross says proudly, "and I love working with my family, love improving our herd, and love helping other Longhorn ranchers buy cattle from us, and I love helping them find stock that can improve their herds as well. I just love the cattle business."

Few Longhorn cattle ranchers or for that matter, anyone else, can match the other sides of Ohlendorf's life. His mother, Patty, retired recently as vice president of legal affairs at the University of Texas at Austin. His father and ranch partner, Curtis, graduated from Texas A&M and retired recently as an information technology technician. An uncle, Norb, played for legendary coach Bear Bryant at A&M, and survived Bryant's brutal, waterless training camp in 1954 at Junction, Texas. Ross picked Princeton because it fit.

"My degree," he explained, "blended my business interests and engineering in a way that sounded like it would be right up my alley. The academic prestige at Princeton is second to none, the campus is beautiful and topping it off, my baseball coach, Scott Bradley, caught in MLB, and I've always said, I became a pitcher my freshman year at Princeton."

Ross in earning his operations research and financial engineering degree, he spent a year working as a volunteer intern in the United States Department of Agriculture during the winter of 2010. He's also a member of Sigma XI, an exclusive international research honor society.

"He's just another Princeton-educated rancher who throws in the mid-nineties and fell one question short of acing the math portion of his SAT," laughed Mark Bechtel of *Sports Illustrated*.

Ivy League education and incredible academic accomplishments aside, Ross Ohlendorf can play the good old Texas cowhand with anyone. Case in point: While pitching for the Texas Rangers in June 2015, Ohlendorf helped the Rangers and their fans celebrate Dairy Month by participating in an old-fashioned, udderly ridiculous, cow milking contest at the Ballpark at Arlington.

Ohlendorf faced off against left-handed Red Sox reliever Wade Miley, a Louisiana native, in a cattle-baron-versus-crustacean-connoisseur free-for-all.

Ohlendorf, in an unsurprising turn of events, out-milked Miley as 35 thousand fans loudly cheered their favorite cow milker.

"Yes, I won," Ohlendorf laughed proudly, "and furthermore, I have the trophy to prove it."

The Arizona Diamondbacks drafted Ross at the end of his junior year at Princeton in 2004. After attending off-season classes to finish his degree, during his Low-A year in the Midwest League pitching for South Bend, Ross began thinking about his thesis.

"The theme kept coming up with my teammates," Ross remembered, "about whether or not signing bonuses were too high for top draft picks. My thesis attempts to answer that question. And I shared it with only one person, Pirates President Frank Coonelly. He appeared impressed."

Cattle ranching and Ivy League aside, a former major-leaguer turned high school coach in Ohlendorf's hometown of Austin, Texas, changed the course of the young man's life a few years before Princeton. Fourteen-year-old Ross loved basketball until the coach, a veteran major-leaguer, spotted the freshman.

"When I first got a look at Ross," said veteran MLB outfielder Keith Moreland, "he was a ninth-grade basketball stud. At six feet, three inches as a freshman, he could run, jump, shoot from anywhere on the court and he dominated."

Moreland served as head baseball coach at St. Stephen's Episcopal School, a private school on Austin's far west side. Moreland played football and baseball for the Texas Longhorns and as an All-American Baseball player drafted by the Phillies, spent thirteen seasons as a big-leaguer. That experience gave him an extremely keen eye for potential talent.

"I mean Ross was all in on basketball," said Moreland, "But when he threw for James Keller [the late assistant coach for

Moreland and an iconic Austin-area baseball figure] and me, Ross opened my eyes."

After Ross' throwing session, Moreland jarred his assistant coach with what later became a profound announcement.

After looking at a dozen Ross fastballs, "I told James [that] from what I've seen, this kid, right here, right now, has all the arm he needs to pitch in the big leagues," Moreland said. "He's a long way from figuring it out, but the arm is there."

While Ross still loved basketball as a high school junior, Moreland upped the ante strongly pressing the baseball message.

"I just told him, Ross you can probably find some place, some college that will allow you to play both," Moreland related. "But I am telling you right now, you have the arm that can lead you to the major leagues, if you go a hundred percent baseball."

"I didn't believe I had a major-league type arm until coach Moreland started talking to me." Ross admitted.

Moreland gave Ohlendorf the "hows" of handling hitters. He quickly realized he was not the man to refine Ohlendorf's pitching mechanics, a profoundly important developmental key. The more Ross heard his coach's "total switch to baseball" mantra, the more he loved the idea. When Moreland asked Triple-A pitching coach Lee Tunnell to work with Ross, that clinched the deal.

"Bringing in Lee Tunnel was great," Ohlendorf remembered. "His career as a Triple-A pitching coach meant a lot to me and his opinion carried a lot of weight."

Before leaving for Princeton, Ross took Moreland's advice and chose baseball.

"Baseball fit me like a glove," he smiled.

By his junior season at Princeton, having been Ivy League Rookie of the Year as a Freshman in 2002 and having pitched summers in the prestigious Cape Cod League, Ohlendorf had seen and spoken with plenty of scouts. In the spring of 2004, the Arizona Diamondbacks signed Ross in the fourth round.

"That was an exciting time," he recalls. "I was ready to see how well I could do against other professionals and ready to see how far I could take the dream."

Within two years and his MLB goals in reach, Arizona promoted him to its Triple-A affiliate Tucson. His assignment? Facing his hometown Triple-A team, the Round Rock Express, in Round Rock (fifteen miles from Austin) in the final game of the Pacific Coast League Championship Series.

"What a day that was," Ohlendorf grinned. "I got the start in front of a hundred family members and friends, and we beat Round Rock and headed on to the Triple-A Championship game."

Ross didn't make his MLB debut with Arizona; they traded him to the Yankees in 2007, transitioning him from starter to reliever. Two great relief appearances and New York placed him on its ALDS roster.

"Anytime you can make a roster like that in your first year," Ross grinned, "it's exciting."

In 2008, Ohlendorf made twenty-five relief appearances in the Yankees bullpen. At the trade deadline, he went to Pittsburgh as part of a six-player deal, and the Pirates shifted him back to the starting rotation.

"I really loved that whole Pittsburgh experience," Ross remembers. "The park itself is great, right on the river; the fans are great. It's just a great place to pitch."

In 2009, Ohlendorf led the Pirates pitchers with eleven wins, a career high. That same season, Pitching Coach Joe Carrigan suggested a change in deliveries.

"He suggested that a big, over the top, old style wind up, thinking it would help my rhythm," Ross remembered. "I was too stiff, and Joe thought that might help give me more flexibility."

Ohlendorf not only led the Pirates in wins that year, but innings pitched as well—a career high 176.2. The next season, he made fewer starts, threw fewer innings but won only one game while losing eleven. Injury problems followed. Ross does not believe the heavier workload caused his injuries.

"No way," he said forcefully. "I was big into game planning and my plan was always to pitch deep into games. My ultimate goal was to be the guy who pitched two-hundred-plus innings a season. That didn't happen, but Joe Carrigan helped me worry less about attacking hitters' weaknesses relying more on my strengths on a particular day."

While the eager righthander listened intently to Carrigan's thoughts, Ross didn't use the big over the top wind up until the 2013 season in Washington, pitching for the Nationals.

"I had challenging seasons in 2010 and 2011 and I spent 2012 between the Padres and a couple of minor-league stops," he remembered. "When I got to spring training in 2013 for the Nationals, I tried the big wind up in bullpen sessions, the ball jumped out of my hand better than it had in years. I liked it so well, I used it for the rest of my career."

Ohlendorf found himself traveling up and down between Washington and Triple A Syracuse that 2013 season, and he was especially effective pitching in D.C. The constant threat of a trip back to the minor leagues didn't especially worry Ross.

"Ross stayed the same," Lex Ohlendorf proudly stated. "He's in control, not allowing the game to control him.

In 2015, Ohlendorf signed with the Texas Rangers, the team he followed as a kid. The deal thrilled his entire family because Ross started his "back home to Texas" journey at Triple A Round Rock. He insists the 2015 campaign was his best, majors or minors.

"Family and friends were there, I had success there," he remembers, "I got to sleep in my own bed a lot, and it all just fit really well. I loved the crowds in Round Rock and then I got the call to the Rangers."

The "call" as he put it, didn't come as simply as one might surmise. Wife Lex immaculately tells the wild tale of Ross' call to the Rangers.

"Ross had a home night game in Round Rock," Lex said, "before a road trip to Colorado Springs, and I went with him."

The couple faced a standard Triple A nightmare—three a.m. wake up call for the Denver flight, and then a rental car ride to Colorado Springs. An hour later, Lex sat in the stands, Ross in the bullpen in thirty-five-degree weather watching the game.

"As we arrived back at the hotel and settled in around midnight, the phone rang," Lex remembers. "It was the Rangers' telling him he'd need to get up early, drive back to Denver, and fly into DFW Airport because he'd be pitching tomorrow night for the Rangers in Arlington."

Unable to sleep, the intrepid couple bounced out and made it to Denver for the early morning flight back to Texas. For the first time in his career Ross would pitch for his favorite home state team.

"Ross was charged with adrenaline," Lex beamed. "He pitched a clean inning that night, but to this day, I do not know how my husband did that!"

Ross made a total of twenty-one appearances for the 2015 Texas Rangers, fashioning a 3-1 record with a 3.72 ERA. But that season meant so much more to Ohlendorf and his family.

"There I was, back at home, first at Round Rock and then with the Rangers," Ross recalled. "Healthy most of the season, it all was about being back in Texas. Every time I drove to the Ballpark at Arlington, I'd pass by that big water park, Wet 'N Wild. I remember my folks taking us to that place twenty years before and then going to watch the Rangers. Those kinds of memories are so special."

Named to the Rangers American League Division Series roster in 2015, Ross entered Game 2 in the fourteenth inning and picked up a save in the Rangers win over Toronto. Texas lost the series to the Blue Jays.

"The emotion of playing for them, I will never forget," he says. "We spend eight months a year traveling all over the place and miss connections with family. Yet there I was with my family the whole year and for any professional or Major League Baseball player that's just the greatest feeling."

Ross played another MLB season with the Cincinnati Reds in 2016, working out of their bullpen, but by 2017, pitching in Japan held an appeal.

"I had known a lot of guys who played there and loved it," Ohlendorf said. "The way my career was going at that point,

I didn't have much in the way of major-league deals, but I did have interest from some teams in Japan.

So, Ross and Lex and their new baby headed off to pitch in Japan for the Yakult Swallows. The new culture, the food, and Japan's different style of play often haunts young players coming over from the U.S. Not Ross.

"It really helped that Lex was there," he said. "Being away from all the family for eight months in a strange land might have been difficult, but she and the baby were there, my parents came over a couple of times, hers as well. And we had great interpreters who really are key to that existence."

Different food choices resulted in Ross eating less and dropping twenty pounds. His first four starts went well, arm troubles developed, and a quick trip to the minor-league club for rehab then back he went to the Swallows.

"I didn't pitch as well as I wanted," Ohlendorf said, "but we had a successful year, the people and the culture we loved, and again I cannot emphasize how important interpreters are to the success of Americans playing in Japan."

Ross gives most of the credit for the success he's had to his wife.

"She's made it so enjoyable," Ross smiled, "She has such a strong emotional foundation and resilience, and better than that, she has always known that baseball wasn't the core of my identity."

Now retired from the game, the Rockin' O Ranch remains a huge Ohlendorf focus. So does Ross and Lex's three children—son Hank Benno Ohlendorf, born in early December 2021, sister Libby and brother Kurt. Having done analytics work for an NFL team and MLB club, Ross might entertain a chance to work for an MLB team in analytics and player development. One other intriguingly interesting career path recently surfaced. Ross has been invited to become the head baseball coach at the Austin private school where he found out he had a future in the game—St. Stephens Episcopal School.

"Gosh, I'd love to do that," he said, "but it would involve finding someone to do my work at the ranch and that kind of person wouldn't necessarily be easy to find."

The only factor lacking, it seems, in Ross Ohlendorf's life right now? Having enough hours in a day to take care of all the opportunities he has in life. If anyone can accomplish all of this, it's the MLB pitcher turned Texas Longhorn rancher who's achieved big dreams and still dreams of other fields to conquer.

RYAN LAVARNWAY, YALE

"Keep Chopping Wood..."

"WE JUST FINISHED our Denver baseball camp for youngsters nine to fourteen, and I'm beat," grinned former Yale record setting catcher and fifteen-year veteran major-league and minor-league catcher Ryan Lavarnway.

Youngsters come to Denver from all over the country to learn from Lavarnway, former major- and minor-league infielder and scout Doug Bernier, and several other professional players living in the Denver area. The camp offers exactly what professional players find when they come into the game. Analytics.

Ryan Lavarnway at the Olympic Village after competing for Team Israel in 2021.
(Photo courtesy of Ryan Lavarnway)

Using varying analytical evaluation, bat speed, swing angles and paths, campers learn the art of hitting. Pitching instruction includes analytics as well, but the heaviest emphasis remains on keeping the game fun.

"It was fun," exhaled Lavarnway, "But we had five inches of snow in Denver two days before the camp started. And once the snow ended, I got on the field by myself and shoveled off all of it. I'm worn out."

The shoveling experience, beyond a shadow of a doubt, cemented the Lavarnway name in The Grinder Hall of Fame.

Past the snow adventure, can you quickly tell me how many Ivy League philosophy students have caught major-league pitching? No answer? Hmmm...Okay...There's one. It's Ryan Lavarnway.

So how does this Ivy League philosophy major take what he's learned in school and translate it to clubhouses, and ballparks?

"Oh, I don't know exactly," said Lavarnway, "but I can argue with anyone, and I can take both sides of an argument and make those arguments with passion, even though I don't believe one side."

Now then, quickly tell me which two Yale graduates became the first battery mates from that school to pitch in a major-league game since 1883. Here's a hint—we've included the other fellow in this chapter as well.

"Of course, it was Craig Breslow," answered Lavarnway. "I caught him when we were with the Red Sox in 2012, and the media came out and made a big deal about it, and sure we understood the Boston connection and how fun it was for everyone in Boston, but heck we were just trying to get outs and keep our big-league jobs."

Lavarnway's MLB debut meant that he'd become the third Yale grad in history to wear a major-league uniform, along with Breslow and former New York Mets pitcher Ron Darling.

Before signing with the Red Sox in 2008, as a sixth-round draft pick, Lavarnway had torn up the Ivy League, winning the batting championship by hitting .467 in his sophomore season. In 2007, he led the NCAA with a whopping slugging percentage of better than .870. He also established an Ivy League all-time best twenty-five-game hitting streak and set Yale all-time records for homers (thirty-three), RBIs (122), and batting average (.384). Ryan also gained semi-finalist honors for the prestigious Johnny Bench Award as the best catcher in collegiate baseball. Coming out of high school in Woodland Hills, California he had interesting choices including Dartmouth, Cornell, and University of California-Davis.

"I made the right choice," Lavarnway grinned.

No doubt.

The Ryan Lavarnway MLB/Triple-A road map looks like this: four seasons split between Boston and Pawtucket, one between Atlanta and Gwinnett, then Baltimore and Norfolk, Oakland and Nashville, Pittsburgh and Indianapolis, Cincinnati and Louisville, and then for good measure throw in Columbus, Ohio, the Indians' Triple-A affiliate. For the 2020 season, it was the Miami Marlins and then back to the Indians in 2021.

Dizzying. That's what it is.

At one point in his career, Ryan estimated he'd been up and down fifteen times. The number of back-and-forth moves he and his wife, Jamie, have made to different clubs and organizations stands closer to thirty, including three in one month alone.

"Really, I lost count," Lavarnway admitted. "The first time up was great, and I will talk about that later, but every other time sucked. It really sucked. Even if I'm not playing well when I am up, or if I am, the question always looms, 'will I ever make it back there again,' and no matter how you cut it, that stuff sucks.

"Look," he continued, "from the outside it looks easy, 'just bide your time, play a little better and you're on your way back,' managers and coaches say. But you have to remember that everyone who makes it to The Show has been the best on the field, whether it's Little League, high school or college, and then they made All-Star teams in rookie ball, Single A, High A, Double A and Triple A, so when you get sent down it hurts. There've been times I've cried, I really have. Think about this. An organization sends up a young guy and he's finally achieved his dream, and just as he begins to think of himself as a big-leaguer, bam, down he goes, and his self-definition as that takes a huge hit."

The mind games are paralyzing, even for brilliant young men like Lavarnway. Few if any professions force young men and their families into such a spiritually exhausting roller coaster. But over the course of his career, he's found ways of dealing.

"I took the self-definition out of it," Lavarnway continued. "I had to remember that baseball's a business, and I have to tell myself, 'They just don't need me now, I have to battle to get better, and maybe I'll go back.' The difficulty here is that the organization loves you one day, you come in, play your very best, work harder than anyone and the next day you're gone," lamented Lavarnway. "That makes it tough, but you have to keep going, and the crazy thing about all of this is that most people outside the game simply do not understand the roller coaster emotions coming with this life. So, we all tend to make friends within the 'former player' base because those guys and their families truly understand."

Ryan and Jamie Niestat began dating in 2010 and married three years later. A chef by trade, Jamie understands Ryan's career better than anyone else besides Lavarnway himself. She wrote a blog called "cookinginredsocks.com," which features pictures of the couple together at the ballparks where Ryan has played, as well as recipes from across the U.S. and its major- and minor-league landscapes, as well as some of her own—appetizers to Asian, Good Eats on the Road, to Mexican, Middle Eastern and Vegetarian, "cookinginredsocks.com" has it.

"[The blog] is a documentary which shows how far we've come," Jamie said. "The one thing that hasn't changed is my love of cooking and food. Every city is a new opportunity to explore something unique in the culinary world. We've eaten at Michelin three-star restaurants, truck stops on the side of the road, and everything in between. If I recommend that you to go to a restaurant, it's your best bet because I take this work very seriously."

Starting in the fall of 2019, Jamie and her sister Calli, created a new epicurean website called "By Tuck and Tate." Named for Ryan and Jamie's West Highland terriers, Tuck and Potato, the site combines Jamie's culinary expertise and her sister's tech background. The Westies often accompany Ryan and Jamie on their food adventures, and during creation time in the kitchen.

"We created a platform to share our passion for cooking, entertainment and food-centric travel," Jamie wrote on the blog. "We create recipes from our travel experiences, family history, and our love of cooking for others."

Outside the world of professional baseball and their epicurean life, both Jamie and Ryan attend Denver's Temple Emanuel regularly, and Ryan played for Team Israel in the World Baseball Classic in 2017 along with former Red Sox teammate Craig Breslow. In 2019, he secured Israeli citizenship allowing him to play for Team Israel in the 2021 Olympics and Lavarnway put on a show, sporting a .565 batting average, two homers and six RBIs.

But more importantly to Ryan Lavarnway, as he told *The Jewish Post*, "It helped me find Jewish identity."

When Lavarnway made his MLB debut with the Red Sox, Jamie, of course, was right there. But not for the first game. Ryan's first call up came with a couple of caveats and remains one for the books. With the Red Sox game on TV inside the Triple A Pawtucket clubhouse in August 2011, PawSox manager Arnie Beyler called Lavarnway into his office for happy news—sort of.

"Don't tell anybody," Beyler said quietly, "But Big Papi [David Ortiz] and Kevin Youklis have both been injured. Depending on doctor visits, one or both might not play tomorrow or the next day, so they want you up."

The more disconcerting conundrum?

"Hey," Beyler finished. "If they both can play tomorrow, you get sent back."

Thanks a bunch, dudes.

Already a lifetime member of Baseball's Intrepid Infantry, Ryan knew that nothing, even calls to the major leagues, ever comes easy. Lavarnway chose to take the positives.

"I'd been crushing the ball for eight weeks in Pawtucket," Lavarnway said. "I sat out the game that night, knowing I'd be taking an early flight the next morning to Kansas City. When I got home…Jamie and I were so excited we couldn't sleep, and in fact we couldn't even talk about it."

Ryan and Jamie overcame "all this nervous energy in the air," Ryan made his flight to Kansas City, and while onboard, he watched the Kevin Costner baseball movie, *For Love of the Game*, in which Costner's character, a veteran major-league pitcher, battles injury and his own demons.

"I cried ugly tears watching that flick," remembered Lavarnway. "I was about to achieve my dream—maybe."

Arriving in Kansas City, Lavarnway learned he wasn't being immediately sent back to Pawtucket. He made dozens of calls to friends and family members, but in the maelstrom of excitement, nerves and focus on the game that night, he left out one extremely important item.

"I forgot to give Jamie my credit card to pay for her flight to Kansas City," lamented Lavarnway.

So, no family members made his major-league debut in Kansas City, although one college friend managed to race in for the game. The next night proved a much different story.

"Oh yeah," Lavarnway said, "they all got to Kansas City and had a chance to see my first major-league hit!"

Off-seasons for grinders always promise worry on top of worry. Who needs a catcher? What will be the location of my next job? How much longer can I play? How hard can I continue working and maintaining my sanity with this process?

"The latest I've had to wait was two days after pitchers and catchers reported in 2021," said Lavarnway stoically. "The waiting absolutely drove me crazy, but fortunately for me, we were remodeling our basement that winter and I'd just go down there, grab a sledgehammer, and start banging down walls. That really releases anxiety as does hammering nails into walls," he laughed.

Ryan Lavarnway still loves the competition, loves finding himself in the middle of the battle between pitcher and catcher. Now an experienced veteran, he has, as have so many grinders, become a mentor to young up and coming players.

"A huge part of my value to clubs now is that I can teach kids how to overcome the ups and down and disappointments," Ryan smiled. "Because I've been there."

And it's not as if Ryan hasn't enjoyed success. Again, in a whirlwind story, Lavarnway opened the 2019 season playing for the Yankees Triple-A affiliate in Scranton-Wilkes Barre, Pennsylvania. Injured in Triple A, the Yankees released him in early July, and he immediately signed on with the Cincinnati Reds, who found themselves needing catching help after two of their backstops went on the injured list. During his mid-July debut with the Reds, Ryan smoked St. Louis Cardinals pitchers for three hits, two home runs, and six RBIs on what was his first start in the big leagues in two seasons and his first MLB home run since 2015.

"I wanted to make a good first impression," he told the *Cincinnati Enquirer*, "I was just trying to keep it simple, and this was fun."

Ryan Lavarnway's fun that night in Cincinnati also turned historic. He became the fourth player since RBIs became an MLB statistic in 1920 to produce a three- hit, two-homer, six-RBI night in his debut. And he became the first Reds player in history to produce more than three RBIs in a debut. Lavarnway had also recorded a two-home run night for the team that drafted him and gave him his first MLB call up, the Boston Red Sox. Still, after the great Cincinnati start, the Reds opted not to re-sign him in 2020.

So, one more time, Ryan hit the weight room, after signing a minor-league contract with an invitation to spring training in 2020 with the Miami Marlins. Several of his Ivy League counterparts have stopped their on-field pursuits and moved into analytics jobs with MLB teams, but not Lavarnway.

"I still want to play," he insists, "and truth to tell, I don't have any idea what I'll do when I'm done."

Two days after pitchers and catchers reported for spring training 2021, Lavarnway signed a minor-league deal with Cleveland. When Manager Terry Francona and General Manager Mike Chernoff asked questions about Ryan's 2021 expectations, the veteran catcher replied emphatically, "Here's how this will work. I will go to Triple A as the backup, because I am the fourth catcher on your planning list for '21, and someone," he continued, "will get hurt and I will get called to the Indians and do a great job."

Both Francona and Chernoff urged Ryan not to sell himself short, that his fate for the season may end up better than his forecast.

"No, no, no," he replied sincerely, "I've been down this road too many times before and I know how it goes, it's happened to me too many times, but I will do a great job."

And Ivy League man, player and now soothsayer he is, Ryan's prediction laid itself out almost perfectly. Starting as Triple-A backup, several days into the season he received his first Triple-A start twenty-seven minutes before game time. Cleveland's starting catcher went down and the Triple-A number one raced to Cleveland. Left as the Triple-A starter, how did Ryan respond?

"Well, I hit homers in back-to-back games," he replied proudly.

As the season moved into June, Cleveland's Assistant General Manager Carter Hawkins, now the Cubs' general manager, called Ryan with the following question:

"Do you plan to play for Team Israel in the Olympics?"
Lavarnway responded: "If you have tangible plans to call me
up, I won't go."

Hawkins replied, "Full cards on the table, you would be the
first call up for a day and not more than a week."

Hearing that less than stirring news, Ryan told his bosses he
would, in fact, play for Team Israel. But before the Olympics
rolled around, Cleveland catcher Austin Hedges took a foul tip
to the head, placing him on the seven-day concussion protocol.
Up to Cleveland went Lavarnway for eleven days, then down
again, and headed to the Olympics for Team Israel.

"Yessir," he beamed proudly. "I hit .350 with a couple of
homers."

After the Olympics in 2021 Ryan went back to Triple A.
Soon, he found himself on the Covid list. But because he'd been
vaccinated and quarantined for ten days, when he came off the
list he went back to Cleveland when a torn anterior cruciate
ended an Indian catcher's season. And again, as always, Ryan
Lavarnway came through.

"First game up, I got a couple of hits," he said proudly.

At season's end, he headed back to Denver with Jamie, whose
life as a food savant continues. The latest for Jamie and Ryan
and Tuck and Tate's food adventures? A twenty-four-hour epicurean excursion to San Francisco, along with a planned week
in London. In an article written for the MLB Players Tribune,
the thirty-four-year-old veteran of fourteen professional seasons answered a question he's heard for years. "Why do you
still do it? Why still play?"

"I simply answered it this way," he said. "My family has a
saying passed along from previous generations that says, 'keep

chopping wood.' So, I'm chopping wood for my baseball life. The call up to Cincinnati in 2019 was my ninth baseball life, the one to the Marlins was my tenth baseball life, and the Indians call up in 2021, my eleventh life. So, as I approach 2022, even though I am thirty-four years old, I love it...I do love it so, so much and I still want to play. Let's leave it like this. I am 'chopping wood,' for my twelfth baseball life."

How can any baseball fan not love Ryan Lavarnway?

CHAPTER 10

CHASE LAMBIN

*"Texas boy to Japanese hero,
with the goose that laid the golden egg..."*

"I TOLD MY FIANCE SARA, I absolutely wouldn't pay fifteen hundred bucks to fly myself to Japan for a tryout," insisted veteran minor-league infielder Chase Lambin. "Sara and I had eight hundred bucks between us."

Weary from playing four Triple-A seasons without a sniff of one MLB call-up, Chase Lambin, like so many other Triple-A lifers, knew rejection well. While playing at the Marlins affiliate in Albuquerque, reality slammed the Houston-area native right in the ego.

"One of the Marlins' special assistants came through to watch us," remembered Lambin. "Uncharacteristically, I asked him where I stood within the organization. The assistant

Chase Lambin fields a ground ball with the Albuquerque Isotopes.
(Photo courtesy of the Albuquerque Isotopes Baseball Club)

responded, 'if we needed someone from Triple A tomorrow, you'd be about eighth on the list.'"

Having, as he said, "the air ripped out of my chest," while later sitting in a Memphis hotel room waiting for that night's game, his phone rang. An international agent asked about Lambin's interest in the Japanese major leagues.

"I listened and I told the guy I was interested," he remembered, "then a couple months after the season ended, they called wanting me to fly to Tokyo, on my own dime, and try out for the Chiba Lotte Marines, managed by Bobby Valentine."

Triple-A veterans know very well that both Japan and Korea represent the "goose that laid the golden egg:" serious guaranteed money, sometimes in the millions, that they most likely would never see playing in the United States. Realizing that fact, Chase followed his fiancée's insistent instructions, paid the money, and climbed aboard a jet headed for Japan. The Lambin audition left the Chiba staff impressed.

"I had the most 'out of body experience' I ever had in my life," he grinned. "In game situational drills, I went twelve for eighteen, four homers and five doubles."

After watching the workout, Valentine's personal words to Chase stunned him.

"Bobby said he had a soft spot in his heart for guys who play the right way and not receive the opportunity they deserve," Chase remembered. "And he said his greatest gift was to empower and promote players who deserved the opportunity."

Praise from the veteran MLB player and manager elevated Lambin's self-confidence. His U.S. agent wasn't convinced, however, that playing in Japan was the correct move.

"He thought maybe I should have taken the invitation to Cubs' major-league spring training," Chase remembered with a smile on his face. "Personally, I couldn't turn down really great, guaranteed money!"

Before leaving for Japan, Chase and Sara married. Chase left for Japan, joined six weeks later by his new bride.

"We had a great set up," Chase said. "We lived in a great apartment on 'Bobby Valentine Way,' near the park where we played. We rode bikes to the train and on off days took trips to spectacular places—and then there were the games!"

Overwhelmed remained the operative word as Lambin settled into Japanese baseball. Accustomed to Triple-A crowds of three to five thousand and topping out at twelve thousand, his life now consisted of crowds upward of fifty thousand, wildly decorated ballparks, never-ending fan celebrations, in-game rather than post-game fireworks, and constant, raucous noise and behavior all overwhelming Lambin's senses.

"Bigger, louder, and noisier than a Duke-North Carolina basketball game," he marveled. "More like a soccer game in Europe, it was."

Two fifteen-minute breaks stood as standard operating procedure during each Japanese game. One break featured the billowing smoke, fire, and noise of fireworks displays. The other included launching hundreds of balloons inside the ballpark.

"You hit a homer—what a celebration," Lambin grinned. "Once back in the dugout, the homer hitter grabs stuffed animals and throws them into the crowd. The 'bleacher creatures' from the outfield stand and scream your name. In response to the screams, the hitter bows expressively to the 'creatures,' because their passion, noise, and energy makes them the twenty-sixth man on your team."

Then there's the celebration for Hero of the Game. Lambin hit a solo homer, and a rocket shot off the wall on Mother's Day against former Yankees starter Darrell Rasner in Chiba's home park. He also turned in two unbelievable defensive plays in the game, the last by executing a 360-degree spin move, throwing out a runner from short right field.

"Yeah, the crowd erupted on that one," Chase laughed. "And I sprinted into the dugout pumping my fist and as I did, the crowd completely lost it."

Named "Hero of the Game," interviewed on a podium above the infield grass, with thirty thousand screaming, cheering fans still there post-game, the "Hero" broke out into a wild dance.

"Yep, it was a heel-slap dance, and it just hit me to go for it," he laughed. "They loved it."

Later, outside the stadium there was more attention for Lambin. Live news trucks lined up as reporters asked Chase about the Lambin Dance. The next day, six national newspapers, television, and radio stations ran pictures and videotape of Chase's dance. A Texas boy became a celebrity all over Japan.

"What the hell are you doing?" Sara asked when she saw the dance.

"Well, I was having fun," Lambin laughed. "And the fun and celebrity continued on the road."

Lambin's legend grew when he hit the first grand slam homer of his career in Yokohoma before fifty thousand screaming fans who were already aware of Lambin and his dance.

"And it got wilder after the game—fans jamming the area near the podium, shouting my name, demanding I dance," Lambin grinned. "I told my interpreter, hey, I'm not gonna dance this time. And he said, 'I think you better dance or some bad stuff could happen.' So, I danced, and again photographers from all the national newspapers recorded it for their papers' front pages the next day."

By the time Chase and the Chiba Lotte Marines arrived in Sapporo, a thousand miles from the Marines' home, the legend grew even bigger and louder.

"Yeah, and next thing you know," Lambin shook his head, "there I am in a video, dancing on top of a Sapporo bar. And listening on the radio, every station carried my dance song. All that commotion for a guy hitting only .192."

Uninvited back to the Marines the next season, Lambin to this day has joyous memories. But, like so many Americans playing in Japan for the first time, Chase ran into major

differences between the game he played in the U.S., and the
Japanese version, including:

- ◆ Strike zones that are much bigger than those in the
  United States

- ◆ Pitchers who have five or six pitches, throwing low in
  the zone, staying away from anything high.

- ◆ Batting practice pitchers using cutters, sinkers, splits,
  two seamers and four seamers, "trying to get you out
  in each one of your four trips into the cage before each
  game. That was exhausting and stressful. So much so,
  Valentine, realizing his hitters were fatigued, tried to cut
  back on batting practice, but "the team climbed the fence
  to the hitting area and had batting practice, anyway."

- ◆ Batter's boxes made of sand rather than clay. "It was like
  trying to hit while standing on the side of a mountain."

- ◆ A diet regimen so lacking in protein Lambin lost twenty
  pounds during the season. Without proper food and
  weightlifting gyms, he couldn't keep muscle or strength.

"It wasn't all simply fun and games," he remembered. "I was
an infielder forced to play other positions and not on a regular
basis, which is difficult. Spot starting and pinch hitting, that's
tough in the U.S. In Japan, it was more so, but thank God I had
a couple of teammates who spoke English and that helped."

The other side of this equation? Chase and Sara not only
had a chance to enjoy the completely fun insanity of Japanese
baseball games but had a chance to tour the country on off days
and grow as a couple.

"I will tell you this," he smiled. "There Sara and I were,
newlyweds on the other side of the world, and being in that

situation made us a hundred percent stronger as a couple and really allowed us to lean on each other for strength."

Returning home and starting a family, the Lambins settled in as Chase finished his career with seven more minor-league seasons, including two with the then-Independent Sugar Land Skeeters, now the Astros' Triple-A affiliate. In a retirement letter he wrote on his last day as a player he said:

> "I don't know what could ever replace the feeling of being completely at home where I work."

He found the answer after coaching young Texas Rangers hitters from Single A to Triple A.

"Playing the game for as long as I did was great," he said. "Playing in Japan that year was wild and wonderful. But the rewards of passing along knowledge to aspiring young professional players, watching them grow and succeed and achieve their dreams, remains more satisfying than simply playing."

SPENCER PATTON

"I saw it in the seventh grade!"

"OUR FAMILY is all about baseball," said gospel songwriter Mark Maxey, "and when we finish dinner, if the weather's good, we go have a catch. That's when I saw it."

Maxey stepped off distances from forty to seventy feet away and watched as his seventh-grade nephew, Spencer Patton, launched missiles bolting into his uncle's leather glove with a resounding "crack."

Spencer Patton pitching for the Round Rock Express.
(Photo courtesy of the Round Rock Express Baseball Club)

"That ball got on me quickly," Uncle Mark said in disbelief. "So, I threw it back with something extra on it, and he said, 'Hey uncle Mark, you trying to play burnout?' I was just trying to throw it back easily."

"Easily?" questioned Uncle Mark, "He thought he threw that one easily? It certainly seemed much harder than easily."

Maxey quickly called Spencer over.

"I told him I was proud of him," exclaimed Maxey. "I told him his grandfather (my dad, who once turned down a minor-league baseball chance) would have been proud too. You, Spencer, have a gift from God."

Years before that day, Spencer's mom, Tracy, experienced her own "ah-ha Spencer can throw" moment. She's an adult national doubles tennis champion, and at age four, caught high pop-ups hit by her dad.

"There he was, at age two and a half," Tracy laughs, "throwing the ball to me from across the yard. Neighbors always used to stop, shaking their heads in disbelief. I thought it was really unusual and really fun to watch."

Competitive genes from his mother and grandfather dominating, Spencer played T-ball, Little League and five seasons of, as his mother described, "very competitive" soccer.

"You name the game, competing lit his fires," Spencer's mom laughed.

Enter Spencer Patton's best friend and spiritual accountability partner, junior high Coach Marty Adams. Adams coached Spencer in the sixth, seventh, and eighth grades. He noticed the "must compete" fire as well.

"And he never settled for losing, ever," Adams said.

Adams' story of an eighth-grade Spencer pitching a road game against his team's biggest rival proves his point.

"Spencer struck out twenty-seven in eleven innings," Adams marveled. "Nowadays, I'd be in trouble allowing any kid to throw that much, but he looked strong, never lost velocity, and was having a ton of fun, so he kept going. He completely took over the game in the eleventh."

Spencer's RBI base hit gave his team a one-run lead into the bottom of the eleventh. Then, loudly telling teammates, "We will not lose this game," he went back to the mound.

"One popup and two strikeouts later," Adams laughs, "Spencer got it done. He wasn't gonna let us lose!"

After high school, Patton pitched in junior college for a year, then went on to Division 1 Southern Illinois University-Edwardsville.

"SIU," Patton remembers, "that's where baseball became more of a reality."

Scouts showed interest.

"He wouldn't tell me they were watching him," mom Tracy remembered. "It was a battle finding out stuff from him in those days."

A knee injury and resultant surgery slowed Patton's senior season progress. Recovering quickly, he signed with a top Collegiate League team, Forest City, North Carolina. After dominating the league and attracting hordes of scouts, Spencer returned for his redshirt senior year at SIU-Edwardsville.

"I saw him," remembers Kansas City scout Scott Melvin, "pitching against a pretty good University of Michigan team. He had a 1-0 lead in the eighth inning, with a couple guys on, and Michigan's best hitter coming up."

Coach Bo Collins came out to remove Patton from the game. After a longer than normal discussion, Spencer talked his way into staying, leaving a lasting impression on Melvin.

"He was outta gas, no doubt," laughed the Royals scout. "Apparently he told Bo, 'Look I can get this guy.' Running on fumes, he shut 'em down in the eighth and ninth, coming away with a complete game shutout. Extremely impressive!"

Melvin's report to the Royals: "Senior sign, extremely competitive, throws strikes, 90-92 fastball with sink, and has no fear."

"On draft day, we got him in the twenty-fourth round," Melvin smiled.

After signing, Spencer credited his late grandfather James Morris Maxey.

"My grandpa repeatedly called the Coastal Plains League, promoting me, telling them I could help the Forest City team win," Patton said. "He lost his legs to diabetes, but he was there for me in Forest City, right behind home plate with his radar gun. He couldn't see the scoreboard readout, so he bought his own gun."

Grandpa Maxey also became a prophet. Spencer won the league's Co-Pitcher of the Year award. And topping it all off, "When we won the League Championship, he came on the field and had his picture made holding the trophy," Patton exclaimed.

Fast-tracking upward with success the next couple of seasons at High A and Double A, Spencer made his Triple-A debut in Omaha in 2013. Triple-A success and a strong Royals MLB spring training, pitching in a couple critical games there, opened eyes.

"One of their pitching gurus, Dave Eiland, told me," Patton recalls, "that the guys who pitch in this type of game will pitch in the big leagues."

Spencer didn't make the Royals twenty-five-man roster out of spring training in 2014, but again dominated Triple-A hitters. Chosen a Pacific Coast League All-Star, with his family in Durham before the All-Star game, Spencer's cell phone rang.

"The Royals told me I'd been traded to the Texas Rangers," Patton remembered. "I had mixed emotions, but I knew I had a chance to pitch in Texas."

With rousing success in his first Triple-A appearances, his work so impressed the Rangers brass that off to The Show he went for his big-league debut.

"I know this sounds strange," he grinned, "but that trade gave me a burst of self-confidence. Somebody else wanted me!"

At the time of his first MLB callup his wife, Jilleta, pregnant with their first son and due that month, was still in Illinois. The Rangers allowed him to head home for the birth of son Bruer, then he rejoined the team in Arlington.

"Spencer had no sleep," mom Tracy laughed, "And my husband and I hadn't either, but early the next morning after Bruer was born, we took Spencer to the St. Louis airport. We were tired, but so excited, and we joined him in Arlington later that day."

After seeing the extreme comfort of the Rangers clubhouse and visiting with fellow players, Spencer walked with teammates to the Texas bullpen, and "dog tired" vanished.

"Tears all over the place, we were crying and hugging, crying and hugging, and high fiving. That started a four-day celebration," his mom said.

As promised, Spencer's uncle Mark, who never attended any of his minor-league games, excitedly showed up for his nephew's MLB debut.

"I almost blew out an artery," Maxey remembered. "When he walked out in a Texas Rangers uniform with his teammates, I thought about my dad's pride in Spencer and all our family experiences watching him grow into an MLB pitcher, and I cried. I cried and cried!"

Once the excitement faded and back to the up-and-down grind from Triple-A to big leagues, reality set in with a trade to the Cubs in 2016.

"I talked to Cubs GM Theo Epstein," Spencer remembered. "I asked him where he saw me in the Cubs plans. He basically said I was an 'up-and-down, Class 4 A kind of pitcher.' That really hurt."

While speaking with Cubs teammates and Japanese baseball veterans Matt Murton and Munenori Kawasaki, both offered advice.

"Murton told me I'd do well there, and I told him, I'm not there yet," Spencer said. "Kawasaki told me if he managed in Japan, he'd make sure I was on his team. I wasn't too keen on it at first, then out of nowhere my agent called telling me a Japanese team was interested."

Several factors weighed in.

"In a sense, my wife felt I was giving up my big-league career," Patton remembered. "She thought I only wanted to go to Japan to make money. When she got to Japan, and as the first season ended, she wasn't sure she was ready to come home."

Signing on as a reliever in the Yokohama Bay Stars' bullpen, Spencer initially went to Japan for spring training without his family. His first thought on arrival? "Wow, this country's really clean," he laughed. "But the best thing that happened, the translator showed up. He took me to the doctor for my physical, to the bank for a bank account, helped me settle into our apartment and get packed for spring training in Okinawa."

Extremely long days mark Japanese spring training. An hour-long stretch warmup included running sprints. "I was already tired," Spencer now laughs, "before I ever picked up a glove and ball!"

Fortunately, Patton's former Triple-A and Rangers team-mate, starting pitcher Phil Klein, also signed with Yokohama.

"He wasn't just an English-speaking friend," Patton grinned. "We'd known each other and having someone like that in a foreign country is great for a lot of reasons."

Two months of spring training included returning to the Japanese mainland for a month of traveling exhibition games "which were tedious," he said.

Once the season began, his family with him, Spencer marveled at Japanese Opening Day.

"It's all one big spectacle," he says. "WWE-type entrances, spotlights shining on each player walking through smoke, pyrotechnics, and loud, loud music. Fans lose their minds cheering so loudly, and they love the whole thing. You're royalty when you play well. Walk down the street in Tokyo with friends and family and a fan asks for an autograph, that's special."

Bullpen differences initially stunned him.

"Unlike U.S. bullpens, in Japan, they're secluded behind a clubhouse or underneath the stadium," he said. "Fortunately, because I worked late innings, I didn't go to the pen until the fifth."

However, the continuing issue between Patton and the Bay Stars regarding his refusal to ride to the mound in the team's sponsored "bullpen car" never really resolved itself. Spencer refused.

"Look, part of my routine involves running in from the bullpen," Patton insists. "The run loosens me up, the heavier breathing helps me focus, and I just didn't want to ride in that car. They didn't like it."

Pitching against most Japanese hitters proved problematic, even though few power hitters exist.

"The hitters go for singles," he noted." So, I pitched inside a lot more because their hitters don't like it. A ball over the plate gets you 'singled' to death. I just kept throwing inside, making them uncomfortable and moving their feet."

During his four seasons with the Bay Stars, Patton, as an eighth inning set-up man, collected more than 130 "holds," in which he held a lead or kept the game in check.

"I didn't realize 'holds' meant that much until I got here," he laughed. "But apparently, they do. They made a big deal about me being one of the best. I thought that was great."

After four excellent seasons, he returned to the Texas Rangers in 2021. Some forty-two appearances out of the Texas bullpen resulted in a 2-2 record, a 3.83 ERA and a 1.20 WHIP.

"I'm excited about 2022," he said. "Looking back, I wasn't ready when I first got the call to the big leagues. After four years pitching in front of big overseas crowds, and coming up with a changeup, becoming better with my slider, I know I can compete in the back of anyone's bullpen."

Would he ever return to Japan?

"I'm never shutting a door," he insists.

Wisely, Spencer remembers his grandpa's love for him and the game, and his family's total support.

"I don't want to be one of these guys," he finished, "who plays on and misses seeing their kids play. I refuse to do that."

JARED HOYING

"Country boy to Korean rock star"

"EVERYWHERE HE GOES in Korea, he's a rock star," Tiffany Hoying said of her husband Jared. "People stop us in the streets, wanting pictures and autographs, as excited as they can be that they've met Jared Hoying, the star of the Hanwha Eagles!"

Hanwha was the first of two Korean Baseball Organizations for which Hoying played. Four seasons in Korea, hitting homers, running down fly balls, doing his best to help the Eagles and KT Wiz win. In 2021, Wiz won the league championship.

"Usually, a year or so before we think a guy is a candidate to play in the Far East," said Hoying's agent Joe Bick, "we begin sowing seeds with the clubs, asking them to put emphasis on scouting him. Jared was a candidate to go over for a couple of years because of his power and the fact he'd been up and down a lot between Triple A and MLB."

"I'm pretty sure I'm not going back," Hoying said. "We have a third daughter, Madison, so I'm probably looking for a Triple-A job with an invitation to spring training, or I'm just gonna hang here in my hometown, Fort Loramie, Ohio, and enjoy life with Tiff, my kids, and my hunting and fishing trips."

Before Korea, watching the six-foot, three-inch, 195-pound Hoying glide smoothly across emerald Pacific Coast League fields, chasing fly balls, stealing twenty bases and drilling twenty homers two straight seasons, one could ask, "Why isn't he in the U.S. major leagues?"

Jared Hoying knocks one out of the park for the Round Rock Express.
(Photo courtesy of "Baseball Jan" Opella)

"They have no money invested in you," Rangers Triple-A hitting coach Justin Mashore told Hoying.

"He was blunt," Hoying remembered, "and he said, 'you need to hit twenty bombs and steal twenty bags every season. They're a big market team and can simply buy someone like you.' That was a tough pill to swallow but 20/20 became my benchmark."

Others in the organization whispered that Hoying couldn't hit major-league pitching. Veteran scouts believe young MLB players need 150 to 200 at-bats before assessing a "can't hit" judgment.

"He has the best, quickest hands you'll see," marveled Brad Snyder, veteran MLB and Triple-A outfielder who played with Hoying in 2014.

Hoying's situation became worse that year. While teammates received September callups to the Rangers, Hoying didn't.

"I thought for sure this was my time," Hoying said. "Then when I was called into the office with GM Jon Daniels, minor-league Coordinator Jace Tingler, and Manager Steve Buechele. The look on their faces said I'd get no call."

The three told Jared he had no spot on the forty-man roster, but after a great season, Jared experienced the business side of baseball and as he said, "I was shell-shocked, always thinking if you play well you move up. That scene haunts me a little to this day."

An invitation to major-league spring training in 2015 led Hoying right back to Triple A Round Rock.

"The wheels fell off," he admitted. "I started slowly, I panicked, nothing felt right when I swung the bat. By midseason I got mononucleosis and walking pneumonia, played through that, angry and not knowing any other way."

He put up another twenty-homer, twenty-steal season, but didn't receive a Rangers spring training invitation in 2016. Then, his dad suffered a major heart attack, which changed his attitude and ultimately his career.

"I remember sitting in his hospital room freaking out because I hadn't hit or worked out in a few days," he said quietly. "Then it hit me. I said to myself, 'Holy shit, Jared, get your priorities straight. Your dad almost died, and you're worried about working out!"

From that day forward, Jared gave up the anger, stopped the worry, and found positives in every situation.

"After the anger left me, I was smiling and actually enjoying baseball again," Jared grinned. "I had played in several big-league games at spring training, went on to Round Rock, raked for six weeks, and on May 23, 2017, got my first call to the Rangers."

Just back from a ten-day, Triple-A road trip and needing a shower, Jared came out to find he'd missed six calls from his manager, Jason Wood. Fearing he'd been traded or released, a call to the big leagues never crossed his mind.

"Woody told me to get my ass to Arlington, I was going to the big leagues," he laughed. "I immediately called Tiff and we cried together because she had been through every minor-league battle with me. Then I called my mom and dad."

Speeding toward Arlington on Interstate 35, Hoying received a call from General Manager Jon Daniels.

"He said, 'hurry up and get here,'" Hoying grinned. "You're starting in left field tonight and I'll pay your speeding ticket if you get stopped.'"

"We were so, so excited and I had an unbelievable day at work," beamed Jared's mom Sue. "We had to book flights, friends called and came by to congratulate us. We couldn't make that night's game but watched it on TV. We flew out the next morning and in that first game we saw he got his first hit."

On May 28, 2017, Hoying got his first MLB hit in a Rangers' win over the Pittsburgh Pirates.

"Tiffany was wound up like a clock, we all were," said Sue. "He got that first hit, which was great and then we met his manager Jeff Banister who told us how great Jared did then handed us the night's scorecard. When he left, we had tons of hugs and tears!"

Later that year, the Rangers chose Hoying for a playoff roster spot against Toronto.

"I was standing there leading off, as we faced elimination against the Blue Jays," Hoying grinned. "That was my grace moment, moment of accomplishment or whatever, and I didn't do anything cool. I struck out facing reliever Roberto Osuna and that 2-1 pitch from him is still low!"

But Hoying didn't stick with the Rangers.

"Through the years, I've looked back on it, and gosh they've had left-handed hitters [Hoying hits from the left] like Joey Gallo and Willie Calhoun, and other outfielders like Delino DeShields, Ian Desmond, Carlos Gomez, and Shin Soo Choo. Long story short, I had left-handed hitters with money in front of me. The fact I even got a small chance against them was big."

Jared, the deer hunting, common sense talking, country boy from the tiny Southwest Ohio burg of Fort Loramie, starred in both basketball and baseball in high school. No professional scouts watched him back then, but he attracted the attention of the University of Toledo. A couple of years before that, Hoying's parents noticed something special.

"As a sophomore in high school," dad Bill said, "Jared hit a homer, a line drive to right center field at about four hundred feet. Not every kid can do that."

Growth and strength came during his last two high school seasons.

"We won the state baseball tournament," said mom Sue. "Toledo saw him there, and in Legion ball that summer they saw him again as a shortstop."

Hoying almost walked away from the University of Toledo, and even considered giving up college baseball until his future wife Tiffany intervened.

"I just told him, 'Hey, look at what you have.' Most of us have to pay for college," Tiffany said sternly, "but they want to pay your way through school by playing baseball. You cannot turn that down."

He stayed at Toledo, as his parents and Tiffany attended as many games as possible.

"Being faithful Catholics, we'd make church, then see his Sunday games at Easter or whenever," Sue said. "One morning we walked in for a seven a.m. mass and walked in on an Easter baptismal. We still laugh about that."

The weekend before Jared's junior year at Toledo, coaches moved him from shortstop to center field, believing a better pro draft spot awaited as an outfielder. As the 2010 draft approached, it became apparent Jared had a chance to go in the top ten rounds.

"I got a text from a female friend," Sue grinned, "Jared got the call to the Rangers in the tenth round, and the celebration started!"

The Hoyings and Tiffany followed Jared on his minor-league journey from rookie ball in the Pacific Northwest to Single A at Myrtle Beach, Double A in Frisco, Texas, and Triple A in Round Rock. When the Rangers' dream failed to materialize, the Hoyings headed for Korea and more baseball.

"It's a peaceful country," Bill said. "Folks in Fort Loramie expressed safety concerns, but we always wanted our kids to take a leap of faith. Jared always smiled, and always received recognition from Korean fans, so small-town USA goes to Korea!"

"The average stay for a foreign player there is a year and a half," Jared said. "I've had four seasons there, so I'm pretty sure I'm not going back."

No matter. The years in Korea provided some financial security, and he's content living life in Fort Loramie, sitting in his deer stand contemplating life, and trying, he said, "to figure out ways I can become a better husband and father." Small-town USA has successfully returned from Korea.

RYAN FEIERABEND

"Fireball to knuckleball, U.S. to Asia...and back again."

"I STARTED PLAYING this game soon as I could walk," Ryan Feierabend said. "My mom and dad played with me, and we used those white plastic baseballs and huge round red plastic bats, and I just couldn't get enough."

At the tender age of four, Ryan played against five- and six-year-olds.

"We didn't play T-ball," he said. "Coaches pitched and that was cool, but past that I was lucky. My dad and uncle played in high school and they, along with my grandfather who later became the top amateur umpire in Ohio, those guys gave me the game."

Let's fast forward. Feierabend advanced past Little League, and one day playing a game of catch with his dad, a knuckleball came flying back to Ryan.

"Now, when I saw that, I thought, 'that's the coolest thing,'" Ryan said. "Of course, I wanted to learn to throw it back to him the same way."

With enough practice, Feierabend mastered the pitch (as much as any high schooler can) and began using it in games. At the end of his senior season, the Seattle Mariners drafted Ryan in the third round in 2003. Seattle brass threw cold water on the knuckleball idea.

"The Mariners told me that because I was left-handed and threw ninety-four, I had no need for the knuckleball," laughed Feierabend. "I still fooled around with it, and used it, but only rarely in a game situation."

Making his MLB debut in 2006, a few days shy of his twenty-first birthday, Ryan learned some lessons the hard way.

"I came into my first MLB game during a huge Mariners loss to Toronto," he recalled. "What I found out was, I didn't have a breaking ball, so I got hit hard."

Splitting time between Seattle and Triple A Tacoma in 2007 and 2008, Feierabend picked up a tight breaking ball, adding it to his two and four seam fastballs and changeup. Pitching in Colorado Springs at altitude in 2008: trouble.

"All of a sudden I felt a twinge in my left, pitching elbow," he grimaced remembering. "Doctors shut me down for two months, the Mariners brought me back on a September callup, but something just wasn't right."

Doctors examined Ryan and concluded he could make another start, believing if he tore elbow ligaments, he'd need surgery anyway. In his last 2008 start, the elbow behaved. Not so much in the next spring training.

"The whole thing tore loose," he said, "And Tommy John followed."

From Tommy John to roller coaster ride: Mariners Single A, Double A, Triple A in 2010, Triple A Lehigh Valley in 2011,

Independent League York and Triple A Louisville in 2012, then Feierabend settled in with the Triple A Rangers in 2013, making six more MLB relief appearances in Texas the next year.

"I just felt like I had done everything I could do at Triple A," he remembered. "So, I had a chat with Colby Lewis with the Rangers, and he had been in the same spot, so he went to Japan and reinvented himself."

After two seasons in Japan, Lewis returned to the Rangers for seven more successful MLB seasons.

"I simply thought I needed something else," Ryan remembered. "Whether it was a new grip, or new approach to pitching, I had to reinvent."

Picked up by the Korean Baseball Organization's Nexen club in 2015 Feierabend posted thirteen wins as a starter. Splitting 2016 between Nexen and KOB's KT Wiz in 2017 and 2018, Ryan found an additional professional tool, returning to his childhood discovery, the knuckleball.

"Hitters at any level just don't see that pitch much, if at all," he says. "But it worked for me."

In 2019, the Blue Jays signed him, sending him to Double A New Hampshire, then to Triple A Buffalo, where he won six games as a starter before he received his third call to the big leagues with two games for the Blue Jays.

"I had lost some velocity, but really began using the knuckleball," he laughed. "But I wasn't invited back."

Feierabend spent the Covid-ridden 2020 campaign in Taiwan, once an outpost for gamblers and outcasts worldwide. Taiwan baseball, as Ryan noted, has cleaned itself up. Plus, it provided work for a thirty-five-year-old battling his way back to the big leagues.

"Look, anyone who's involved in any kind of competition needs to stay sharp," Ryan insists. "They really liked what I offered in Taiwan and while I missed my family, especially with Covid tearing up the U.S., being there gave me a chance to stay alive as a professional pitcher."

At age thirty-six, with no overseas or U.S. offers on the table, the intrepid, left-handed Feierabend found work as a starter in independent ball in his home state of Ohio for the Lake Erie Crushers.

"I won eight games, had a decent ERA, and I went six and two-thirds' innings on my last start," he grinned. "After the game I told the team and an interviewer that I was ninety-nine percent sure this was my last game."

After a whirlwind lasting almost twenty years, Ryan Feierabend may or may not be done with professional baseball.

"It would take a great minor-league offer with a major-league invitation to spring training," he said. "So far that hasn't happened."

Ninety-nine percent sure also means something else: as intrepid a grinder as he is, Ryan Feierabend will gladly become an everyday husband and father unless baseball bowls him over. Either way, Ryan finds his passion.

CHAPTER 11

★

"It's a war out there..."

FOR YEARS, most likely you've heard adrenaline-charged football and baseball coaches and managers from high school through college and even some professionals misuse that refrain as a motivating tactic. Obviously, coaches aim their war-based rants at young players, readying them for what they call "battle."

Speaking and listening to those who've truly been in real combat, and some who've covered such conflict, they'll tell you unequivocally that no football field scrimmage or baseball or basketball game skirmish compares to wartime combat... not even closely.

"Any coach or player who thinks playing football or baseball comes anything close to combat has lost his mind," said Bill Mercer, a World War II veteran and sports broadcaster for sixty years. "Comparisons of sports and war zone combat don't hold water. War zones mean life and death."

Mercer, at age seventeen, piloted a Navy landing craft in the Pacific, ducking and dodging Japanese machine-gun fire while delivering hundreds of Marines to beachhead warfare. After World War II, he broadcast ten seasons of Dallas Cowboys football, later became the Texas Rangers original voice, and then, the voice of the Chicago White Sox. He also was an accomplished news reporter for the CBS-TV and radio affiliate in Dallas-Fort Worth and was integral to its coverage of the assassination of President John F. Kennedy in 1963, later co-authoring *When the News Went Live*, a fascinating story told by reporters and photographers who covered Kennedy's tragic death. He also authored *Play by Play,* the story of his life as a broadcaster. A member of the Texas Radio Hall of Fame, Mercer's also a member of the Texas Sports Hall of Fame's Media Section and a member of the Oklahoma Sports Hall of Fame.

"I had such admiration and respect for every one of those Marines on our boats," Mercer said. "Besides facing machine gun, mortar, and automatic rifle fire, these guys—every single day—faced deadly snipers and a fanatic enemy dug deeply into beaches and jungles. What they did took tons of guts."

Hundreds of young men set aside baseball dreams in struggles against Germany, Japan, North Korea, and North Vietnam. Some came back, readjusted to life in America, and pursued their baseball dreams. Some weren't so fortunate. They all represent the best of what being a grinder and an American is all about. We honor such names from World War I as 373-game winning, Hall of Fame pitcher Christy Mathewson, who died seven years after the end of the World War I from the effects of breathing mustard gas while battling German soldiers.

From World War II, a former minor-leaguer, Joe Pinder, posthumously earned the Congressional Medal of Honor, suffering multiple wounds while charging on shore during D-Day, strapped down with radio communications gear. According to reports, German machine gun fire hit Pinder numerous times as he delivered the much-needed equipment to the beach at Normandy. His face torn apart by enemy bursts and refusing medical attention, Pinder delivered the equipment to the beach as a volley of Nazi machine gun fire tore open his chest, ending the ballplayer's spectacularly courageous, heroic life.

Players, managers, and team executives knew Ralph Houk, New York Yankees backup catcher, manager and general manager who later became manager of the Boston Red Sox, as "The Major." Houk earned that moniker from World War II for his ironclad leadership and for his Silver Star, Bronze Star, and Purple Heart bravery at Bastogne and The Battle of the Bulge. Houk always believed his military service and combat leadership served him well as a baseball skipper.

Left-handed knuckleballer Gene Bearden fashioned a seven-year MLB career for himself after World War II with the Cleveland Indians, Chicago White Sox, St. Louis Browns, Washington Senators, and Detroit Tigers. Bearden survived serious injuries suffered in the Navy while battling the Japanese in the Pacific. His Navy cruiser took three torpedo blasts in an April 1943 battle with the Japanese. Bearden survived a crushed kneecap and fractured skull, undergoing surgeries to place metal plates in his head and knee. Bearden, pitching for Cleveland, fashioned twenty wins in his rookie season of 1948, and an AL ERA championship, and pitched a complete game shutout win for the Indians in the 1948 World Series against the Boston Braves.

Future Hall of Fame catcher Yogi Berra served on a rocket assault boat during D-Day, shortly after beginning his professional career. And Hall of Famer Bob Feller walked away from a $100,000 multi-year deal with the Indians six years into his career to join the Navy. Feller basically lost five prime career years defending his country as a Navy gunnery officer fighting Japanese.

Future Hall of Famer Warren Spahn and knuckleballer Hoyt Wilhelm both earned Purple Hearts while battling Nazis in the Battle of the Bulge. And up-and-coming Cardinals shortstop Tom Woodruff, after becoming a Navy fighter pilot, flew forty-four combat missions before being shot down over the Philippines. His body was never recovered.

In the Korean War, future Hall of Famer Ted Williams flew thirty-nine combat missions as a Marine jet fighter pilot. Korean small arms fire shot down Williams, who recovered and came home to finish his brilliant career. The only MLB player killed during the Korean War, former St. Louis Brown Bob Neighbors, was shot down in a night raid while flying a B-26B Invader bomber.

Others served and came home. All made sacrifices, and some provided impressively heroic stories, as you will read.

HANK BAUER — WORLD WAR II

"Sergeant Rock"

I F YOU GREW UP as a male child of the 1950s or 1960s and you were a comic book fan, you'll remember Sgt. Rock—a grizzled giant of a man, a soldier's soldier, who aggressively led his men in battle against the Nazis all over Europe. Equipped with a Thompson submachine gun, Sgt. Rock never lost a battle, while eliminating the enemy and sending them straight to hell with a snarl on his face. We have no tangible proof that comic book authors picked Hank Bauer as the prototype for Sgt. Rock, but if they didn't it's a magical coincidence. Sgt. Rock always got it done, and so did Hank Bauer.

With the sixth and what turned out to be the final game of the 1951 World Series, the New York Giants had a sparse, 2-1 lead over their East River rivals the New York Yankees. At the end of seven and a half innings, World War II Marine Sergeant, combat vet, and rock-jawed Yankees outfielder Hank Bauer stepped to the plate in that fateful bottom of the eighth. With the bases loaded, Bauer torched a pitch served up by Giants' lefty Dave Koslo into the right centerfield gap, clearing the bases. Those three runs gave the Yankees a 4-2 lead.

The battle-scarred Bauer, well aware this World Series skirmish's outcome still wasn't decided, continued taking his personal fight to the New York Giants. In the top of the ninth, the Giants loaded the bases and their pinch hitter, Sal Yvars, ripped a line drive into the same right center field gap. Bauer, with uncanny speed for a man his size, yet burdened by shrapnel lodged in his legs and back from World War II battle wounds, sprinted for all he was worth, slid on his knees, making a grass-top catch and preserving the Yankees' 4-2 World Series win—one of seven the Bronx Bombers notched during Hank Bauer's eleven seasons in the Big Apple.

But let's digress.

At the tender age of eighteen, East St. Louis, Illinois, resident Hank Bauer already looked the part of the Marine Drill Sergeant he soon became. At six feet, two inches and 195 pounds, Bauer was a square-jawed, rock-hard young man sporting a buzz cut. He signed a professional baseball contract right out of high school in 1941 and set off for the Oshkosh Giants in the Wisconsin State League. Young Hank showed an ability to hit against more experienced professionals and even in his first professional foray, hit with some power. With the season ended in Wisconsin, Bauer headed back to East St. Louis, and as almost all professional ballplayers of his era, found off-season work. Good, steady, union work it was, as Hank became an apprentice installing and repairing furnaces in the St. Louis area.

Before he ever bought Christmas presents for friends and family in 1941, Hank Bauer's life changed.

On December 7, 1941, Bauer's world—and the world of hundreds of thousands of young men in the United States—took a sharp, life-threatening turn. As caffeine- and adrenaline- charged radio announcers bellowed the dreaded news, Bauer sat for hours, stunned in disbelief, locked intensely to the reports on his family's Philco radio. Bulletin after bulletin streamed over the air. Reports from Pearl Harbor, Hawaii, describing in great detail the relentlessly vicious Japanese air strikes on the American Fleet poured out over the radio airwaves. The deaths of thousands of American sailors and the crippling of the Navy fleet based in Hawaii plunged the United States into World War II. That night, Bauer slept restlessly. The next morning, he awoke knowing what he had to do. Dressing, then downing a cup of coffee, Bauer found himself on a mission as he hustled himself to the local Marine Corps recruiting office in East St. Louis and immediately signed up for service. Bauer enlisted knowing full well he might have played his last professional baseball game.

Completing basic training in California while playing baseball for the camp team, his drill instructor watched the savage physicality Bauer used in attacking the baseball while at the plate and witnessed the speed and dexterity he exhibited in the outfield. The DI issued the following challenge:

"Hey, big man, why don't you get more involved in this war? With your size and strength, you should sign up for a Marine Raider battalion."

Never one to avoid a challenge, Bauer, always the aggressor, met the charge, becoming a Raider and heading out to his first combat assignment in the Pacific. Once in theatre, malaria, however, laid him low for a week. Bauer battled through, then began the life-and-death task of learning how to grind with bullets flying and bombs exploding. Knowing the horrors Hank Bauer and thousands of Marines faced in the Pacific, one can argue with absolute certainty that Marines are born grinders.

Let's think about that for a second.

Imagine yourself jammed aboard a U.S. Navy landing craft, the sun searing the back of your neck on a brutally hot, humid day in the Pacific theater. You're staring straight ahead at a fiery island nightmare, the beachhead representing your destination. Hell actually might have held an appeal in comparison. Rolling seas and well-frayed human nerves caused fully equipped Marines to vomit repeatedly amidst the curses they screamed at the awaiting Japanese. Then, as even the toughest of the tough Marines all but refuse to admit; fear sets in. That fear, a vivid Armageddon-based mindset, enveloped Marines watching intently as enemy machine gun fire ripped across crashing waves above coral reefs and beachheads lying straight ahead. Add to that the terror of deadly Japanese mortar and artillery barrages gouging deep, black smoky holes in the sandy beaches while blowing to bits any human being nearby. Those lead and fire death agents aimed to take the life out of Marines intent on taking the bloody battle to the enemy.

"Having gone over in my mind numerous times the impossible situations Marines faced on those islands," said Bill Mercer, who piloted a landing vessel in World War II when he was seventeen, "the actions those guys had to take time and again, while facing grenades, mortar, and machine gun fire, in merciless heat and humidity were so valiant. I have absolutely no idea how they found the courage time and again to face that kind of hell. But somehow, they did it. It's astounding."

A battlefield promotion raised Bauer's rank to Sergeant, leading groups of Marines on hell-bent beachhead assaults on Guam, Guadalcanal, and Okinawa.

The most vicious? Okinawa. Easter Sunday, April 1, 1945.

Sergeant Bauer couldn't have known, as he readied sixty-four fellow Marines for a landing that day, that he and his men would ultimately find themselves all but overwhelmed in the largest amphibious landing in World War II's Pacific theater. Obviously, they knew they'd be headed into a bloodbath, opposing a furiously suicidal group of more than 150,000 Japanese ground, naval, and air forces. They could not, however, have possibly known they were about to begin combat ultimately lasting two and a half months. The Japanese no doubt knew their backs were to the wall against pig-iron-tough Allied forces, determined to end the war in the Pacific. Once onshore,

Bauer and thousands of Marines found themselves pinned down and badly overmatched. Anchored to the beach while facing a Japanese military, all but five of Bauer's sixty-four Marines were cut down by enemy fire. Bauer himself survived but suffered shrapnel wounds to his left leg. (He'd already suffered, in previous landings, shrapnel wounds to his legs and back.)

Still, over the near three-month bloodbath, two U.S. Marine Divisions and two U.S. Army Divisions, aided by unbridled air support raining fire from above, killed about 110,000 Japanese, while only 8,000 surrendered during the Allied onslaught. U.S. and allied forces suffered 12,000 killed and 38,000 wounded. The raw viciousness and bloodiness of Okinawa proved to American military brass just how difficult and deadly island landings could be.

Some historians remain convinced the Okinawa carnage most likely played a major role in forcing American military leaders to forget invading Japan in an attempt to end the war. Those same historians also believed the Okinawa bloodbath may have played an integral role in a new strategy—unleashing the atomic bomb.

While on duty in the Pacific, no death or destruction or shrapnel wounds ever swayed Hank Bauer's love for baseball. Thirty-two months of combat yielded Bauer eleven Campaign Ribbons, two Bronze Stars for bravery, and two Purple Hearts for shrapnel wounds in separate battles on Okinawa.

After the war, Bauer returned to East St. Louis, joining the pipefitters union, wondering if his wounded body would ever be strong enough to return to baseball. Before he could settle into the pipefitter's trade, however, a New York Yankees scout provided what turned out to be a life-altering moment for the World War II hero. The Yankees offered Bauer the following:

> "Come play Class A ball for us for $175 a month," said the scout, "And, we'll pony up an additional $250 bonus, plus $50 a week in additional money if you make our Double-A club by season's end in 1946."

No surprise to anyone, Hank Bauer made it to Double A in 1946.

Buoyed by his rediscovered physical strength and baseball muscle memory, and his military experience—looking death face to face and returning home alive—Hank Bauer set an extremely high standard for Yankees teammates first in the minors and then with the big club.

After three seasons in the Yankees minor-league system, Bauer made his major-league debut in September 1948. His on-field demeanor, passion and pride for the game gave fans a look at Charlie Hustle well before anyone ever heard of anyone else carrying that nickname.

"He was," Yankees teammate and future Hall of Fame catcher Yogi Berra told a New York newspaper, "first in the clubhouse, and last out."

As a starting right fielder, and sometimes fourth outfielder on Casey Stengel's Yankees in the late 1940s through the late 1950's, Bauer led with hard-core, straight arrow Marine rigidity. While he demanded maximum effort from himself on every play in the field and every at bat, Bauer also had no problem calling out teammates who spent too much time with the lights, liquor, and ladies on Broadway. When bleary-eyed rookie Mickey Mantle sauntered into the clubhouse nursing a hangover after a bacchanalian tour of New York gin joints, Bauer, according to a newspaper report, was furious at the youngster's weaving countenance.

"He grabbed me by the collar," Mantle told a reporter, "And shouted at me, 'rookie, don't mess with my money,' and that was a huge wake up call for me."

Make no mistake, Bauer didn't lead simply with a blistering tongue and rugged physical strength. He did whatever it took to complete the job, be it drunken rookie or game-saving play. One afternoon, playing in right field against the Detroit Tigers in the 1950s, behind right-hander Bob Turley at Yankee Stadium, Bauer took off on a dead run chasing a titanic drive off the bat of All-Star outfielder Harvey Kuenn.

Sports Illustrated later interviewed Turley.

"God knows how he did it," marveled Turley. "As he was racing across the grass, he just managed to get his right [throwing] hand on a line drive as it was about to hit the turf in deep right center. He tipped it off his hand and right into Mickey Mantle's glove."

Still in the midst of a furious dead run, Bauer's out of control momentum slammed him full force, with a loud crash, into the metal scoreboard anchored to the right center field wall.

"But, as I watched," said a disbelieving Turley, "he just picked himself up, shook his head a bit, and trotted back to right field. Amazing."

No sweat for Bauer. The speed and defensive genius seemed like child's play and truly represented a happy day at the ballyard, given where he'd been and what he'd seen and experienced over four years dodging hot lead aimed at his skull. Bauer played an integral role on nine Yankees pennant winners and seven World Series champions, and he still holds the World Series record for the longest hitting streak, seventeen games. Traded to the Kansas City Athletics in 1959 in a deal that brought outfielder Roger Maris, who later broke Babe Ruth's single-season home run record with sixty-one in 1961, Bauer later became player-manager of the A's. In 1964, Bauer took over the reins of the Baltimore Orioles and two years after that welcomed a future Hall of Famer, Jim Palmer, to an Orioles rotation featuring names like Dave McNally, Steve Barber, and Wally Bunker.

"He was strictly a player's manager," Palmer told the Associated Press. "He had our respect from his days with the Yankees, and he brought us Baltimore's first World Series Championship team."

"When you were on the field against Hank Bauer, he was your opponent and enemy," said Yogi Berra. "But [he was] the nicest guy off the field you'd ever meet."

Baseball or military it mattered not. Hank Bauer set a standard for Marines, for baseball players and managers, and for all Americans, as perhaps the toughest grinder ever.

BOBBY JONES – VIETNAM

DREAMS, as we've all experienced, come and go. When dreams come true, sometimes they're only achieved by walking into hell and back. That's how it went for Maryland native and Baltimore Orioles fan Bobby Jones. Like so many kid players through childhood and beyond, Jones fancied one career and one career only for himself—professional baseball.

"We didn't have much going on in my hometown in Maryland," said Jones, "I didn't have any college offers and I thought if baseball didn't somehow work out, I'd find a job at the local mobile home factory like everyone else."

Having received no college baseball offers, Jones strongly believed no one was watching. In June 1967 he learned he was wrong. Very wrong. The Washington Senators, a team he'd

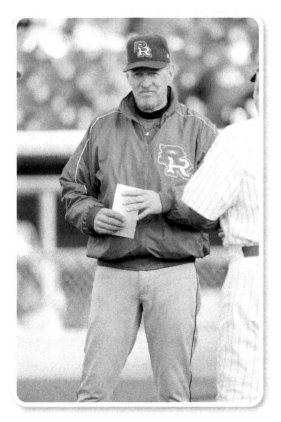

Bobby Jones with the Round Rock Express at Iowa in 2011.
(Photo courtesy of the Round Rock Express Baseball Club)

never really followed as a youngster, drafted him in the thirty-sixth round as a first baseman/outfielder. He and a lifelong friend and American Legion teammate found out they were drafted to professional baseball on the same day.

"You know how we found out about that, how we'd been picked?" laughed Jones. "We were heading off to play an American Legion game and it came on the radio station in my hometown. That's right. No one from either the Senators or his team called us. We found out on the radio. Can you believe that?"

After the game that night, Jones and his buddy celebrated by driving around town talking about their newly found fates, and simply dreaming the dream.

"All we could talk about was the big money, big cars, and big homes we were gonna get," Jones said, laughing. "Boy, did we find out differently. What a rude awakening it was, finding out exactly what professional baseball was really all about."

Once contracts were signed and the Senators gave him his first assignment (with the lingering threat of Vietnam on a lot of young men's minds) reality for Bobby Jones set in. Assigned by the Senators to Geneva, New York, in the short season (seventy-six games) New York-Penn League, his life's work as it turns out, began.

"Well, that team and that league were more like what we now call extended spring," said Jones. "According to league rules only twenty-five guys could compete each night and ten others had it sit it out, and that was disappointing. We worked out very hard in the mornings but sat in the stands at night unless someone at our position got hurt and that's just the way it was. It was tough, because all any of us wanted to do was play and succeed and we didn't always get to do that, but at the end of the day we were in professional baseball."

Things changed in 1968. Jones received more playing time in Single-A ball, but in early 1969, two years into a fledgling baseball career, a very different set of greetings came in the mail.

"Yep, the Army, basic training, artillery school, and trips to Germany and Korea," Jones said. "Next thing you know, hello Viet Cong."

As the leader of an artillery group of mostly fuzzy-cheeked soldiers and their 105-millimeter Howitzers, Jones, like so many others of his baby boomer generation, found themselves locked into combat truly not knowing from hour to hour whether they'd live or die.

"They used helicopters to drop us off at our fire base in what amounted to the thickest, hottest, most humid jungle you ever saw," said Jones. "We were wet behind the ears to this stuff. It was eerily quiet a lot of the time and then in June [1969] the Viet Cong began knocking the hell out of us."

Experienced Viet Cong soldiers repeatedly and relentlessly pummeled Jones and his flak-jacketed mates with mortar fire, rockets, and grenades, as Jones and his group returned artillery fire.

"Full-scale, fiery hell, no other way to describe it," according to Jones. "Every day, day after day in that hot, nasty, humid jungle they came after us, and then all of a sudden it became really quiet, sometimes for eight or nine hours at a time, and then just as suddenly, here came the noise and chaos and fire from the skies again."

The oddity of combat, it's been said by Bobby Jones and countless other combat veterans, is that fear never seems to strike in the heat of a battle.

"Nah," laughed Jones. "It's the craziest damned thing. When you're in the middle of it, it's loud as hell, you hear wounded screaming, you hear gunfire, artillery fire, mortar fire, hellish chaos describes it best."

"In the midst of that," Jones continued, "you're well aware you have a job to do. Whether ordering fire, or moving your batteries into position, or whatever it is, you yourself have to concentrate and lock in to get your job done. It might be a few minutes, it might be a few hours, and then boom...it ends...and back to silence."

The silence for some including Jones brought its own issues.

"After the fighting ends and you sit there in your bunk and think about what happened," Jones remembered, "you say to yourself, 'what in the hell did I just go through and how in hell did I ever survive that?' Then you force yourself to sleep, and somehow wake up and start it all over again. It's a crazy, crazy way to live and for some, to die."

Jones earned a Bronze Star for Vietnam battle heroics, but the medal came with a price—partial hearing loss. To him, simply surviving and having the chance to come home and immerse himself in his lifelong love and dream—baseball—kept him going in Vietnam.

"Being in the middle of all that in 'Nam and knowing a lot of guys never came back, I always appreciated baseball more than I might have otherwise," Jones said. "You better believe me, I got a gift from above!"

That said, and as excited as he was heading home, he and his fellow soldiers ran into some serious trouble in the form of anti-war protests in airports in Seattle, Chicago, and Philadelphia.

"Oh, we'd all read *Stars and Stripes,* so we knew it was going on," said Jones, shaking his head. "But I don't think any of us realized how nasty and ugly it was going to be until we landed in Seattle. All the cursing and screaming and demonstrations really upset us. Hell, we put our lives on the line for this country. But our superiors were smart. They marched us off those planes two by two and we avoided any kind of physical confrontation. [I] was ready to get back to playin' some ball!"

The Washington Senators welcomed Jones back to spring training in Plant City, Florida, in March 1971. He returned to baseball much stronger mentally and physically at six feet, three inches and 200 pounds than his signing weight of 185. Jones tore up Single-A ball in 1971, did the same thing in early 1972, as the Senators changed locales and became the Texas Rangers. The Rangers loved the way Jones played and advanced him two levels the next year to Triple A. In 1973, with the Oklahoma City 89ers, found himself one step from Major League Baseball.

"I switched to center field in Triple A, and loved it," smiled Jones. "Then, our club won the Pacific Coast League Championship playing in Spokane, Washington, in 1974, and in September of that year, I got my first big-league call up."

He and five other teammates flew into Dallas-Fort Worth International Airport that September on their way to the old Arlington Stadium. The group received no royal treatment from the Rangers upon arrival. No one from the Rangers met the Triple-A group at the airport, so Jones and his buddies rode to Arlington Stadium in the back of a pickup truck in the ninety-five-degree Texas heat and humidity.

"One of my teammates had a girlfriend in Texas with a pickup truck, an older Chevy, and she volunteered to pick us up and deliver us," Jones said. "Two guys jumped in the front, the other three of us stacked all the bags and ourselves in the back and we took us a windblown ride to the big time. We didn't care; we'd *made* it!"

That first trip to The Show launched the roller coaster ride back and forth between Triple A and the major leagues with the Texas Rangers and California Angels. Certainly not to be dismissed, Jones also spent two seasons with the Japanese Major League's Chunichi Dragons.

"That was a completely different experience while I was there in 1979 and 1980," said Jones. "I just never really felt challenged by their best pitchers a lot of the time. I thought they pitched around me a lot, especially with runners on, so that wasn't much fun. That said, the overall experience was well worth the time and effort."

Even before his playing career ended, Rangers' brass recognized Bobby Jones as a strong, solid leader. They saw how well he worked with younger players, explaining the game's nuances and tricks of the trade. So, the next step for Jones became managing Rangers' farmhands. Turns out his bosses correctly assessed Jones talent, as he quickly went to work developing talent for Texas.

"When you take a long, realistic look at players, you turn to your own experience," Jones said. "By that I mean, you use where you've been and what you've seen as a player to make talent judgments. If you've paid attention at all, it's relatively easy to see who can and who can't play. So, all those years playing in the major leagues, in the minors and in Japan, helped me in switching from playing to managing an entire ballclub."

Jones credits his Rangers bosses with supplying him with some outstanding up-and-comers to work with through his thirty-plus years managing in the minors.

"Pudge Rodriguez who turned out to be a Hall of Famer, for starters, are you kidding me?" Jones said. "Sammy Sosa, Juan Gonzalez, Billy Haselman, and grinders like Jeff Frye, well, they had it. The It Factor. What a thrill watching all those guys grow up and become big-leaguers."

Managing in Single A, Double A, and Triple A, Jones the skipper notched almost 1,700 wins in the Rangers system. Added to that he served three separate stints as a coach at the major-league level. Now retired, Jones still does occasional work for the Rangers as a special assistant in player development. Retiring from the playing field in 2016, Jones loves his lifestyle.

"My wife Debbie deserves so much credit," Jones smiled. "She stayed home a lot of the time for all those years I was managing. She stayed home in Tulsa raising our daughter and joined me when she could on the road, and when I managed in Oklahoma City and Round Rock, she was there. She loved that, but I love being with her all the time now."

Any career regrets from this man who dodged death in Vietnam as an American soldier, grinder's grinder, and baseball lifer?

"Well, just one time in the nine-plus years I was in the big leagues as a bench player I wish the manager had said to me, 'hey, Jones, left field is yours. Play great, you keep the job. Play lousy, you lose it,'" Jones said. "That's fair, and I would have loved that chance. It didn't happen, but...I am so fortunate to have the career I had. When all is said and done, I appreciate all that I have, all I experienced, and I absolutely have no regrets."

CHAPTER 12

JACKSON RYAN

"He's just an inspiration."

BASEBALL DNA races through your veins like rolling, foaming, cascading Niagara Falls waters. It's deeply embedded in your soul, and at twenty years old, you simply cannot get enough of the game you love, and you love it more and more each day you walk this earth.

Every single day of your life, you awaken to the fact that your father served the Houston Astros as the club's president of business operations. Before Houston, he created the Round Rock Express, an extremely successful Triple-A team north of Austin. And don't forget, your grandfather, Hall of Famer Nolan Ryan, may have been the best ever.

"I realize how lucky I am," said Jackson Ryan. "My very first memories come from being at Dell Diamond [the Express's

Jackson Ryan pitching for the University of Mary Hardin-Baylor.
(Photo courtesy of the University of Mary Hardin-Baylor)

home park] with my parents and grandparents, running up and down, having a blast, visiting the manager, Jackie Moore's office, and just loving being at the ballpark."

"Jackson's owned that place since he was a little guy," said Moore, the baseball veteran of more than fifty years. "Even when he was maybe three or four years old, he always came by my office and told me who should be playing that night and who shouldn't, and why. His observations always were spot on, simply because he watches the game so intently. He got so good at it I said what the hell, and I just let him fill out a lineup every time he came in to see me."

Yes, Jackson Ryan's pores ooze baseball.

Yet, unlike most children of athletes coming into the game, Jackson entered life a different way—with cerebral palsy, a condition that impairs muscle coordination, typically caused by brain damage before birth. From the moment he was born, Jackson's grind and battle to play the game, and to make a huge positive difference in the lives of others, represented an all-out, 'game-on' effort by everyone in his life.

Most especially his mom and dad.

"When Jackson was born," remembered his dad, Reid, "we could tell something was wrong. The nurses took him away to put him on oxygen and a short time later moved him into the ICU."

Fortunately for Jackson, he didn't suffer the cognitive effects some cerebral palsy kids battle their entire lives. He had no learning disability or speech disorder.

"We didn't know much about CP when Jackson was born," said his father. "And doctors told us he might not talk or walk, but he did have issues with coordination, balance and fine motor skills."

That never stopped Jackson and his friends from racing up and down the concourses at Dell Diamond, enjoying the ecstatic childhood joy of being the ballpark. His cerebral palsy simply turned out to be a hurdle he leaped with passion and conviction. CP never kept him from playing in Little League through the collegiate ranks. With his parents' support, Jackson never let the use of only one hand or stiffness and immobility in one leg and one arm stop him or slow his unquenchable thirst to simply play.

"I just loved it," Jackson said. "Always have and always will. I had to prove to myself and others that I could play, no matter what, and to show others with CP that they can do anything they want to do, too."

Reid and his wife, Nicole, worked for years to make sure Jackson had the proper treatment—the physical work giving him as much mobility as possible. They drove him countless times, and miles, between Austin and a treatment center in San Antonio, making sure they left no physical stone unturned, assuring their son as full and normal a life as possible.

"We went at this like rehabbing an athlete," Reid said. "Doing all we can yet taking it one day at a time. Nicole and I could not look at ourselves in the mirror if we didn't do everything we could to give him the best chance for a fully normal life. I think most of the things we did really helped maximize Jackson's God-given gifts."

Both Jackson's parents come from athletic backgrounds. Nicole was a collegiate basketball player at Texas Christian University, and Reid pitched at TCU and for a couple of seasons of professional baseball. The two dreamed that Jackson would be a great athlete, a Little League and high school sports star, winning state titles.

"When your kid has CP," Reid said, "you stop thinking about winning state titles and [you] just want him to be like other kids. When he was little, we always thought of what he might not be able to do. While that might have been a low mark, the high marks have been so many and have exceeded all expectations."

No matter his age or developmental stage, Jackson figured out ways to compete with kids his age. While he dearly loved to play baseball, he also had success in another sport.

"He was a little guy playing flag football and made a great one-handed catch for a touchdown," Reid said. "That was a special time."

"I just wanted to play every sport I could," Jackson said. "I played some basketball, and I really liked flag football and that touchdown was a bunch of fun."

While Jackson's mom and dad gave it their all, aiming to give their kid every chance at his dreams, they also found common ground with other parents whose children had cerebral palsy. One night at a game at the then, Ryan-owned Corpus Christi Hooks ballpark, a man named Jack Todd stopped Reid with the question "does your kid have CP?"

"That pissed me off at first, like who do you think you are?" Reid said. "Then I realized CP parents can see other CP kids from a mile away."

Todd's son, Jake, several years older than Jackson, was a high-functioning CP kid, which helped Reid and Nicole immensely.

"Jake's experiences gave us a sneak peek at what the future could look like," Reid recalled. "We shared experiences with Jake and his dad, and as Jackson got older, we realized what a godsend Jake and Jack Todd were to us."

Jake went on to pitch at a community college in the Dallas-area and worked on the Texas A&M football program.

Buoyed by Jake's experiences, and full of his own fire and drive, Jackson still found plenty of challenges playing baseball. Playing first base as a Little-Leaguer was fine, but he loved to pitch. So, Reid, seeing the passion in his son's eyes for work on the mound and knowing Jackson's love of the game, diligently went to work—with one critically important caveat.

"We never pushed Jackson to baseball," Reid said. "He loved all the sports when he was a little guy. But the beauty of baseball is that people have been successful playing with one arm."

With only one hand, his left, sturdy enough for heavy athletic duty, and with a lack of flexibility on his right side, Jackson couldn't extend his pitching arm and whip the ball toward home plate like most other youngsters. So, he learned to keep the ball low in the zone, and pitch to soft contact. He and his father studied videos of Jim Abbott, a first-round draft pick and successful MLB lefty in the 1990s, and Reid pointed out how Abbott switched his glove and caught and threw with the same hand.

"He practiced and practiced and kept working at it so hard," Reid said of his son. "And as he began catching the ball and got better at it that motivated him to work harder."

Reid originally helped Jackson start his mound adventure, allowing his son to pitch without a glove. But Little League officials and umpires refused to allow the youngster to take the field without a glove, simply for safety's sake.

"I argued," Reid remembered, "that a glove would be useless for protection, but the league insisted."

The father of one of Jackson's teammates worked in the medical supply industry and suggested Velcro wrist bands, allowing Jackson to throw the ball with his left hand, then quickly grab his glove with his pitching hand. The wrist bands held the glove in place as he came through his delivery, allowing him to field his position. The system worked through Little League, high school and into the collegiate ranks.

"I had Velcro wrist bands that ran from my forearm and around my right hand," he explained. "The glove went down on my hand with the pocket, which also had the Velcro sticky stuff, attached the Velcro on my hand. While it got sweaty sometimes, it worked."

Jackson also found another way to celebrate baseball, besides playing, at the age of eight.

From the time he was four, Jackson would excitedly run into the press box at Dell Diamond and spout worlds of knowledge about each Pacific Coast League player who either played for the Round Rock Express or came through to play against the E-Train.

Jackson always offered loud, crystal clear, astute opinions to anyone listening. He propelled his thoughts into the air with his standard passion and conviction. Jackson also showed no hesitancy in sharing his feelings with whoever was in ear-shot—me, Express manager Jackie Moore, or the dozens of MLB scouts visiting our press box. Everyone loved hearing from Jackson simply because he loved the game, and wanted it played correctly. More impressively, experienced baseball people marveled at his insight and found it difficult to argue against Jackson's school of thought.

"Jackson simply watches the game like an experienced adult," said former Round Rock Express and MLB reliever Travis Driskill, who served as color analyst for Express radio games for seven seasons. "And he doesn't miss much. Believe me he's got it going on!"

By age eight, with his parents' permission, we sat him on a tall wooden stool with a back, placed headphones on him, and encouraged him to provide color commentary on our radio broadcasts. We found out right away what a long-time radio and television star from the 1950s, Art Linkletter, always said: "Kids Say the Darndest Things." Jackson showed star potential.

One of his first games pitted Round Rock against the Portland Beavers, then the affiliate of the San Diego Padres. A Beavers' infielder stood as perhaps the top prospect in the Padres organization and most assuredly one of the top ten in baseball. Unfortunately for the infielder—and fortunately for Round Rock Express fans listening to our broadcast—the top prospect badly mishandled a ground ball. Jackson's passion-ately vivid response?

"Wait, wait a minute, you can't do that," Jackson proclaimed in loudly righteous indignation over the airwaves. "You're sup-posed to be one of the best in baseball, and this is Triple-A ball, and you're kicking a ground ball. Ahhh. Come *on!*"

From the outset at Dell Diamond, fans seated in the rows below our booth wore head seats, and still do. When they heard Jackson's rant, they turned and looked upward in a wave of unification, smiling, laughing, nudging each other, and as the young boy looked down, his fans gave him thumbs-up for his stout-hearted comments.

Young Jackson, one year later, also learned an uncomfortable lesson about the power of radio and especially the power of radio sponsors, and the importance his father placed on those who paid the freight. A pizza sponsor spent mega bucks on sponsorships with the Express and three scoreboard updates per night made up part of the radio sponsorship package.

With nine-year-old Jackson standing by, I came out of the scoreboard package saying by saying it was sponsored by the pizza maker, adding it was a favorite of Express fans. And then I added, "and Jackson Ryan's favorite as well."

Jackson's response?

"Nope, nope, no nope...Oh, no sir...nope, nope, nope." He threw back his head and laughingly sang, "Not my favorite, not by a mile, nope, nope, *nope.*"

Jackson didn't realize his parents and grandparents, seated in their open-air porch below the owners' booth and adjacent to our radio booth, could hear the broadcast.

Reid flew out of his seat, insisting loudly that the pizza was indeed Jackson's favorite. With panic on his face, Jackson climbed down from his chair, and as he removed his headsets, said quietly on the air, "Uh, I think I gotta go now. I think my dad's coming, and I will *try* to see you tomorrow night."

Fans loved it, and still do. More than a decade later they often ask Jackson or me about his favorite pizza.

In May 2013, the Houston Astros named Reid Ryan president of business operations. Off went Jackson to Houston, becoming an Astros fan, absorbing himself in a club that, while cellar dwellers, were moving up.

Pitching in the youth leagues and then as a young high schooler, Jackson's parents enrolled him at the prestigious, private, Second Baptist Academy. There, he found familiarity with his coaches, former Astros outfielder Lance Berkman and his pitching coach, former Yankees and Astros lefty Andy Pettitte. Pettitte told Houston TV station KTRK they were amazed at Jackson's work ethic and the fact he took nothing for granted.

"He's the first one out here," Berkman said, "and the last to leave. Now, he's a pitcher, but at the end of the workout when everyone's tried and ready to go in, you look up and there he is trying to improve his base running skills. That says a lot."

"He's just an inspiration," Pettitte added. "He proves to anyone that if you work hard you can achieve. Lance and I laugh and say if we had a team of Jackson Ryans, we could accomplish all we wanted as coaches and as a team."

"Look, I never expected anything to be handed to me," Jackson said softly. "I've never taken anything for granted. I know this is a tough game and I know I have to earn my own way."

Jackson bounced between the junior varsity and varsity during his career at Second Baptist. But he had some great moments playing for a summer league team, Spring Spirit Toros. With his team down by a run, Jackson stood as the third batter up in the inning, with the game on the line and a runner on. Thinking they could handle Jackson, who swings the bat with his left hand and uses his stiff right hand as a guide, opponents walked the two hitters ahead of Jackson so they could face him.

Father and son have slightly different takes on what happened next.

"He came up with the bases loaded," Reid grinned broadly, "and lined the ball to right, two runs scored, and we won! He ran down the baseline pumping his first up and down, in pure satisfaction and the joy on his face. Well, that was awesome and one of my favorite memories."

"Well," Jackson said haltingly, "First thing was, I didn't think it was so cool that they walked two guys ahead of me. Then I thought, 'oh yeah, okay watch this.' Bang, into right field, two ribbies and we win—Ha!"

Jackson holds his summer league team, the Spring Spirit Toros close to his heart. He calls his coach, Ben Vigil, "one of the greatest guys and mentors ever, and he treated us players like men, which I loved. I owe him a lot."

After graduation from Second Baptist in 2018, Jackson moved back to Central Texas, choosing the University of Mary Hardin-Baylor in Belton over his parents' collegiate home, TCU in Fort Worth.

"Jackson always told us he wanted to attend a small Texas school," his father said. "And we wanted him to go to a place where he felt he fit. Attending Second Baptist in Houston, he was raised in a Christian school environment. He had that at Mary Hardin-Baylor, and when he met the school's President Randy O'Rear and the sports management counselor Mickey Kerr, Jackson knew it was a fit."

Jackson pitched one season for UMHB, then decided the time had come to bear down on his ultimate professional career choice. Studying hard, and interning with his childhood heroes the Round Rock Express, Jackson practiced what his dad preached.

"It's all about the fans."

"He's right," Jackson smiled. "Everything we have in this game, all of us in this game, is because these great folks come out to see our team and let us take care of them."

Watching him from the press box, on nights he wasn't helping us with his oftentimes bitingly accurate insights about the play of the Express or their opponents, became an absolute treat. Jackson patrolled the seating bowl, just like his father did before he went to the Astros. There he was, moving steadily through the stands, shaking hands, and hugging longtime season ticket holders and introducing himself to fans new to the Express experience.

"I love visiting with everyone, and I am serious," Jackson smiled, "they really need to know how much they mean to us."

Long time season ticket holder "Baseball Jan" Opella first laid eyes on Jackson Ryan as a baby in the Express' first season.

"Wow, has he grown up to be some kind of a young man," Jan said. "But boy does he know how to work the fans, and you can tell, he's his dad's son, and he's learned his lessons well."

When asked about passing his "The Fans Mean Everything to Us," mantra along to his son, Reid's response is, "I guess this proves your kids are listening even when you think they are not."

Listening, indeed. And watching. Locked onto every word describes Jackson's attention to what his father says.

"My dad just offers me so much wisdom," Jackson said. "And I have always listened and done my best to learn his lessons."

As he's grown up, Jackson's talked about perhaps running his own minor-league team, or maybe a major-league team at some point. But now, with three semesters of school left for a sports management degree and shadowing his dear family friend and Kansas City Royals special assistant to the general manager, Gene Watson, Jackson's vision for his future focus turned crystal clear.

"I believe in God's plan for my life," he said. "And I know I had cerebral palsy for a reason. And I know part of that reason is telling anyone who has CP and who will listen that 'hey, you can be whatever you want to be. Do not ever give up!'"

Okay. So, what's his true career path? How does Jackson Ryan envision the life ahead for himself?

"There's no doubt in my mind, now," Jackson beamed. "I want to be a general manager in Major League Baseball. I can see myself doing that job."

Jackson loves and appreciates his dad's former role with the Houston Astros.

"My dad is my all-time hero," he grinned. "He means the world to me, but unlike him, I don't want to be on the business side of the game. Don't get me wrong, I know it takes a team, business side and baseball side, to make a successful major-league franchise. For instance, I know that the Astros could not have acquired Justin Verlander for the stretch run in 2017 without my dad's business sense that gave the Astros the financial means to get him, nor could they have done it without owner Jim Crane having the courage to do his job and pay

Verlander what it took. It all comes down to the business side working with the baseball side as a team."

Jackson realizes the dream he's dreaming will not be handed to him.

"I never want anything to be handed to me," he said. "I didn't when I played, and I know I have a lot of hard work ahead moving up to where I want to go in MLB, but I intend to do it."

"He's relentless," said Watson, who continually allows Jackson an inside look at the way an organization works as a front office team.

"As a thirty-year veteran of this game, a scout, and now an executive," Watson notes, "I wake up every morning with baseball, and it's there and I take it on. But, at times I allow my thought process to slip away from it just a bit, but not Jackson. He never stops thinking about it—thinking about what players could be moved to make us better, thinking about rosters and how they are made up and how they could be improved. I ask him who he likes and doesn't like, player wise, and we play mental games with that. Such as, 'Jackson, you say you don't like player X, why?' And he tells me, and he's fired up about why he doesn't like that player. And I come right back and say, 'Well, what if he was hitting .320 at the trade deadline, and we needed say, a catcher, would you trade this guy for a catcher straight up?' And we bat that around. Royals bench coach Pedro Grifol and I challenged Jackson, genuinely trying to help him make those kinds of judgments, watching his fire and determination, yet making sure he learns to look at all the angles, look at players from all sides, hear what others—managers, coaches, and scouts in the organization—think about that player before rushing to judgment. This way he learns that the job he ultimately wants is way more difficult than simply one opinion."

Jackson has a huge phone bank of trusted baseball names he can call for answers to his question about anything in the game. Watson gave him the chance to see and hear some true "inside" baseball beginning in April 2020.

"I got to sit in on Zoom calls with Gene and Pedro, and the general manager, scouts, and other player personnel," Jackson said. "I thought the whole thing was cool. Not only did they teach me so much about how player evaluation, acquisition, and trades work, they helped me expand my contact network throughout baseball, and seeing the inner workings of the game really made me more intent than ever to become a general manager in Major League Baseball."

One other important factor rounds out Jackson's emerging baseball management skills.

"Jackson's authentic," said Tom House, the biomechanics coach who trained a thousand MLB pitchers, including Jackson's grandfather, Nolan. "Jackson knows so many people in the game and is so well connected. Young people like him are so hard to find."

House invited Jackson to become a part of the Mustard app, which allows up-and-coming players to receive the same training House imparts to older players.

"At first, when we'd hold Mustard seminars and Jackson showed up in his booth," said House, "a lot of folks really didn't understand who Jackson is, and his role. But, by the time we got to the second day, a lot of players jammed around his booth, and on the third day, Jackson was like the Pied Piper, leading the charge, helping players improve."

"Because of Tom House I understand what players need to do with elite physical drills, proper mental preparation, and with their nutrition and sleep habits, allowing them to be the best they can be on any one of a number of levels," Jackson said.

On the cutting edge of the Mustard program, Jackson saw how dramatically House's comprehensive program works its magic. Early in 2021, with Jackson Ryan looking on, House and his staff began work with a young right-handed pitcher named Justin Courtney. Courtney certainly looks the part of a potential major-league pitcher. At six feet, four inches and 225 pounds, Courtney is a former starting pitcher at the University of Maine whose career shut down with Tommy John surgery in 2018.

"Training for baseball never stopped," Courtney told the paper in Bangor, Maine. "But the path to professional baseball was unclear at times. The past few years have been a grind, but it has turned into a great story."

Did it ever.

When House and his Mustard staff began work with Courtney, the young man's fastball topped out at eighty-eight miles an hour. Hard work, and a complete buy in to House's program turned Courtney from a passable collegiate pitcher to a sure-fire professional prospect. Changes in Courtney's body, his mechanics, and mental makeup took his pedestrian fastball to a consistent ninety-eight miles an hour and topping out at 101.

With House helping him track Courtney's progress, Jackson called his friend and mentor Watson, who had briefly taken a job as the Angels' assistant general manager. Angels' scouts loved what they saw and immediately signed Courtney to a minor-league deal.

That just makes me so happy to be able to help connect the dots and help a deserving guy get a professional shot," Jackson said.

Somehow, friends have the feeling Jackson's just beginning to scratch the surface of helping other people achieve their dreams in baseball. Even at age twenty, an extremely motivated, extremely serious and immersed Jackson Ryan sees his future in baseball and prepares for all phases of it as he pursues his goals. Saying baseball stands as his lifelong love and passion is an understatement.

That said, dad Reid still puts no pressure on his son to continue in the game of baseball.

"Baseball is a funny business," Reid said. "I just want Jackson to be happy. If that is in baseball, great. If it's doing something else, great. I know whatever he does he will work hard and do a good job."

Jackson himself couldn't be happier. As he finishes his college degree, he plans more work with House and his friends in the player development business in Major League Baseball. When he lays his head on his pillow at night, Jackson knows he's extremely fortunate to have such friends to help him, and a family DNA that screams baseball. As importantly, he also appreciates the fact that he wants to spend his baseball life helping others achieve their dreams.

All those factors make it easy to say: The biggest and best for Jackson Ryan awaits.

MEET THE AUTHORS

Clockwise from bottom left: Mike Capps, Karen Phillips, Chuck Hartenstein, and Bill Mercer, the original voice of the Texas Rangers.
(Author photo)

MIKE CAPPS

Grinders: Baseball's Intrepid Infantry represents the second literary effort for baseball broadcaster and former CNN Correspondent Mike Capps. Capps wrote his first, *The Scout: Searching for the Best in Baseball,* with legendary scout Red Murff, who discovered Hall of Fame pitcher Nolan Ryan. Murff also signed more than seventy players who made the major leagues, including other members, besides Ryan, of the 1969 World Champion "Miracle" New York Mets: Jerry Grote, Kenny Boswell, and Jerry Koosman.

Capps began broadcasting professional baseball in 1996, and for twenty-one seasons he's been the play-by-play voice of the Triple a Round Rock Express. He's also done fill-in major-league work for ESPN Radio, the Texas Rangers, and the Houston Astros. Twice in his career, he's been named Minor League Broadcaster of the Year by Ballparkdigest.com and Minor League News.

Capps spent twenty-two years in the radio-television news business, working for ABC and CNN, as well as WFAA-TV in Dallas-Fort Worth and KPRC-TV in Houston. As a correspondent for CNN, he covered the first Gulf War, the overthrow of President John Bertrand Aristede in Haiti, the Branch Davidian siege in Waco, and the Midwest floods. In management at ABC News as Midwest assignments manager/deputy bureau chief, he was responsible for executing all network coverage of twelve Midwest states.

As a reporter for two Texas television stations, KPRC-TV in Houston and WFAA-TV in Dallas, he covered the return to earth of the Skylab space station in 1979, as well as sixteen Space Shuttle missions including the Challenger disaster. He also covered Hurricane Alicia's devastation of Houston and Galveston in the early 1980s, which led ABC World News Tonight broadcasts on both the East and West Coasts—the first time in ABC history a local correspondent's work led both World News Tonight broadcasts. And in the mid-1980s, Capps and producer John Sparks broke the story of the "pay for play" scandal within the Southern Methodist University football program. The stories resulted in the only time the NCAA has ever shut down an athletics program with its "death penalty."

For his work in television news Capps has won the following awards:

- ◆ National Emmy Nomination for coverage of the bloody 10-hour end to the Branch Davidian siege in Waco, Texas

- ◆ Cable Ace Award for Branch Davidian siege-ending coverage

- ◆ Alfred I. duPont-Columbia Award for coverage of the SMU scandal

- ◆ George F. Peabody award for SMU Coverage

Capps and his wife, Karen, live in Austin, Texas. Their family consists of daughter Dr. Christa Lows, husband, Kent, and grandson and granddaughter, Grayson and Avery Lows of Atlanta, Georgia; daughter Kelli Wetsel, husband Reagan, granddaughter Cameron and grandsons Carter, Reese, and Rex of Corsicana, Texas; daughter Karli of Austin; son Brice, wife Caitlin, and grandson Sam of Austin. The family rescues dogs and cats including their dogs Archie and Molly and cats Penny, Sid, and Lylah, and supports Austin Humane Society and Austin Sheltie Rescue.

Capps is on the board of directors of Capital Area Crime Stoppers and Williamson County Fellowship of Christian Athletes.

CHUCK HARTENSTEIN

A native of Seguin, Texas, Chuck Hartenstein pitched and won both a state-semifinal match-up, and a no-hitter the next day, giving his Seguin Matadors a state championship in 1960.

Watching that day was legendary Texas Longhorns Baseball Coach and former Chicago White Sox outfielder Bibb Falk, who offered Hartenstein a scholarship. Hartenstein pitched the University of Texas to back-to-back appearances at the College World Series in Omaha in 1962 and 1963, and still ranks among the all-time ERA leaders for starting pitchers at the College World Series.

Signed as a free agent by the Chicago Cubs, Hartenstein went on to pitch as a reliever for the Cubs, Pirates, Cardinals, Red Sox, and Blue Jays. His best season took place in 1967, as he compiled a 9-5 record, including eleven saves and a 3.08 ERA for Chicago.

Before his major-league debut, however, Hartenstein pitched one of the most incredible games in the history of the Texas League. On June 17, 1965, Hartenstein, pitching for the Dallas-Fort Worth Spurs, facing the Austin Braves at old Turnpike Stadium in Arlington, went eighteen innings against Austin, surrendering only one run. Unfortunately, long after Hartenstein left, the game went a whopping twenty-five innings with the Spurs losing to Austin 2-1.

After fifteen years of pitching and 187 major-league appearances, Hartenstein became a pitching coach, serving in the minor and major leagues for both the Cleveland Indians and Milwaukee Brewers. After his coaching career ended, Hartenstein served three seasons as a scout.

In 2004, the legendary Texas hurler, known as "Twiggy" for his slight, 155-pound build, was voted into the University of Texas Athletics Hall of Honor.

Chuck is survived by his wife of sixty years, Joyce Engleke Hartenstein, his son Greg and his wife Susan of Austin, Texas; son, Chris and his wife Michelle, also of Austin, Texas; his five granddaughters: Macy, Ashley, and Emma Hartenstein, Megan Bassinger and her husband, Brandon, and Michelle Wilson, her husband Jack, and their son Jack. Jack Wilson, Chuck's great-grandson, inherits his grandfather's baseball glove, which Chuck saved for thirty years for the first male descendant of his children.

ACKNOWLEDGMENTS and THANK YOUS

From Mike

FOR ANYONE in baseball, true success begins at home. The love of my life, wife, sweetheart, and partner Karen Phillips understands our industry and with love and care paves the way for whatever success comes our way. Our children, Dr. Christa Lows (a grinder herself, gamely whipping Stage 3 breast cancer in 2019 and Covid 19 in late 2020), son-in-law Kent Lows, daughter Kelli and son-in-law Reagan Wetsel, daughter Karli Capps, our son Brice and daughter-in-law Cait Kindred give us feedback (Cait also assembled this book), a plethora of ideas and support. Our incredible seven grandchildren range in age from nineteen to six. Carter, Cameron, Reece, and Rex Wetsel, Avery and Grayson Lows, and Sammy Kindred, give us big smiles, big laughs, and joyful tears as they mature. Keeping us sharp and on our toes, they're a source of pure, utter joy!

Loren Steffy, an outstanding business news writer for the *Houston Chronicle* and *Texas Monthly* and author-turned-publisher, gave us this huge chance. Special words of thanks to longtime friend and news compatriot Olive Talley for connecting us. Owe you much for that!

To the longtime TV voice of the Houston Astros, Bill Brown. Also a published author, Brown edited this book while passing along encouragement and patience, keeping us out of many literary ditches along the way.

To former Astros President Tal Smith, a great friend, who set us on the right track when we started this book, provided guidance along the way, and wrote an extremely flattering preface. We could never have done this without your incredible expertise.

Former Pacific Coast League President Branch B. Rickey, also a great friend, greatly aided our thought process and came up with the title. Former minor-league president Pat O'Conner pep-talked us through some difficult days, and former Astros General Manager Tim Purpura did the same, also helping us fill in the blanks on a couple of our player profiles.

Most profound gratitude goes to Bill Mercer, my mentor and father-confessor. He stepped into my life in so many ways after my father died when I was seventeen. We've been down a helluva lot of roads together. Bill counseled while listening to me drone on about successes and failures and ultimately molded and shaped my life as a broadcast correspondent and baseball broadcaster. A twice-published author himself, he's a member of three Halls of Fame. He sure is in mine.

To The Rogers Hornsby Chapter of Society for American Baseball Research, for your friendship, encouragement and help in piecing together some of the profiles in this work. You are amazing!

The late Hall of Fame Detroit Tigers broadcaster Ernie Harwell patiently listened to tapes of my broadcast work, offering criticism and advice, while making me feel a part of his baseball life.

To all our friends who helped us with player pictures, a huge tip of the hat in thanks.

- Baseball Jan Opella, Round Rock Express Season Seat holder
- Laura Fragoso, Sr. VP/Marketing, Round Rock Express
- Michael Coffin, broadcaster, Corpus Christi Hooks
- Ryan Posner, Sugar Land baseball club
- Kraig Williams, Communications Manager, Salt Lake Bees
- Brian Carroll, Assistant General Manager/VP Public Relations & Baseball Ops, Tulsa Drillers

Special thanks to a vast cadre of radio partners through the years at ESPN Radio, the Houston Astros, and Texas Rangers, as well as the Round Rock Express, along with my Texas League and Pacific Coast League cohorts. My friend Steve Selby readily accepted me into his Triple-A booth in Nashville my second year in the game and we made a pretty good team. Kudos to incredibly gifted friends and Texas Leaguers Bob Hardge and Michael Coffin, and fellow outstanding Pacific Coast League broadcasters Mark Nasser, Michael Curto, Johnny Doskow, Deene Ehlis, Randy Wehofer, Tim Grubbs, Steve Klauke, Russ Langer, Alex Freedman, Jeff Hem, Doug Greenwald, Josh Suchon, Tim Hagerty, Dan Karcher, Dick Calvert, Jerry Reuss, Ron Swoboda, Rob Portnoy, Bob Socci and Zac Bayrouty— thanks to each and every one of you guys for turning my baseball broadcast life into a wild and crazy joy ride!

Talk about blessings? What a cast of greats have joined me on Round Rock, ESPN, Rangers, and Astros broadcasts. Names like Harold Reynolds, Tim Kurkjian, Chris Chambliss, Kevin

Kennedy, Keith Moreland, Ross Ohlendorf, Kirk Dressendorfer, Marty Esposito, Spike Owen, Bruce Ruffin, Travis Driskill, Val Majewski, Jerry Grote, Steve Sparks, Kelly Wunsch, Kevin Millar, John Flannery, Bill Brown, Mike Hardge, Robert Ford, and Eric Nadel made us sound better than we are. We cannot leave out Mark Saccomanno, Jim Raup, college coaches Ben Shipp, Tommy Boggs, Rob Penders, Chase Almendarez, J.C. Bunch and David Pierce, as well as All-American and professional softball pitcher Cat Osterman and one of the greatest high school coaches of all time, John Langerhans.

To the Ryan family, Nolan and Ruth, and especially to Reid Ryan for his support of our work through the years and his willingness to share thoughts on his son Jackson, who by the way will one day become a general manager in Major League Baseball. To Reese Ryan, Don, Brett and Brad Sanders, and Eddie Maloney, undying gratitude for all the encouragement and belief you've shown in me. To Jay Miller, one of the best operators in baseball... *ever*... and a great friend for forty years. And to Jay's brother Gregg for wise counsel through the years. To Austin sports psychologist Dr. Hillary Cauthen for her spot-on assessments of grinders minds. *And a special, huge thank you* to the staff of the Round Rock Express Baseball Club and Ryan-Sanders Baseball; Reese Ryan, J.J.Gottsch, Chris Almendarez, Tim Jackson, Laura Fragoso, Dave Fendrick, Missy Martin and a myriad of other top flight professionals, and especially to the best clubbie in minor-league baseball, Kenny Bufton.

And finally, I owe the deepest debt of gratitude to a multitude of my trusted friends—veteran scouts. Talk about grinders! Unfortunately, some of these top-flight professionals have been forced to the back of the bus by "modern knowledge."

In reality, professional baseball at all levels would not have reached the pinnacle it did without these veterans who've given heart and soul to the game. They're wise eyes who played the game, succeeded, and failed. They know the hearts and minds of young players, how the game should be played correctly and who can and who can't. Veteran scouts have always been irreplaceable, no matter the crazes of the day. They'll always be integral to the game's success.

Speaking of veteran scouts. To the family of the late Billy Capps, my cousin and longtime scout for the Cubs, your dad and granddad set an incredible example as a humble man of God, family man, scout, and friend. Thanks also to the family of the late Red Murff, who gave me back this game. To the family of great friend and scout Buzzy Keller who spent hours on the phone with me, laughing, and ripping on each other, yet forming an incredible bond, and was always there with encouragement. To the families of the late Jim Hughes, the late Doug Gassaway, and the late Al LaMacchia, dear friends who constantly encouraged and challenged. And, to the memory of Michael Point; an extraordinary mind, writer, and baseball brother who died way too young.

To valued friends and compatriots, Agent Joe Bick and his son Brett, Royals Vice President Gene Watson, former MLB GM Dan Evans, once my agent, and remains to this day a dear friend, and Bobby Heck, special assistant to the GM in Tampa Bay, a go-to guy and trusted friend and ally, humble thanks. To former MLB GM Dan Jennings, a great friend, great scout and great man. And to Bruce Tanner, a great scout and former pitcher. To GMs in the old Pacific Coast League who I absolutely admire: Oklahoma City's Michael Byrnes, Las

Vegas' Don Logan, Salt Lake City's Mark Amicone, dear friend John Traub in Albuquerque, Iowa Cubs legend Sam Bernabe and his owner, former NBC News President Michael Gartner, thanks for all the hospitality and discussion about our industry through the years, and to Martie Cordaro in Omaha...blessings and thanks.

Veteran scouts, still with us, and still looking for *those who can*, remain incredible friends. Names like Tom Allison, Bill Wood, Jay Robertson, Randy Smith, Sandy Johnson, Marty Scott, Greg Smith, Mike Basso, Dick Egan, Rudy Terrasas, Sonny and Clint Bowers, Jeff Stewart, Ralph Garr (senior and junior), Paul Scott, Kyle Van Hook, Todd 'Tiny' Thomas (who assisted us with this book), as did great friend and retired Twins and Marlins scout Marty Esposito. More who meant so much, Ben McClure, Marv Thompson, Gerald Turner—a great friend and former amateur baseball teammate—as well as Dennis Cardoza, Steve Riha, Randy Taylor, Jeff Edwards, Ty Coslow, Jeff Morris, Mike Anderson, Jason Karagennis, Ron Toenjes, Ken Kravec, Keith Staab, Pat Murphy, Ray Corbett, Ray Crone (senior and junior) Tim Holt, Jim Skaalen, Andrew Lorraine, and Sal Butera. We cannot forget our friends who scout for Asian clubs; Kevin Hodges, DJ Houlton, Tony Yates, Al Hargesheimer, Dave DeFrietas and Nate Minchey. All great men, great professionals, and even greater friends.

And to the memory of great friends and former college teammates Jim Callendar and Bobby Price. Plus, special thanks to my former teammates from Hill Junior College who still show up for reunions at Dell Diamond: Mike Anderson, Raul Zamora, David Armstrong, Keith Randall, Pete Gill, Tom Ladusau, Mike Chitty, John Dawson, Terry Headrick, Wayne

Taylor, and Wayne Hopson. This book, gentlemen, would not have happened without you.

And a special word of thanks to you—baseball fans—for hooking into our passion. You make our dreams a reality, and as Jackson Ryan always says, "You fans make it possible for us to do what we do!" Amen.

Blessings from Austin!

—Mike Capps

From Chuck

T HIS IS LENGTHY, so bear with me.

First, my thanks goes to my partner in this book Mike Capps and to perhaps the best friend I have in the radio and TV broadcasting business, Bill Mercer, for creating this book and being such great friends and compatriots.

Thanks to my high school coach, the late Bill McElduff, who gave me everything he had, providing knowledge a lot of young high school pitchers and players had never received. And thanks to high school pitching coach Ray Erxleben for the knowledge he implanted.

I played college baseball at the University of Texas for a legendary coach, the late Bibb Falk, a former major-leaguer who could do anything on a baseball field, including pitch batting practice with a fungo bat. Coach gave us so much of himself, and truly taught us the big-league way to play this game. He gave all of us who played for him with the Longhorns, a huge advantage when we got to professional baseball.

The late Fred Martin, a worldly baseball man if there ever was one, taught me, late in my minor-league career in the White

Sox organization, a very important lesson. In fifteen minutes, Fred taught me how to change my grip to his grip, putting my fingers on the top of the baseball, coming out of my glove. That corrected what I was doing which was flipping the ball behind my back with my wrist. Making that correction, Fred helped me make the ball sink in a more dynamic downward spin, and it gave me much better control. Some pitchers learn that quickly, some never learn it at all. Fred was one hell of a teacher, and he understood the game, and most especially its people.

My second father, Roy Hartsfield, a veteran player and manager in the big leagues took me with him when he became the first manager in Toronto Blue Jays history. I pitched for Roy in Hawaii, and he knew what I could do. He also knew I needed some additional time in MLB to qualify for a pension, but he also wanted me to ultimately become a pitching coach in the Blue Jays' minor-league system because he knew I'd teach pitchers the right way to conduct their business. He's one of my all-time heroes for helping me that way.

Former Houston Astros player and MLB manager Doug Rader and I first met playing in a collegiate league in Illinois in the early 1960s. We crossed paths coming and going in the big leagues and I was his pitching coach in Triple-A ball in Hawaii. Rader remains one of the most intelligent men I ever met in any walk of life. In his third time up against me in a game in Illinois, I threw him a nasty, nasty pitch eight inches outside and four inches high, and he pulled that pitch, blasting it over the left center field wall. As he rounded third, I walked over and yelled, "How in the hell did you hit *that*?" He yelled back, "I was looking for it." I laugh every time I think about that, and Doug and our friendship.

When Tom Trebelhorn finished his minor-league catching career, he caught a great break and became the Milwaukee Brewers manager in 1986, and I went with him as his pitching coach. As Roy Hartsfield gave me the time needed for my pension, Trebelhorn gave me additional MLB time as a coach, and I thank him every first of the month when the pension check arrives!

After ten MLB seasons as an outstanding catcher (he caught Sandy Koufax' perfect game for the Dodgers in 1965, which was my first game in the big leagues), Jeff Torborg switched to managing with the Cleveland Indians, and he took me with him. Thank you so much Jeff!

Tony LaRussa won three World Series titles and 2,278 games, which ranks him behind two legends, Connie Mack and John McGraw. A Hall of Famer since 2014, he's also a true friend and I thank him for that friendship.

When I left Cleveland as pitching coach, Dave Duncan took over in what turned out to be his first pitching coach job in the big leagues. Ultimately four of his pitchers won Cy Young Awards, as he and Tony La Russa worked together for the White Sox, Cardinals, and St. Louis. Thanks, Dave.

A backup outfielder for the Twins, Joe Nossek started most of the 1965 World Series against the Dodgers. The Twins lost the series, but baseball gained THE best sign-stealer of all time. I don't mean using cameras set up all over the ballpark. Joe could sit and study the pitcher and the third-base coach, and pretty much tell you what was about to happen. Plus, he's a great friend.

Former MLB manager with the Royals and bench coach in San Diego, Tony Muser and I played Triple-A ball in the White

Sox organization in the early 1970s and the friendship has lasted that long.

Voted Pacific Coast League Manager of the Year in 1984 for the Hawaii Islanders, Tommy Sandt and I worked together. I'm proud of my days as his pitching coach and proud of our friendship. We lost Tommy recently and it broke my heart.

Former Pittsburgh Pirates General Manager Joe Brown always helped me find my place as a mediocre player at contract discussion time. When I'd grimace at him for the numbers on his offer sheet he'd say, "Best I can do, best I can do."

The consummate professional pitcher, Ferguson Jenkins, became the first Canadian to win a Cy Young Award, and the first Canadian in the National Baseball Hall of Fame. That was in 1991, and the best part? He's my friend.

The man who beat the Yankees with a home run in the 1960 World Series, Bill Mazeroski, and I played a lot of golf at his nine-hole course in Pittsburgh when I was with the Pirates. He's a friend to this day.

One of the greatest gifts about playing for the Pirates in the 1970s was my friendship with the late Willie Stargell. We had no controversy in the clubhouse in those years and Willie saw to it. Baseball saw to it. He's a Hall of Famer in many, many ways.

Roberto Clemente. Hall of Fame ballplayer. Hall of Fame human. God rest his soul.

Lefty pitcher with the Pirates Bob Veale had the longest arms I ever saw. One night at spring training, his roommate refused to get off the phone, as he laid in the top bed of a bunk bed configuration, talking to his wife. After repeated pleas by Veale to release the phone went unheard, the six-foot, seven-inch giant showed that his arms were not only long but strong, as he reached under the lower level of the bed, picked up the entire bunk bed, player and all, which resulted in the room-mate releasing the phone to Big Bob. Wow! Did I mention how proud I am that Bob and I are still friends?

Hall of Famer Billy Williams with the Chicago Cubs remains a friend to this day. Anyone who would nickname a skinny guy like me, "Twiggy," should always receive open arms as a friend and plenty of credit.

Another Hall of Famer, former Red Sox second baseman, the late Bobby Doerr for many, many reasons was my idol. God bless him for who he was and what he was in this game.

I taught Hall of Famer Tony Gwynn to hit. Well, here's what happened. When the Padres signed him, they sent him to Walla Walla, Washington. The Padres created special sessions, me versus him in game situations. There, they used me to pick out and throw to his weaknesses as a hitter (he had very few even as a rookie), and pound away at those weaknesses, until he learned how to handle pitches he was weak on. Boy did he ever learn and learn quickly! I miss him.

Veteran player and then minor-league manager Rocky Bridges may have chewed the largest wads of tobacco I ever saw. And as manager, he used his "chaws, and juice," to have fun with his players, including me. Sometimes between innings when I pitched, he'd cram that wet mess between the fingers of my glove. I don't know if you've ever gripped a used chewing tobacco wad, but the only way I can describe it is, *disturbing* to say the least. Another fun Rocky Bridges stunt? When he pitched batting practice, he'd sometimes, and all at once, throw his glove, hat, and ball at the hitter. Talk about nuts. What a great chaos creator. What do you hit, the glove, hat, or ball? Well, the last day of the season when I was on the mound, I told my catcher, Mike Sadek, I was going to pull Rocky's "unload the glove, hat, and ball" stunt on the hitter. Sadek laughed and said okay. Home plate umpire Terry Cooney had no idea the trick was coming. So, with a guy on second, I let go of it all—glove, hat, and ball—flying in all directions. The runner at second stayed at second laughing his backside off, the hyena-laughing Sadek, never came close to handling any of the projectiles coming his way. Lucky for me, umpire Terry Cooney never saw that pitch before and didn't know what the hell was going on. Fortunately, he didn't kick me out, so I quickly got another ball, fired a slider, the hitter popped it up, season over, see ya next year! Thank you, God, for Rocky Bridges!

Bob "Monk" Miller served as my pitching coach with the Toronto Blue Jays. What a great friend he was, helping me secure some jobs that kept me and my family going.

Jay Miller, one of the best operators in MLB of minor-league baseball and a dear, dear friend.

To the grandson of the legendary Branch Rickey, Branch B. Rickey, longtime president of the Pacific Coast League, and the only person who ever fired me who I still like as a friend.

My certified public accountant all the years I was in baseball, and still my accountant today, Ernst "Juno" Druebert. He made sure my taxes were done correctly and kept me out of the IRS shame corner. Bless him and his friendship.

And bless you, dear baseball friends and fans, for being loyal to all of us who've played, coached, and managed this game throughout the years.

—*Chuck Hartenstein*

Check out the Grinder podcast on the Stoney Creek
Network or major podcast hosting sites
StoneyCreekPublishing.com/podcasts

LOOKING FOR YOUR
NEXT BOOK?

Check out our other titles,
including audio books, at
StoneyCreekPublishing.com.

*For author book signings, speaking engagements
or other events, please contact us at
info@stoneycreekpublishing.com*

A Member of the Texas Book Consortium

CPSIA information can be obtained
at www.ICGtesting.com
Printed in the USA
BVHW030047050622
638843BV00004B/4

9 781736 839041